PRENTICE HALL
CHEMISTRY
THE STUDY OF MATTER

LABORATORY MANUAL
Fourth Edition

Maxine Wagner

D1530417

Prentice Hall, Inc.
Needham, Massachusetts
Englewood Cliffs, New Jersey

Credits

About the Author
Maxine Wagner has earned academic degrees at both Cornell University (B.A. with distinction, Chemistry) and Hofstra University (M.S., Secondary Education in Chemistry and General Science). She has worked in various fields of research and development and in technical writing. Mrs. Wagner is formerly a Chemistry Instructor and Coordinator at St. John the Baptist Diocesan High School in West Islip, New York, where she taught for 15 years.

Staff Credits

Editorial Development	Robert J. Hope, Diana G. Kessler, Lois B. Arnold, Julia A. Fellows
Design Coordination	Jonathan B. Pollard
Production Editor	George Carl Cordes
Book Manufacturing	Bill Wood
Art Direction	L. Christopher Valente
Marketing	Arthur C. Germano, Paul P. Scopa, Michael D. Buckley

Outside Credits

Editorial Services	A. H. Drummond, Jr.
Book Design	Sandra Rigney, The Book Department, Inc.
Illustrations	Leonard Boylan & Associates Boston Graphics, Inc.
Production Services	The Book Department, Inc., Elizabeth A. Jordan
Laboratory Safety Consultant	James A. Kaufman

Cover

Cover Design	Martucci Studios
Art Direction	L. Christopher Valente

A Simon & Schuster Company
© Copyright 1992, 1989 by Prentice Hall, Inc.

Previous editions were published by **Cebco·Allyn and Bacon, Inc.** © 1982 and **Allyn and Bacon, Inc.** © 1987.

ISBN 0-13-127358-2

Printed in the United States of America

34 17

To The Student

Chemistry is a laboratory science. In the laboratory, you become actively involved in the process of investigation and will develop an appreciation of the scientific method of inquiry. As a result of some laboratory activities, you will "discover" important chemical concepts before they are introduced in the classroom. In other activities, concepts learned in class will be reinforced or clarified.

As with any new undertaking, success in the laboratory requires a basic knowledge of the "tools of the trade" and how to use them. A descriptive section is included at the beginning of this manual to help familiarize you with the techniques and equipment you will use in the laboratory. The first few experiments are designed to help you develop competency in laboratory techniques and procedures.

Laboratory work should be an interesting and meaningful part of any chemistry course. It is my wish that this book will help give you the satisfaction and enjoyment that come when a subject is well understood. Thanks go to my family, friends, and students, all of whom encouraged me in the writing of this laboratory manual.

Maxine Wagner

To The Teacher

The content of the experiments in this lab manual is universal to any introductory chemistry course. The order of presentation can be easily rearranged to conform to any order you desire.

Several experiments in this lab manual are designated as "demonstrations." These designations are made for one or more of the following reasons: the experiment may have a relatively high potential for accident; preparation for one or more classes of student teams may be unusually time-consuming; the experiment may require expensive equipment that may not be available in sufficient quantity. The format in these suggested demonstrations is identical to that used in the student-conducted experiments.

This annotated Teacher's Edition (TE) is an expanded version of the student lab manual. It contains all of the student pages plus additional Teacher's Edition pages.

In this TE, all of the information, teaching suggestions, sample data and calculations, art, and answers to questions are located at points in the manual where they will be used. A brief description of these materials follows.

The following topics are found in the TE notes beginning on the first page of an experiment: **Pre-Lab, Lab Time, A Shorter Lab Period, Safety, Advance Preparation,** and **Quantities** (per student lab team or demonstration).

Pre-Lab: This section suggests the course material to which the lab exercise is most closely related. It contains material that should be discussed before students start their lab work. This may include concepts, definitions, and simulated situations that students will encounter in their lab work. Some teaching hints and suggestions also might appear in this section.

Lab Time: This section suggests the time a lab should normally require.

A Shorter Lab Period: This section suggests modifications to the laboratory procedures to permit completion of the experiment within a 40-minute period.

Safety: This section gives specific precautions that should be taken when performing the lab.

Advance Preparation: This section describes preparations that should be made prior to class. Such preparations include mixing of solutions, cutting and bending of glass tubing, apparatus set-ups, etc.

Quantities (per student lab team): This section lists the quantity of each reagent needed for each lab team.

The following appear as annotations to the student lab manual pages: **sample observations and data, sample calculations, sample art,** and **answers to "Conclusions and Questions."** These annotations are located in the spaces provided for the student to enter this information.

Contents

Appendices

Correlation of Student Text with Laboratory Manual

Safety in the Chemistry Laboratory

Chemistry is a laboratory science. In the laboratory, you become actively involved in the process of investigation and will develop an appreciation of the scientific method of inquiry. As a result of some laboratory activities, you will "discover" important chemical concepts before they are introduced in the classroom. In other activities, concepts learned in class will be reinforced or clarified.

Following General Safety Guidelines

1. Be prepared to work when you arrive at the laboratory. If instructed to do so by your teacher, familiarize yourself with the lab procedures before beginning the lab.

2. Perform only those lab activities assigned by your teacher. *Never* do anything in the laboratory that is not called for in the laboratory procedure or by your teacher.

3. Work areas should be kept clean and tidy at all times. Only lab manuals and notebooks should be brought to the work area. Other books, purses, briefcases, etc. should be left at your desk or placed in a designated storage area.

4. Clothing should be appropriate for working in the lab. Jackets, ties, and other loose garments should be removed. Long sleeves should be rolled up or secured in some manner.

5. Long hair should be tied back or covered, especially in the vicinity of an open flame.

6. Jewelry that might present a safety hazard, such as dangling necklaces, chains, medallions, or bracelets, should not be worn in the lab.

7. Follow all instructions, both written and oral, carefully.

8. Safety goggles and a lab coat or apron should be worn at all times.

9. Set up apparatus as described in the lab manual or by your teacher. Never use makeshift arrangements.

10. Always use the prescribed instrument (tongs, test-tube holder, forceps, etc.) for handling apparatus or equipment.

11. Keep all combustible materials away from open flames.

12. Never touch or taste any substance in the lab unless instructed to do so by your teacher.

13. Never put your face near the mouth of a container that is holding chemicals.

14. When testing for odors, use a wafting motion to direct the odors to your nose. Never smell any chemical unless instructed to do so.

15. Any activity involving poisonous vapors should be conducted in the fume hood.

16. Dispose of waste materials as instructed by your teacher.

17. Clean up all spills immediately.

18. Clean and wipe dry all work surfaces at the end of class. Wash your hands thoroughly.

19. Know the location of emergency equipment (first-aid kit, fire extinguisher, fire shower, fire blanket, etc.) and how to use them.

20. Report all accidents to the teacher immediately.

Handling Chemicals

21. Read and double-check labels on reagent bottles before removing any reagent. Take only as much reagent as you need.

22. Do not return unused reagent to stock bottles.

23. When transferring chemical reagents from one container to another, hold the containers out away from your body.

24. When mixing an acid and water, *always add the acid to the water.*

25. Avoid touching chemicals with your hands. If chemicals do come in contact with your hands, wash them immediately.

Handling Glassware

26. Glass tubing, especially long pieces, should be carried in a vertical position to minimize the likelihood of breakage and to avoid stabbing anyone.

27. Never handle broken glass with your bare hands. Use a brush and dustpan to clean up broken glass. Dispose of the glass as directed by your teacher.

28. Always lubricate a piece of glassware (tubing, thistle tubes, thermometers, etc.) with water or glycerine before attempting to insert it in a stopper.

29. Never apply force when inserting or removing glassware from a stopper. Use a twisting motion. If a piece of glassware becomes "frozen" in a stopper, take it to your teacher.

30. Do not place hot glassware directly on the lab table. Always use an insulating pad of some sort.

31. Allow plenty of time for hot glass to cool before touching it. Hot glass can cause painful burns. (Remember: Hot glass *looks* cool.)

Heating Substances

32. Exercise extreme caution when using a gas burner. Keep your head and clothing away from the flame.

33. Always turn the burner off when it is not in use.

34. Do not bring any substance into contact with a flame unless instructed to do so.

35. Never heat anything without being instructed to do so.

36. Never look into a container that is being heated.

37. Never heat a closed container.

38. When heating a substance in a test tube, make sure that the mouth of the tube is not pointed at yourself or anyone else.

39. Never leave unattended anything that is being heated or that is visibly reacting.

Identifying Caution Alert Symbols

The symbols shown below are used throughout this lab manual at points where extra caution should be exercised. Whenever you see one of these symbols, stop, read the material carefully, and proceed with extra care. If you have any questions, ask your teacher before going on.

SAFETY CLOTHING/SAFETY GOGGLES
These two symbols appear at the beginning of each experiment. They are to remind you that safety goggles and a lab apron (or coat) are to be worn *at all times* when working in the lab. For some activities, your teacher may also instruct you to wear protective gloves.

FIRE
This symbol indicates the presence of an open flame. Loose hair should be tied back or covered, and bulky or loose clothing should be secured in some manner.

CORROSIVE SUBSTANCE
This symbol indicates a caustic or corrosive substance—most frequently an acid. Avoid contact with skin, eyes, and clothing. Do not inhale vapors.

BREAKAGE
This symbol indicates an activity in which the likelihood of breakage is greater than usual, such as working with glass tubing, funnels, etc.

DANGEROUS VAPORS
This symbol indicates the presence of or production of poisonous or noxious vapors. *Use the fume hood* when directed to do so. Care should be taken not to inhale vapors directly. When testing an odor, use a wafting motion to direct the vapor toward your nose.

EXPLOSION
This symbol indicates that the potential for an explosive situation is present. When you see this symbol, read the instructions carefully and *follow them exactly.*

POISON
This symbol indicates the presence of a poisonous substance. Do not let such a substance come in contact with your skin and do not breathe its vapors.

ELECTRICAL SHOCK
This symbol indicates that the potential for an electrical shock exists. Read all instructions carefully. Disconnect all apparatus when not in use.

RADIATION
This symbol indicates a radioactive substance. Follow your teacher's instructions as to the proper handling of such substances.

DISPOSAL
This symbol indicates that a chemical should be disposed of in a special way. Dispose of these chemicals as directed by your teacher.

Laboratory Equipment and Skills

In the chemistry laboratory, you will be using equipment, handling materials, and performing certain unfamiliar tasks. The purpose of this section is to introduce you to the equipment and to describe some of the skills you will be required to use in this laboratory course. A few of the "dos" and "don'ts" necessary for safe and effective laboratory work also are included.

Recognizing Lab Equipment

The equipment you will be using most frequently in the laboratory is illustrated in Figure 1. Study this figure carefully and familiarize yourself with each item.

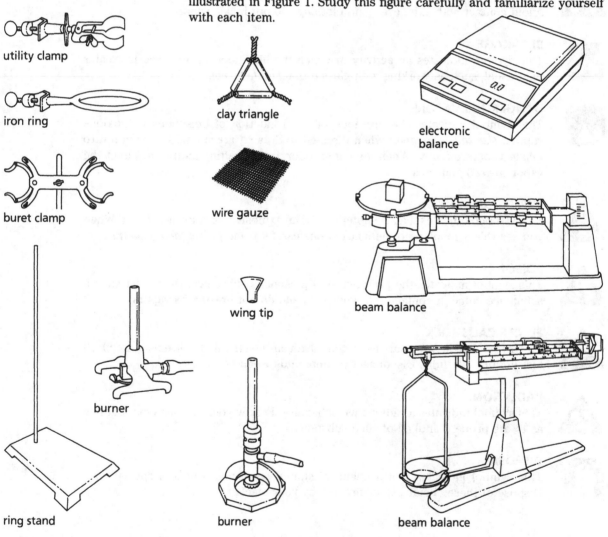

Figure 1 Laboratory equipment.

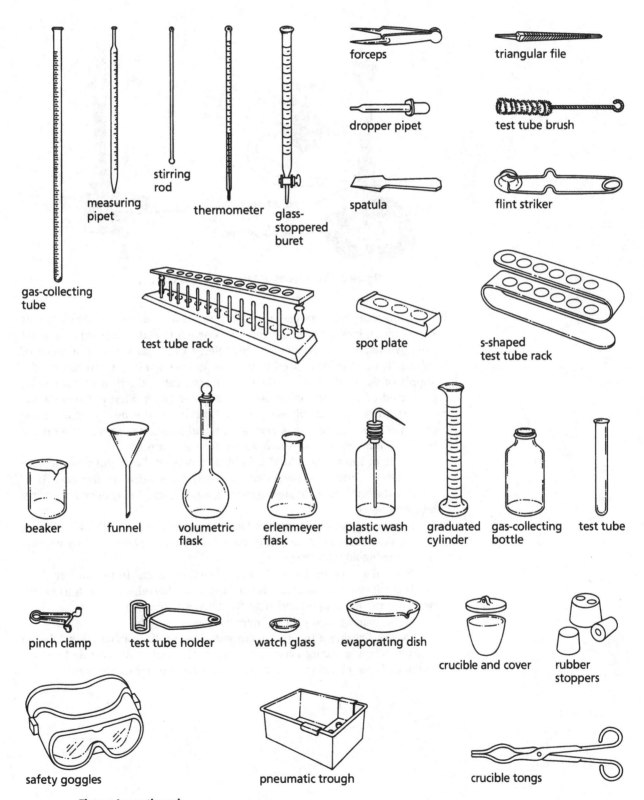

gas-collecting tube

measuring pipet

stirring rod

thermometer

glass-stoppered buret

forceps

triangular file

dropper pipet

test tube brush

spatula

flint striker

test tube rack

spot plate

s-shaped test tube rack

beaker

funnel

volumetric flask

erlenmeyer flask

plastic wash bottle

graduated cylinder

gas-collecting bottle

test tube

pinch clamp

test tube holder

watch glass

evaporating dish

crucible and cover

rubber stoppers

safety goggles

pneumatic trough

crucible tongs

Figure 1, continued

Using the Laboratory Burner

One of the most frequently used pieces of equipment in the chemistry lab is the laboratory burner. Although laboratory burners differ somewhat in appearance and construction, they all have several features in common. Figure 2 shows two typical laboratory burners.

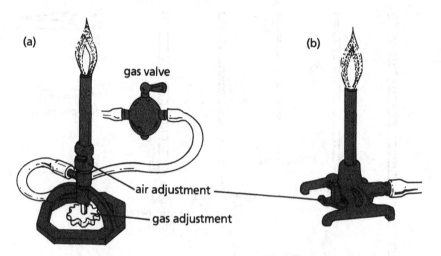

Figure 2   Two types of laboratory gas burners.

Laboratory burners use a mixture of gas and air as fuel. The amount of gas that mixes with the air must be correct in order to obtain the most effective flame. The burner is connected to the gas valve by a piece of tubing. The gas valve is used to turn the gas on and off and to control the supply of gas to the burner. By adjusting the valve, the flow of gas can be increased or reduced. Some burners, such as (**a**) in Figure 2, have a gas adjustment knob that allows you to "fine tune" the flow of gas to the burner. The supply of air is regulated by adjusting a vent or valve on the burner. All burners have some device for this purpose.

To light the burner, hold a lighted match or flint lighter to the side and slightly above the barrel of the burner and turn on the gas. After lighting the burner, make any adjustments necessary to produce a properly adjusted flame.

A properly adjusted burner flame is nonluminous, with two distinct cones, as shown in Figure 3. Improper flames can be corrected by making the following adjustments:

If the flame is too large, decrease the flow of gas to the burner.

If the flame "disappears" down the burner barrel, turn the burner off, decrease the air supply, and light the burner again.

If the flame is too yellow, increase the air supply.

Before lighting a burner, make sure that no flammable materials are nearby. When working around a burner, tie back long hair and secure bulky or loose clothing. Never leave a lighted burner unattended.

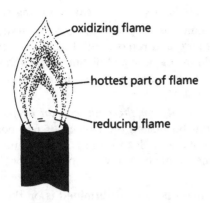

Figure 3 A properly adjusted burner flame.

Using the Balance

Beam balances are the most common type used in high school laboratories. The two balances shown in Figure 4 are (**a**) a triple-beam platform balance and (**b**) a four-beam pan balance.

(a)

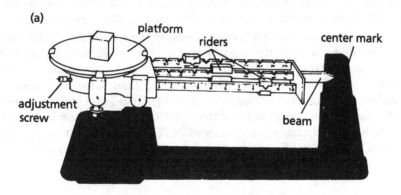

(b)

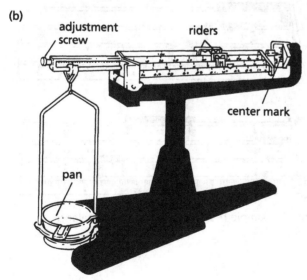

Figure 4 Two types of beam balances.

The proper use of the balance is described in the following steps:

1. Check to see that the balance is properly adjusted, or "zeroed." To do this, set all of the riders at zero and remove all objects from the pan or platform. The pointer should swing an equal distance on each side of the zero point on the scale. If it does not, use the adjustment screw to obtain an equal swing of the pointer.

2. *Never place chemicals directly on the balance pan or platform.* Samples to be measured should be placed on a piece of pre-measured paper or in a pre-measured container. Clean up any spills immediately. Never place hot objects on the balance. Allow samples to cool before measuring their mass.

3. Once the object whose mass is to be determined is on the pan or platform, move the rider of greatest mass along this beam, one notch at a time, until it causes the pointer to drop. Then move the rider *back* one notch. Repeat this procedure with each succeeding rider of smaller mass. If the beams are notched, make sure each rider is securely in its notch. The front beam, which is marked off in the smallest increments, is not notched. Slide the rider on this beam until the pointer swings an equal distance on each side of the zero on the scale.

4. When the pointer is zeroed, sum up the masses shown on the beams. The mass of the object is equal to the sum of the masses shown on the beams *minus the pre-measured mass of the paper or container.*

The precision of a balance depends on the size of the smallest increments on the scale of the front beam. On some triple-beam balances, this scale is divided into 10 1-gram increments. This scale can be read to the nearest ±0.1 gram. On a four-beam balance (and some triple-beam balances), the scale on the front beam is divided into 10 0.1-gram increments. This scale can be read to the nearest ±0.01 gram. Some sample readings of this type of balance are illustrated in Figure 5. The reading on balance (**a**) is 24.56 grams. The reading on balance (**b**) is 107.08 grams.

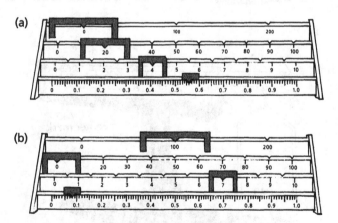

Figure 5 Sample readings of a four-beam balance.

Handling Chemical Reagents

When conducting an experiment, it will be necessary for you to obtain chemical reagents, both liquid and solid, from some central supply area. The chemicals in this supply area have a degree of purity that must be maintained. In order to avoid contaminating these chemicals, the following rules should be strictly adhered to:

1. Take only as much reagent as you need.

2. If a scoop (or spatula) is used to remove a solid reagent from its container, use *only* that scoop for that reagent. Do *not* use your own scoop. Do *not* use the same scoop to remove reagents from two different containers.

3. Once a reagent has been removed from its container, *never return any portion of it to its container*. All excess materials should be discarded as instructed by your teacher.

Solids. Whenever possible, solid reagents should be poured, rather than scooped, from their containers. Figure 6 illustrates the most satisfactory method for pouring solid reagents.

Figure 6   Pouring solid reagent.

By gently rotating the bottle back and forth and tapping the side of the bottle with your finger, you can make the reagent come out in a controlled, steady flow.

When transferring a solid reagent to a test tube or other small-mouth container, it is best to use a piece of paper. Using the method shown in Figure 6, the desired quantity of reagent is first poured from its container onto a piece of paper. The paper is then used to pour the reagent into the test tube, as shown in Figure 7.

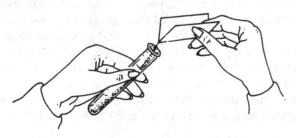

Figure 7   Using a creased paper to transfer a solid.

Liquids. When transferring liquids from a reagent bottle, remove the stopper from the bottle by grasping it between the forefinger and middle finger, as shown in Figure 8.

Figure 8 Removing the stopper from a liquid reagent bottle.

Do not set the stopper down. While still grasping the stopper, pour from the side of the reagent bottle away from the label, as illustrated in Figure 9.

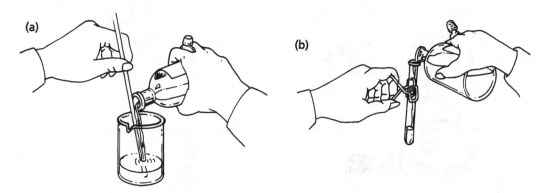

Figure 9 Proper methods of pouring liquid reagents

When pouring a liquid into a large-mouth container, pour the liquid down a glass stirring rod [Figure 9(a)] to avoid spattering. If pouring into a test tube, stand the tube in a test-tube rack, or use a test-tube holder [Figure 9(b)].

Measuring Liquids

The most commonly used instruments for measuring liquids in the laboratory are graduated cylinders, burets, and measuring pipets. Each of these instruments has a scale marked on its side. In most cases, the larger the measuring device, the less precise the scale. Graduated cylinders are designed to measure the volume of liquid they are *holding*. Thus, the 0-mL mark is at the bottom of the scale. Burets and pipets are designed to measure the volume of liquid they *deliver*. On the scales of these instruments, the 0-mL mark is at the top. This permits the user to read the amount of liquid that has been delivered from the zero mark.

In all of these instruments, the surface of the liquid will be slightly curved. This curved surface is called a *meniscus*. The curvature is caused by the combined effects of the pull of gravity on the liquid and the attraction (or nonattraction) of the liquid for the glass of the instrument. Most liquids are attracted to the glass and are said to "wet" the glass. The meniscus formed by such a liquid is concave (curved downward). Such liquids as mercury, that do not wet the glass, form a convex meniscus.

When reading the scale of an instrument containing a liquid, you read to the *bottom* of a concave meniscus and to the *top* of a convex meniscus. Figure 10 shows the correct and incorrect lines of sight in reading a concave meniscus.

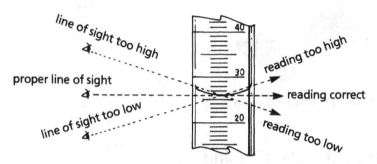

Figure 10   Reading a concave meniscus.

Filtering a Mixture

Filtration is a procedure commonly used to separate liquids from insoluble solids. In this procedure, the solid-liquid mixture is poured into a funnel in which a paper filter has been fitted. The filter traps the solid particles and allows the liquid to pass through, where it is collected in a container.

The paper filter is formed by folding a piece of filter paper as illustrated in Figure 11. Tearing off a corner of the filter paper, as shown in step (3) of the figure, prevents air from leaking down the fold of the filter. Once the filter is formed, place it in the funnel and "tack" it into position by wetting it slightly with distilled water and pressing it against the walls of the funnel until all air bubbles are removed.

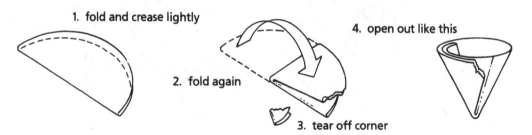

Figure 11   Folding a filter paper.

Figure 12 shows the proper setup for carrying out a filtration. Slowly pour the mixture down a glass stirring rod into the filter, making sure that none of the mixture rises above the edge of the filter in the funnel. After all the liquid has been poured from the container, use a wash bottle to rinse out any solid that remains in the container. Then wash the solid trapped in the filter with small amounts of water from the wash bottle.

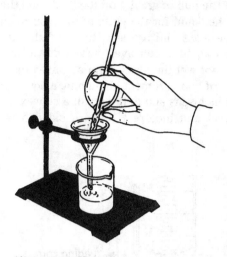

Figure 12 Filtration setup.

Working with Glass Tubing

The glass tubing most commonly used in the laboratory is made of a "soft" type of glass that is easily cut and shaped. To cut a piece of tubing, place it on a flat surface. Place one edge of a triangular file on the tubing at the spot where you wish to make your cut. While holding the tubing with one hand, press down firmly with the file and make one firm stroke away from you. Before trying to break the tubing at the cut mark, protect your hands by wearing gloves or wrapping a piece of cloth around the tubing. Pick up the tubing and place your thumbs on opposite sides of the scratch, as shown in Figure 13(a). Holding your thumbs firmly against the glass, snap the tubing at the scratch, as shown in Figure 13(b).

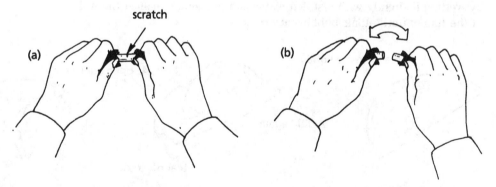

Figure 13 Cutting glass tubing.

After a piece of tubing has been cut, the cut edges are very sharp and should be polished. To do this, place the cut end of the tubing into the hottest part of a burner flame. Rotate the glass as you heat it (Figure 14), and continue heating it until the flame becomes a bright yellow. If you examine the cut end, you will see that the sharp edges have become smooth.

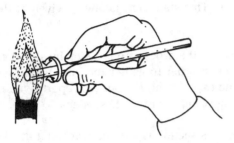

Figure 14   Fire-polishing glass tubing.

Place the tubing on an insulated pad to cool. DO NOT TOUCH THE HOT GLASS.

If you wish to bend a piece of glass tubing, first place a flame spreader, or "wing tip," on the burner. Light the burner and rotate the glass in the flame, as shown in Figure 15.

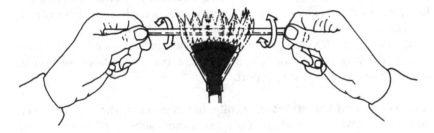

Figure 15   Heating glass tubing prior to bending.

As the glass heats, the flame will become yellow and the glass will soften. Remove the glass from the flame and lift the ends of the tubing with a smooth, even motion. When the glass has been bent to the desired angle, place it on an insulated pad to cool.

Preparing Laboratory Reports

A laboratory report is a written record of an investigation. Such a report is an integral part of any laboratory experiment. The names and brief descriptions of the sections of a laboratory report are given below.

Purpose. The purpose is a brief statement of the goals to be achieved by conducting the experiment. This statement is always given at the beginning of the experiment.

Procedure. In the lab manual, the procedure is a step-by-step description of the activities to be done in order to gather the information needed to achieve the purpose of the experiment. In your lab reports, you might be asked to summarize the most important of these steps.

Observations and Data. This section is a running account of what takes place during the course of an investigation. All of your observations, qualitative and quantitative, must be recorded in this section *at the time the observation is made.* Entries in the final two sections of the lab report will be based on the information recorded here. Thus, it is vital that this information be complete, well-organized, accurate, and properly labeled.

Calculations. In many cases, the "raw" data collected during the course of an experiment must be "processed" before valid conclusions can be reached. Processing data can include making mathematical calculations. the results of these calculations then are used as a basis on which to draw conclusions.

In some experiments, the raw data are all that is needed for the purpose of drawing conclusions. In such cases, the calculations section is omitted from the laboratory report.

Conclusions and Questions. Basically, this section is where you answer the question: "Was the purpose of this experiment achieved?" In answering this question, you must provide evidence to support your answer.

The pages of this laboratory manual are designed to be used as a laboratory report. The purpose is stated, and space is provided for recording observations and data and for making calculations. In cases where data are to be graphed, grids are provided. The "Conclusions and Questions" section consists of a series of questions and/or problems related to the experiment. However, your teacher might prefer that you prepare your own laboratory reports on separate sheets of paper.

Qualitative Observations of a Chemical Reaction

Lab 1

Text reference: **Chapter 1**, pp. 2–4

Pre-Lab Discussion

Scientists rely heavily on experimentation. A good scientist must observe and interpret what is happening. Observing means using the senses: seeing, smelling, touching, hearing, and *sometimes* tasting. NEVER TASTE CHEMICALS UNLESS INSTRUCTED TO BY YOUR TEACHER.

When scientists make observations, they try to be objective. Being objective means putting aside any preconceived notions. Scientists are interested in what *really* occurs, not in what they *wish* would occur.

After observations are made, scientists must make interpretations. Interpretations are based on previous knowledge and experience. Because people have different experiences, one scientist may interpret observations in one way while another may interpret the same observations to mean something else. When we interpret, we attempt to make sense out of observations. Scientists never assume that their interpretations are correct until they test them fully and repeatedly. After complete testing, scientists then come to their conclusions.

In this investigation, you will make some qualitative observations of a chemical reaction. That is, no measurements will be made. During a chemical reaction, one or more substances change into one or more other substances. The burning of wood, wax, oil, gasoline, and coal are examples of a chemical reaction known as combustion. The reaction you will study in this investigation is a combustion reaction.

Purpose

Carefully observe and interpret a chemical reaction.

Equipment

beaker, 250-mL
Erlenmeyer flask, 125-mL
glass square
microspatula
metric ruler

microslide
rubber stopper
safety goggles
lab apron or coat

Materials

candle (2-cm diameter)
matches, 2 or 3
toothpicks, 2
limewater solution

string
aluminum foil
cobalt chloride paper

Safety   ⚠

In this experiment, you will be working with an open flame. Tie back long hair and secure loose clothing. Also, wear safety goggles and a lab apron or coat at all times when working in the lab. Be sure all matches and burned materials are completely extinguished before they are discarded.

Procedure

Record observations *for each step*.

1. Note appearance, odor, and feel of the unlighted candle.

2. Heat the bottom of the candle and secure it to a glass square on your lab bench. Light the candle and allow it to burn for several minutes. Note any changes. Briefly describe the burning candle.

3. Blow out the flame and immediately place a lighted match in the "smoke" about 2 cm above the wick. See Figure 1-1. Note the result.

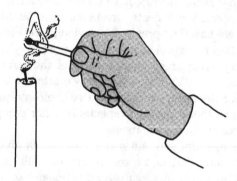

Figure 1-1

4. Use a microspatula to transfer a small amount of liquid from the bowl of the candle onto a microslide. Try to light it and note the result.

5. Place a toothpick into the soft candle next to the unlighted wick to form a wooden wick. Light the toothpick and note the result.

6. Place a length of string about 4 cm long on the glass square. Light it and observe its behavior.

7. Make a slit in a small piece of aluminum foil. See Figure 1-2. Light the candle. Place the foil between the base of the flame and the liquid in the candle bowl. Note the behavior of the flame.

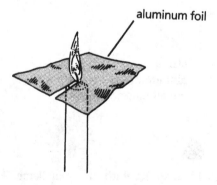

aluminum foil

Figure 1-2

1 Qualitative Observations of a Chemical Reaction (continued)

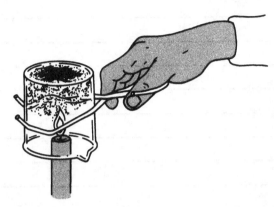

Figure 1-3

8. Invert a 250-mL beaker over the lighted candle. See Figure 1-3. Note any substance that collects on the inside of the beaker. Test the liquid with cobalt chloride paper.

9. Invert a 125-mL Erlenmeyer flask over the lighted candle for several minutes. Remove the flask, turn it right side up, and add about 10 mL of the clear limewater solution. Stopper and shake the flask. Note any change in the limewater solution.

Observations and Data

_____

_____

_____

_____

_____

_____

_____

_____

_____

_____

_____

_____

_____

_____

_____

_____

_____

_____

_____
_____
_____
_____
_____
_____
_____
_____
_____
_____
_____
_____
_____
_____
_____
_____
_____
_____
_____

Conclusions and Questions

1. What phases (solid, liquid, gas) are present in the unlighted candle? In the burning candle? Which phase appears to take part in the chemical reaction?

_____
_____
_____
_____
_____

1 Qualitative Observations of a Chemical Reaction (continued)

2. What part does the wick play in the burning of the candle? What properties should the wick have? Explain the result when aluminum is placed between the liquid and the wick. Is the wick part of the chemical reaction?

_____
_____
_____
_____
_____
_____
_____

3. What two substances are indicated by the cobalt chloride and lime-water tests? Is it possible that other substances are produced when the candle burns? Explain.

_____
_____
_____
_____
_____
_____

4. A source of energy is needed to start the burning of the candle. What energy source is used? Did the reaction give off or absorb heat?

_____
_____

5. Give an example illustrating the difference between observation and interpretation.

_____
_____
_____
_____

Quantitative Observations of a Chemical Reaction

Lab 2

Text reference: **Chapter 1**, pp. 2–4

Pre-Lab Discussion

Most experiments require the investigator to make some quantitative observations, or measurements. The numerical values of these measurements are called *data*. The most frequently measured quantities in the chemistry laboratory are mass, volume, and temperature.

When conducting an experiment of a quantitative nature, the first step in the procedure is to make and record measurements of the materials that are being investigated. If the materials take part in a chemical reaction (undergo chemical change), many, if not all, of the initial measured values probably will change. The nature and extent of these changes often help the investigator to understand what is taking place. Some of these changes, such as temperature change, can be measured and recorded as the reaction is taking place. When the reaction is ended, measurements again are made and recorded. The collected data from all of these measurements provide an overall record of what quantitative changes took place during the reaction.

When making measurements, you should keep in mind that the numerical values can be only as accurate as the instruments used to make the measurements. These values also are affected by the care and skill of the person using the instruments. As you gain more experience in the laboratory, you will become more familiar with the limitations and accuracy of the various instruments you use. You also will become more skillful in the use of these instruments and in carrying out various activities that are essential to a successful investigation.

Scientists must be imaginative. In many cases, they must devise their own experiments and decide what measurements will provide useful information. In this investigation, you will make measurements to determine the effects of a chemical reaction (combustion). You then will be asked to decide how these measurements can be used to extend your understanding of the reaction.

Purpose

Make a quantitative investigation of a chemical reaction.

Equipment

laboratory balance	graduated cylinder, 100-mL
ring stand	watch or clock with second hand
iron ring	glass square
wire gauze	safety goggles
thermometer	lab apron or coat
beaker, 250-mL	

Materials

candle (2-cm diameter)	matches, 2 or 3

Safety

In this experiment, you will be working with an open flame. Tie back long hair and secure loose clothing. Also, wear safety goggles and a lab apron or coat at all times when working in the lab. Be sure matches are completely extinguished before they are discarded.

Procedure

1. Find the mass of the candle.

2. Measure exactly 100 mL of tap water in a graduated cylinder. Pour the water into a 250-mL beaker and place the beaker on a wire gauze as shown in Figure 2-1. Measure the temperature of the water

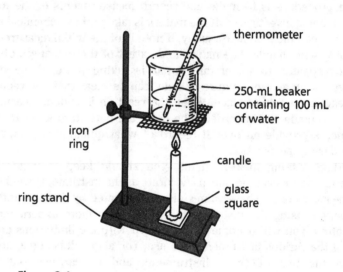

Figure 2-1

 3. Light the candle and place it on the glass square, as shown. Adjust the height of the ring so that the flame is 2 cm below the base of the beaker. Using the candle, heat the water for exactly 10 minutes. Extinguish the flame and measure the temperature of the water and the mass of the candle.

4. Relight the candle and repeat steps 1–3 for a second trial.

Observations and Data

	Trial 1	Trial 2
Original mass of candle	_____	_____
Mass of candle after burning	_____	_____
Time candle burned	_____	_____
Original temperature of water	_____	_____
Final temperature of water	_____	_____
Time water heated	_____	_____

Name _____

2 Quantitative Observations of a Chemical Reaction (continued)

Calculations

For each trial, find:	Trial 1	Trial 2
1. The change in the mass of the candle	_____	_____
2. The change in the mass of the candle per minute	_____	_____
3. The change in the temperature of the water	_____	_____
4. The change in the temperature of the water per minute	_____	_____

Conclusions and Questions

1. Compare your trial results and calculations with those of other lab teams. Are your results exactly the same? How do you account for any differences in data? If one set of data differs from another in an experiment, does this mean that one or both sets are wrong? Explain your answer.

_____
_____
_____
_____
_____
_____
_____
_____

2. What does the term rate mean? **a.** What was the rate of burning of the candle? **b.** What was the rate of heating of the water?

_____

_____

_____

_____

_____

3. Explain how the heat from the combustion reaction is related to the temperature change of the water.

_____

_____

_____

_____

4. Outline a laboratory procedure that would determine which produces more heat—a gram of candle wax or a gram of alcohol. How could this type of experiment be used to decide which substance would make the better fuel? What other factors might enter into choosing a fuel?

_____

_____

_____

_____

_____

_____

_____

_____

_____

_____

_____

_____

_____

_____

Measuring Mass

Lab 3

Text reference: **Chapter 2,** pp. 15–17

Pre-Lab Discussion

For laboratory work in a general chemistry course, three basic types of measurement using the lab balance should be mastered. These are: measuring mass directly, "measuring out" a specific mass of a substance, and determining mass by difference. These three types of measurement and the techniques for making them are briefly described in the following paragraphs.

1. Measuring mass directly. Direct measurement is used to determine the mass of a beaker or flask or similar object. This is the simplest type of measurement made with the balance. In a direct measurement, the object with a mass to be measured is placed on the balance pan, and the appropriate riders are moved into positions along the beams until the pointer is balanced at the zero point. The mass of the object is read directly from the positions of the riders on the beams.

2. "Measuring out" a substance. This technique often is used to obtain a desired mass of a solid chemical, such as table salt, that exists in a granular or crystalline state. To do this, the balance riders are preset to the desired mass reading. The substance being measured out then is added to the balance pan until the pointer is balanced at the zero point. Keep in mind, however, that chemicals should never be placed directly on the balance pan. A piece of paper or a container of some kind should be placed on the pan to receive the substance being measured. The preset mass must then be equal to the mass of the paper or container *plus* the mass to be measured out. This technique can be used for liquids as well as solids. The liquid is poured into a container resting on the balance pan with the preset mass equal to the mass of the empty container plus the mass of the liquid to be measured out.

3. Determining mass by difference. Finding mass by difference is an important laboratory technique. As the name suggests, this technique involves subtraction. One common use for this technique is to determine the mass of a quantity of a substance, such as a liquid, that is in a container. In a case of this sort, it is necessary to subtract the mass of the empty container from the combined mass of the container and the substance. Another important use of this technique is to measure changes in mass that occur during a chemical reaction.

In this experiment, you will learn how to perform all three types of measurement described here. In addition, you will gain valuable practice in using the laboratory balance and in handling different materials and apparatus.

Purpose

Practice the various techniques of measuring masses using the lab balance. Gain experience in the techniques of handling laboratory materials and equipment.

Equipment

lab balance   graduated cylinder, 100-mL
watch glass   timer (watch or clock)
beaker, 150-mL   safety goggles
beaker, 50-mL   lab apron or coat
microspatula

Materials

sodium chloride (NaCl)   toy balloon
calcium chloride ($CaCl_2$)   coins (1 penny, 1 nickel)
filter paper

Safety

Do not allow lab chemicals to come in contact with your skin. Calcium chloride ($CaCl_2$) removes moisture from the skin and can produce irritation and a burning sensation. If contact should occur, immediately flush the area with cold water. Always wear safety goggles and a lab apron or coat when working in the lab.

Procedure

PART A MEASURING MASS DIRECTLY

1. Check your balance to make sure that the pointer is properly "zeroed." If an adjustment is necessary, consult your teacher.

2. Place a penny on the balance pan. Move the rider(s) until the pointer is balanced (zeroed). Record the mass of the penny.

3. Repeat step 2 for objects listed below. Record the mass of each object.
   a. a nickel
   b. a watch glass
   c. a 150-mL beaker
   d. a 100-mL graduated cylinder

PART B MEASURING OUT A SUBSTANCE

4. Place a piece of filter paper on the balance pan. Move the rider on the front beam until the balance is zeroed. Record this reading.

5. Move the riders until they read exactly 7.50 g *more* than the reading you obtained in step 4. Record this setting.

6. Obtain a quantity of sodium chloride (NaCl) on a piece of paper. Using your microspatula, add this substance to the filter paper on the balance pan until the pointer is balanced. (If you add too much, remove enough with your microspatula to make the pointer balance.) Discard the NaCl and filter paper as instructed by your teacher.

7. Place a dry 50-mL beaker on the balance pan. Move the riders until the pointer is balanced. Record this reading.

8. Move the riders until they read exactly 22.0 g more than the reading you obtained in step 7. Record this setting.

3 Measuring Mass (continued)

9. In a 100-mL graduated cylinder, obtain exactly 30.0 mL of cold tap water. *Slowly* and *carefully* pour water from the graduated cylinder into the beaker on the balance pan until the pointer is balanced. Avoid splashing water onto the pan. Note and record the volume of water remaining in the graduated cylinder. Discard the water and dry the beaker.

PART C DETERMINING MASS BY DIFFERENCE

10. Measure and record the mass of a watch glass.

11. Using the procedure described by your teacher, obtain 20–25 crystals of calcium chloride ($CaCl_2$) on a piece of paper. Carefully transfer the crystals to the watch glass.

12. Measure and record the combined mass of the watch glass and calcium chloride. Note and record the time you make this measurement.

13. Using your microspatula, spread the crystals out on the watch glass. Study the crystals and record your observations. Set the watch glass and crystals aside to be reexamined later.

14. Measure and record the mass of a piece of filter paper.

15. Obtain a quantity of sodium chloride (NaCl) on a piece of paper. Using your microspatula, place one heaping scoop of the NaCl on the filter paper. Measure and record the combined mass of the filter paper and NaCl.

16. Add a second heaping scoop of NaCl to the sample on the filter paper. Measure and record the combined mass of the filter paper and the two scoops of NaCl.

17. Add a third heaping scoop of NaCl to the sample on the filter paper. Measure and record the combined mass of the filter paper and the salt. Discard the salt and the filter paper.

18. Measure and record the mass of a 150-mL beaker.

19. In a 100-mL graduated cylinder, obtain exactly 30 mL of cold tap water. Carefully pour this water into the beaker. Measure and record the combined mass of the beaker and water.

20. Inflate a toy balloon and tie off the open end so that no gas can escape. Measure and record the mass of the inflated balloon.

21. Puncture the balloon and allow all the gas to escape. Measure and record the mass of the deflated balloon. Discard the balloon.

22. Reexamine the calcium chloride crystals on the watch glass that you set aside earlier. Record your observations.

23. Measure and record the combined mass of the watch glass and its contents. Note and record the time of this measurement. Discard the calcium chloride and clean and dry the watch glass.

Observations and Data

PART A

1. Mass of a penny   _____ g

2. Mass of a nickel   _____ g

3. Mass of a watch glass   _____ g

4. Mass of 150-mL beaker   _____ g

5. Mass of 100-mL graduated cylinder   _____ g

PART B

6. Mass of filter paper   _____ g

7. New setting (filter paper + 7.50 g)   _____ g

8. Mass of 50-mL beaker   _____ g

9. New setting (50-mL beaker + 22.0 g)   _____ g

10. Volume of water remaining in graduated cylinder   _____ mL

PART C

11. Mass of watch glass   _____ g

12. Mass of watch glass + $CaCl_2$ _____ g

13. Time of measurement 12   _____

14. Mass of filter paper   _____ g

15. Mass of filter paper + 1 scoop of NaCl   _____ g

16. Mass of filter paper + 2 scoops of NaCl   _____ g

17. Mass of filter paper + 3 scoops of NaCl   _____ g

18. Mass of 150-mL beaker   _____ g

19. Mass of 150-mL beaker + 30 mL of water   _____ g

20. Mass of inflated balloon   _____ g

21. Mass of deflated balloon   _____ g

22. Mass of watch glass + $CaCl_2$ (after sitting)   _____ g

23. Time of measurement 22   _____

3 Measuring Mass (continued)

Observations

Calcium chloride crystals

a. initial examination (step 12):

b. later examination (step 22):

Calculations

1. Calculate the volume of water added to the beaker in step 9.
(initial volume − volume remaining in graduated cylinder)   _____ mL

2. Calculate the mass of 1 mL of water.
(mass of water ÷ volume of water)   _____ g

3. Using the mass-by-difference technique, calculate the mass of:

    a. $CaCl_2$ crystals added to the watch glass
    (step 12 − step 11)   _____ g

    b. NaCl (1 scoop) (step 15 − step 14)   _____ g

    c. NaCl (2 scoops) (step 16 − step 14)   _____ g

    d. NaCl (3 scoops) (step 17 − step 14)   _____ g

    e. 30 mL of tap water (step 19 − step 18)   _____ g

    f. moisture absorbed by $CaCl_2$ crystals
    (step 22 − step 12)   _____ g

4. Calculate the difference in mass between the inflated balloon and the deflated balloon
(step 20 − step 21).   _____ g

5. Calculate how much time, in minutes, elapsed between the two measurements of the $CaCl_2$
(step 23 − step 13).   _____ min

Conclusions and Questions

1. In steps 15–17 of the procedure, you measured the combined masses of a piece of filter paper plus one, two, and three heaping scoops of NaCl, respectively.

    a. From Calculation 3(b), what was the mass of the *first* scoop of NaCl?

    b. From your data, calculate the masses of: the second scoop of NaCl (step 16 − step 15) and the third scoop of NaCl (step 17 − step 16).

    c. Compare the masses of each individual scoop of NaCl as determined in (a) and (b) above. Are the three values identical? If not, how do you account for the differences?

_____

_____

_____

_____

_____

_____

_____

_____

2. What measurements would you make to determine the *average* mass of a heaping microspatula of NaCl? How would you use these measurements to arrive at an average mass?

_____

_____

_____

_____

_____

_____

_____

3. The difference between the mass of the balloon when inflated and its mass after being punctured is not an accurate determination of the mass of the gas in the inflated balloon. Why is this?

_____

_____

_____

_____

_____

_____

_____

Name _____

3 Measuring Mass (continued)

4. Suppose you were asked to measure out 5 grams of calcium chloride. Briefly describe how you would make this measurement.

_____

_____

_____

_____

_____

_____

5. Suppose that you wanted to know the mass of a quantity of orange juice that was poured into a drinking glass. Describe how you would determine this mass.

_____

_____

_____

_____

_____

_____

6. A beaker contains a quantity of a liquid. You want to know the combined mass of the beaker and the liquid. Describe how you would go about making this determination.

_____

_____

7. Suppose you were asked to compare the mass of a nickel and a sample of NaCl crystals.
    a. Which method would you use to determine the mass of the nickel?
    b. Which method would you use to determine the mass of the NaCl crystals?
    c. Which of the two measurements is likely to be the more accurate one? Explain.

_____

_____

_____

_____

_____

_____

_____

_____

Uncertainty in Measurement   Lab 4

Text reference: **Chapter 3,** pp. 50–55

Pre-Lab Discussion

Laboratory measurements are never exact. The uncertainty of a measured quantity depends on the skill of the researcher and the limitations of the measuring instrument. These two factors determine the *accuracy* of a measurement. Accuracy reflects the nearness of a measurement to the actual or accepted value. When reporting experimental data, researchers record all digits they are certain of plus one digit they are uncertain of. These are known as *significant figures*. The uncertainty of the measurement too is indicated. This depends on the size of the smallest increment on the scale of the instrument.

When gathering data to solve a problem, skilled experimenters select instruments that will produce the desired level of accuracy. Thus, they must know the level of accuracy possible with calibrated instruments commonly found in laboratories. By studying some simple laboratory equipment, a better understanding of uncertainty in measurement can be achieved.

Purpose

Examine some calibrated measuring instruments, make some measurements, and record data. Report data using the correct number of significant figures and scientific notation. Indicate the uncertainty of the measurements.

Equipment

laboratory balance, four-beam
centimeter ruler
thermometer (0°–120°C)
graduated cylinder, 100-mL
calibrated pipets, burets, 10-mL

graduated cylinder, triple-beam
  balance, meter stick
safety goggles
lab apron or coat

Materials

a coin, such as a nickel
piece of paper, less than 10-cm square
water

Safety

Handle glassware with care, especially thermometers, pipets, and burets. They are fragile and easily broken. Always wear safety goggles and a lab apron or coat when working in the lab.

Procedure

Record all measurements in the data table. Report data to the correct number of significant figures and using scientific notation. Indicate the uncertainty of the measurements.

1. Using the four-beam balance, measure and record the mass of the coin.

2. Using the centimeter ruler, measure the length of one side of the piece of paper.

3. Using the thermometer, measure and record the temperature of the air in the laboratory.

4. Using the 100-mL graduated cylinder, measure and record the volume of a sample of water between 0 and 100 mL.

5. Make additional measurements, as time permits, using calibrated pipets, burets, a 10-mL graduated cylinder, a triple-beam balance, a meter stick, and other devices provided.

Observations and Data

DATA TABLE

Instrument	Measurement	Data	Uncertainty
four-beam balance	mass of coin		
centimeter ruler	paper edge		
0°–120°C thermometer	temperature of room air		
100-mL graduated cylinder	volume of water		

4 Uncertainty in Measurement (continued)

Conclusions and Questions

1. What is the difference between precision and accuracy? Is a precise measurement always accurate? Explain.

_____

_____

_____

_____

_____

_____

_____

_____

_____

_____

_____

_____

2. A square piece of paper has an edge measuring 7.06 cm (using a centimeter ruler). How many significant figures should appear in the calculated surface area ($A = S^2$)? Write the result correctly.

_____

_____

_____

_____

_____

_____

3. Why do liquid vitamins for babies come with a dropper pipet rather than a container marked with graduated lines, as on a graduated cylinder? Explain in terms of accuracy.

_____

_____

_____

_____

_____

_____

_____

Density Determination

Lab **5**

Text reference: **Chapter 4,** pp. 69–74

Pre-Lab Discussion

Chemistry is the study of matter, which usually is defined as anything that has mass and volume. You already have some experience determining mass in the laboratory. In this experiment, you will measure volumes of different materials, using direct and indirect methods. You also will use the relationship between the mass and volume of a substance to find its density.

Volumes of liquids are measured directly in a graduated cylinder. Liquid quantities dealt with in the laboratory usually are expressed in milliliters (mL), although larger quantities may be expressed in liters (L). Volumes of regularly shaped geometric solids can be calculated from direct measurements of their dimensions. For example, the volume of a rectangular solid is calculated by multiplying its length, width, and height ($V = l \times w \times h$). Volumes of solids usually are expressed in cubic centimeters (cm^3).

Many solids do not lend themselves to direct measurement of their dimensions. These include irregularly shaped objects, such as rocks, and regular solids that are too small to be measured with accuracy. Volumes of such solids can be measured by water displacement. If a solid is immersed in a liquid, such as water, the solid will push aside, or *displace*, a volume of water equal to its own volume. Thus, each milliliter of water displaced by a solid represents one cubic centimeter of solid volume.

Density is an important property of matter. By itself, or in conjunction with other properties, density can be used to identify substances. Density is defined as the quantity of matter in a given unit of volume. This relationship, expressed mathematically, is

$$\text{density} = \frac{\text{mass}}{\text{volume}} \qquad \text{or} \qquad D = \frac{m}{V}$$

You will be expected to use the measuring skills and techniques developed in earlier laboratory sessions and in the first part of this experiment to find the mass and volume of different substances. You will use these data to calculate the densities of these substances.

Purpose

Learn and practice techniques and calculations for determining volume and density of a substance.

Equipment

laboratory balance	scissors
centimeter ruler	thread
graduated cylinder, 10-mL	safety goggles
graduated cylinder, 100-mL	lab apron or coat
beaker, 50-mL	

Materials

distilled water
regularly shaped metal object
metal pellets

unknown liquids (liquid A, liquid B, ...)
2 irregularly shaped solids (rocks or
   metals)
section of glass rod (about 5 cm long)

Safety

Always wear safety goggles and a lab apron or coat when working in the lab. Handle glassware with care to avoid breakage and possible flying glass fragments.

Procedure

PART A   SOLIDS

1. Measure and record the dimensions (diameter and length) of the section of glass rod. (±0.05 cm)

2. Measure and record the mass of the section of glass rod. (±0.01 g)

3. Fill a 10-mL graduated cylinder with tap water to the 7.0-mL mark. (±0.2 mL)

4. Tie a piece of thread around the section of glass rod as shown. Lower the glass into the water in the cylinder until it is completely submerged. (See Figure 5-1.) Do not allow it to touch

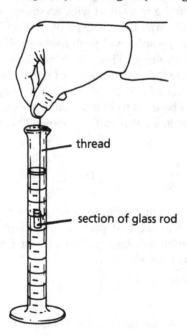

thread

section of glass rod

Figure 5-1

the sides or bottom of the cylinder. Read and record the new water level.

5. Repeat steps 2 to 4 with two different, irregularly shaped objects.

6. Obtain and describe a regularly shaped metal object. Measure and record its dimensions and its mass.

24

5 Density Determination (continued)

7. Add exactly 25.0 mL of tap water to a 100-mL graduated cylinder.

8. Immerse the metal object in the water and record the new water level.

9. Remove the metal object and refill the graduated cylinder to the 25-mL mark with tap water.

10. Measure and record the mass of a 50-mL beaker.

11. Add 50 metal pellets to the beaker. Measure and record the combined mass of the beaker and pellets.

12. Carefully pour the pellets into the water in the graduated cylinder. Record the new water level. Remove the pellets and set them aside to dry.

PART B LIQUIDS AT ROOM TEMPERATURE

13. Measure and record the mass of a clean, dry 10-mL graduated cylinder.

14. Add exactly 10.0 mL of distilled water to the cylinder. Measure and record the combined mass of the cylinder and water. Dispose of the water. Clean and dry the cylinder.

15. Repeat steps 13 and 14 for two unknown liquids.

Observations and Data

PART A

1. Dimensions

a. glass rod: diameter_____ length _____

b. regularly shaped metal object: shape _____

dimensions _____

2. Mass and water displacement

Sample	Mass	Original water level	Final water level
a. glass rod	_____ g	_____ mL	_____ mL
b. 1st irregular solid	_____	_____	_____
c. 2nd irregular solid	_____	_____	_____
d. regular metal object	_____	_____	_____
e. beaker	_____		
f. beaker + pellets	_____		
g. metal pellets		_____	_____

PART B

1. Mass of 10-mL graduated cylinder _____ g

2.   Sample   Mass (cylinder + 10-mL sample)

a. distilled water   _____ g

b. unknown liquid _____   _____ g

c. unknown liquid _____   _____ g

Calculations

1. a. From the measured diameter and length of the glass rod, calculate its volume.   _____ cm^3

b. From the measured dimensions of the regularly shaped metal object, calculate its volume.   _____ cm^3

2. Determine the volumes of the following solid objects by calculating how much water they displace (final water level − original water level).

a. glass rod   _____ cm^3

b. 1st irregularly shaped solid   _____ cm^3

c. 2nd irregularly shaped solid   _____ cm^3

d. regularly shaped metal object   _____ cm^3

e. metal pellets   _____ cm^3

3. Calculate the mass of the metal pellets.   _____ g

5 Density Determination (continued)

4. Calculate the densities of the section of glass rod and the regularly shaped metal object, using their measured masses and the volumes calculated from their dimensions. (Remember: $D = m/V$)

Sample	Mass (g)	Volume (cm³)	Density (g/cm³)
a. glass rod	_____	_____	_____
b. metal object	_____	_____	_____

5. Using their measured masses and the volumes calculated from their water displacements, calculate the densities of the solid samples.

Sample	Mass	Volume	Density
a. glass rod	_____	_____	_____
b. 1st irregularly shaped solid	_____	_____	_____
c. 2nd irregularly shaped solid	_____	_____	_____
d. regularly shaped metal object	_____	_____	_____
e. metal pellets	_____	_____	_____

6. Using mass-by-difference, calculate the masses of the liquids.

Sample	Mass (cylinder + sample)	− Mass (cylinder)	= Mass (sample)
a. distilled water	_____	_____	_____
b. unknown liquid _____	_____	_____	_____
c. unknown liquid _____	_____	_____	_____

7. Using the calculated masses and the measured volumes, calculate the densities of the liquids.

Sample	Mass (g)	Volume (mL)	Density (g/mL)
a. distilled water	_____	_____	_____
b. unknown liquid _____	_____	_____	_____
c. unknown liquid _____	_____	_____	_____

Conclusions and Questions

1. Compare the value of the volume of the glass rod calculated from its dimensions with that attained by measuring its water displacement.

Make the same comparison for the values attained by these two methods for the volume of the regularly shaped metal object.

_____

_____

_____

_____

_____

_____

2. Of the two methods used to determine the volume of a solid, which is more accurate? Explain your answer.

_____

_____

_____

_____

3. From your observations and data, are the metal object and the metal pellets composed of the same metal? Give evidence to support your answer.

_____

_____

_____

_____

4. The density of glass ranges from 2.4 to 2.8 g/cm^3. That of distilled water at 20°C is approximately 1.0 g/mL. Compare your experimental results with these values. What errors might account for differences between your results and these accepted values?

_____

_____

_____

_____

5. Why is it necessary to indicate temperature when giving density values of liquids?

_____

_____

_____

_____

_____

_____

5 Density Determination (continued)

6. The table below lists the densities for several different substances. (Liquids are at 20°C.) Using this table and your data, try to identify the following:

    a. composition of the regularly shaped metal object;

    b. composition of the metal pellets;

    c. unknown liquid _____ ;

    d. unknown liquid _____ .

Sample	Density
lead	11.34 g/cm^3
copper	8.93 g/cm^3
aluminum	2.70 g/cm^3
ethanol	0.79 g/mL
vegetable oil	0.92 g/mL
ethylene glycol	1.11 g/mL
glycerine	1.25 g/mL

a. _____

b. _____

c. _____

d. _____

Physical and Chemical Change   Lab 6

Text reference: **Chapter 4,** pp. 74–78

Pre-Lab Discussion

Chemistry is the study of matter and the changes it undergoes. These changes can be broken down into two classes—physical changes and chemical changes. In a physical change, one or more physical properties of a substance are altered. Examples of such physical properties include size, shape, color, and physical phase. Grinding, melting, dissolving, and evaporating all are physical changes. No new substance or substances are formed as a result of a physical change.

A chemical change results in the formation of one or more "new" substances. These new substances differ in chemical properties and composition from the original substance. The rusting of iron and the burning of paper are two examples of chemical change.

This experiment will help you to understand the difference between physical and chemical change and to recognize each type of change when it occurs.

Purpose

Recognize and distinquish between chemical and physical changes.

Equipment

lab balance
lab burner
5 test tubes (18×150-mm)
test tube rack
test tube holder
watch glass
glass square

microspatula
dropper pipet
mortar and pestle
magnet
insulating pad
safety goggles
lab apron or coat

Materials

copper sulfate pentahydrate
    ($CuSO_4 \cdot 5H_2O$)
sodium chloride (NaCl)
hydrochloric acid (6 M HCl)
silver nitrate (0.1 M $AgNO_3$)
sulfur (S), powdered

iron filings (Fe)
magnesium ribbon (Mg)
paper (5 cm × 10 cm)
birthday candle
matches

Safety

Note the caution alert symbols here and beside certain steps in the "Procedure." Refer to page xi to review the precautions associated with each symbol.

When heating a substance in a test tube, be sure the open end of the tube points *away from* yourself and others.

Handle all acids with *extra caution*. Always wear safety goggles when handling acids. Report all acid spills to your teacher, and flush with cold water and a dilute solution of sodium bicarbonate ($NaHCO_3$).

Give heated glass ample time to cool before handling it. *Glass retains heat.* Tie back long hair and secure loose clothing before working with an open flame. Wear safety goggles and a lab apron or coat at all times when working in the lab.

Procedure

Note and record all observations in your data table.

1. Place a small amount of wax from a birthday candle into a test tube. Heat gently over a burner flame until the wax melts completely; then allow the sample to cool. Next, light the candle, secure it to a glass square, and allow it to burn until it extinguishes itself. Proceed with the rest of the experiment while the candle burns.

2. Tear a piece of paper (about 5 cm × 10 cm) into small pieces. Set a watch glass on an insulating square and place the pieces of paper on the glass. Ignite the paper with a match and allow to burn.

3. Add a microspatula of NaCl (sodium chloride) to a small quantity of water (about 5 mL) in a test tube. Shake the contents of the tube. Next, use a dropper to add 10 drops of 0.1 M $AgNO_3$ (silver nitrate) to the NaCl-water mixture.

4. Obtain a piece of magnesium ribbon about 5 cm long. Tear the ribbon into 1-cm pieces. Place two of the pieces into a test tube and add a few drops of 6 M HCl (hydrochloric acid). **CAUTION:** *Use extreme care in handling this acid. It will cause severe burns if allowed to come in contact with the skin.* Touch the bottom of the test tube with your fingertip.

5. Use a mortar and pestle to grind several crystals of $CuSO_4 \cdot 5H_2O$ into a uniform powder. Place one microspatula of the powder into a test tube. Heat gently over a burner flame for 5 minutes. Allow the sample to cool and then add a few drops of water.

6. Using a lab balance, measure out the following samples: 0.50 g of iron filings and 0.50 g of powdered sulfur. Test each sample with a magnet. Mix the two samples thoroughly in a test tube. Run the magnet along the bottom and sides of the test tube (Figure 6-1).

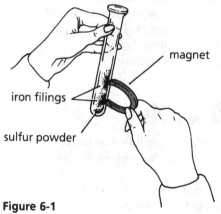

magnet

iron filings

sulfur powder

Figure 6-1

Name _____

6 Physical and Chemical Change (continued)

7. Heat the iron-sulfur mixture in a burner flame for several minutes until the mixture "glows." Allow the sample to cool and examine it by probing it with a microspatula. Run the magnet along the test tube again.

Observations and Data

Record all qualitative observations for each step of the procedure.

_____
_____
_____
_____
_____
_____
_____
_____
_____
_____
_____
_____
_____
_____
_____
_____
_____
_____
_____
_____
_____
_____
_____
_____
_____
_____
_____
_____

Conclusions and Questions

1. Indicate whether the following changes are physical or chemical. Support your conclusions.

- **a.** melting candle wax
- **b.** burning a candle
- **c.** tearing paper
- **d.** burning paper
- **e.** dissolving NaCl
- **f.** mixing NaCl and $AgNo_3$
- **g.** tearing Mg ribbon
- **h.** adding HCl to Mg
- **i.** grinding $CuSO_4 \cdot 5H_2O$
- **j.** heating $CuSO_4 \cdot 5H_2O$
- **k.** mixing Fe and S
- **l.** heating a mixture of Fe and S

_____

_____

_____

_____

_____

_____

_____

_____

_____

_____

_____

_____

_____

_____

_____

_____

_____

_____

_____

_____

_____

_____

_____

_____

_____

_____

6 Physical and Chemical Change (continued)

2. Name two possible indications that a chemical change has taken place. Give examples from this experiment.

_____
_____
_____
_____

3. Chemical change involves the formation of "new" substances. Briefly describe the "new" substances that formed as a result of each chemical change in this experiment.

_____
_____
_____
_____
_____
_____
_____
_____
_____
_____

4. The following changes do not always indicate chemical change. Give examples in which they might be the result of physical change.
  a. change of color
  b. apparent loss of mass
  c. apparent disappearance of a substance

_____
_____
_____
_____
_____
_____
_____
_____

5. How can substances in a mixture be separated? How can substances in a compound be separated? Use an example from this experiment in your explanation.

_____

_____

_____

_____

_____

_____

_____

_____

_____

Calorimetry: Heat of Fusion of Ice

Lab 7

Text reference: **Chapter 5**, pp. 95–100

Pre-Lab Discussion

When a chemical or physical change takes place, heat is either given off or absorbed. That is, the change is either exothermic or endothermic. It is important for chemists to be able to measure this heat. Measurements of this sort are made in a device called a calorimeter. The technique used in making these measurements is called calorimetry.

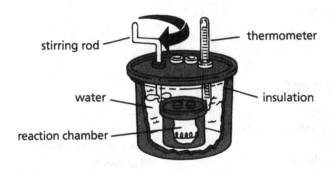

stirring rod — thermometer

water — insulation

reaction chamber —

Figure 7-1

In simplest terms, a calorimeter is an insulated container made up of two chambers (see Figure 7-1). The outer chamber contains a known mass of water. In the inner chamber, the experimenter places the materials that are to lose or gain heat while undergoing a physical or chemical change. The basic principle on which the calorimeter works is that when two bodies at different temperatures are in contact with one another, heat will flow from the warmer body to the colder body. Thus, the heat lost by one body will be gained by the other. This exchange of heat will continue until the two bodies are at the same temperature. In a calorimeter, heat is exchanged between the water and the materials undergoing change. The experimenter makes a direct measurement of the temperature change of the water. From this information, the heat gained (or lost) by the water can be calculated. The experimenter then uses these data to determine the heat lost (or gained) by the materials undergoing change.

Unlike most calorimeters, the simple Styrofoam-cup calorimeter used in this experiment will have only one chamber. The ice will be placed directly into a measured amount of water. The heat required to melt the ice will be supplied by the water. By measuring the temperature change (ΔT) of the water, you can calculate the quantity of heat exchanged between the water and the ice. Using these experimental data, you will calculate the heat of fusion of ice.

The following relationships will be used in this experiment:

a.
$$\begin{pmatrix} \text{heat lost (or gained)} \\ \text{by the water in} \\ \text{the calorimeter} \end{pmatrix} = \begin{pmatrix} \text{original mass} \\ \text{of water in} \\ \text{the calorimeter} \end{pmatrix} \times \begin{pmatrix} \text{change in} \\ \text{temperature} \\ \text{of the water} \end{pmatrix} \times \begin{pmatrix} \text{specific heat} \\ \text{capacity} \\ \text{of water} \end{pmatrix}$$

In symbols, this word formula becomes:

$$\Delta Q = m \times \Delta T \times c$$

b. heat given off by the water = heat absorbed by the ice

c. $\dfrac{\text{heat needed to melt the ice}}{\text{mass of the melted ice}}$ = heat of fusion of ice

The *specific heat capacity* of a substance is the quantity of heat energy needed to raise the temperature of 1 gram of the substance by 1°Celsius. The specific heat capacity of water is 4.2 joules per gram per degree Celsius (4.2 J/g°C).

Purpose

Using a simple calorimeter, find the heat of fusion of ice.

Equipment

beaker, 250-mL
graduated cylinder, 100-mL
lab burner
cup, Styrofoam
thermometer
ring stand

iron ring
wire gauze
tongs or perforated spoon
safety goggles
lab apron or coat

Materials

water
ice cubes

Safety

Note the safety alert symbols here and beside certain steps in the "Procedure." Refer to page xi to review the precautions associated with each symbol.

Handle the thermometer with care. It is fragile and easily broken.

Tie back long hair and secure loose clothing before working with an open flame. Always wear safety goggles and a lab apron or coat when working in the lab.

Procedure

1. In a 250-mL beaker, heat about 125 mL of water to a temperature of 50°C.

2. Measure exactly 100 mL of this heated water in a graduated cylinder and pour it into a Styrofoam cup. Record this volume of water, V_1.

3. Measure accurately and record the temperature of the water, T_1. Immediately add 2–3 ice cubes. See Figure 7-2.

7 Calorimetry: Heat of Fusion of Ice (continued)

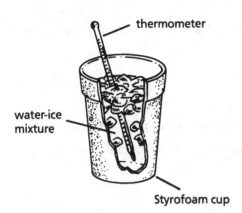

thermometer

water-ice mixture

Styrofoam cup

Figure 7-2

4. Stir the ice-water mixture carefully with the thermometer. **CAUTION:** *Thermometers break easily.* The cup should contain ice at all times. Therefore, if the last of the ice appears about to melt, add another ice cube. Monitor the temperature of the ice-water mixture as you stir. Continue stirring (and adding ice, if necessary) until the temperature evens off (no longer drops). Record this final temperature, T_2.

5. Carefully remove the unmelted ice. Allow any water removed to drain back into the cup. Measure and record the volume of water in the cup, V_2.

Observations and Data

$V_1 = $ _____ $T_1 = $ _____

$V_2 = $ _____ $T_2 = $ _____

Calculations

1. Using the known density of water, find the mass (m_1) of the original volume of water (V_1).

2. Find the volume of water resulting from the melted ice. ($V = V_2 - V_1$)

3. Find the mass (m_2) of this volume of water.

4. Find the change in temperature of the water. ($\Delta T = T_1 - T_2$)

5. Find the heat lost by the original mass of water. $(\Delta Q = m_1 \times \Delta T \times c)$

6. Find the heat of fusion of ice. $\left(\dfrac{\Delta Q}{m_2} = \text{heat of fusion of ice} \right)$

7. Find your percent error.
(The true value for the heat of fusion of ice is 336 J/g.)

$$\text{percent error} = \frac{(\text{true value} - \text{experimental value})}{\text{true value}} \times 100$$

Conclusions and Questions

1. List possible sources of error in this experiment. How might the use of a calorimeter such as the one shown in Figure 7-1 reduce some of these errors?

_____

_____

_____

_____

_____

_____

_____

2. One source of error is the flow of heat between the water in the cup and the surroundings. Explain how this error is reduced by starting with water at about 50°C.

_____

_____

_____

_____

_____

_____

_____

_____

_____

_____

_____

7 Calorimetry: Heat of Fusion of Ice (continued)

3. In what way does calorimetry make use of the law of conservation of energy?

_____
_____
_____
_____
_____
_____
_____

4. Define the following terms: **a.** exothermic; **b.** endothermic; **c.** heat of fusion; **d.** specific heat capacity.

_____
_____
_____
_____
_____
_____
_____
_____
_____
_____
_____
_____

5. Is the process of melting exothermic or endothermic? Give evidence to support your answer.

_____
_____
_____
_____

6. What is the difference between heat and temperature?

_____
_____
_____
_____

7. Try this problem in calorimetry: A solid substance with a mass of 200 g is at its melting point temperature in a calorimeter. While the substance changes from a solid to a liquid at the same temperature, the 400-gram mass of water in the calorimeter goes from an initial temperature of 80°C to a final temperature of 30°C.

    a. How much heat did the water lose while the substance melted?

    b. What is the heat of fusion of the substance that melted?

Calorimetry: Heat of Crystallization of Wax

Lab 8

Text reference: **Chapter 5,** pp. 95–99

Pre-Lab Discussion

The process of crystallization (solidification) is the exact opposite of the process of fusion (melting). When a substance undergoes a phase change from liquid to solid, heat is released by the substance. Crystallization, then, is an exothermic process. The principles used to determine the heat of fusion of a substance (Lab 7) can be applied to find the heat of crystallization of a substance.

When the process of crystallization takes place in a calorimeter, the heat released by the process is absorbed by the water in the calorimeter. As a result, the temperature of the water increases. Using mathematical relationships similar to those in Lab 7, the temperature change of the water can be used to calculate the heat of crystallization of the substance undergoing the phase change.

Purpose

Using a simple calorimeter, find the heat of crystallization of wax.

Equipment

test tube, 25×200-mm	iron ring
beaker, 250-mL	test tube holder
lab burner	wire gauze
graduated cylinder, 100-mL	cup, Styrofoam
thermometer	safety goggles
ring stand	lab apron or coat

Materials

wax sample, 10.00 g   water

Safety

Note the safety alert symbols here and beside certain steps in the "Procedure." Refer to page xi to review the precautions associated with each symbol.

Tie back long hair and secure loose clothing before working with an open flame. Handle the thermometer with care. It is fragile and easily broken. Always wear safety goggles and a lab apron or coat when working in the lab.

Procedure

1. In a 250-mL beaker, heat about 200 mL of water to boiling using the apparatus setup shown in Figure 8-1.

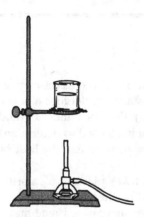

Figure 8-1

2. Obtain a 25×200-mm test tube containing the 10.00-g sample of wax. Place the test tube into the beaker of boiling water and rotate the tube until the wax is completely melted.

3. Measure 100 mL (±0.5 mL) of cold tap water into a graduated cylinder and pour it into a Styrofoam cup.

4. Using a test tube holder, remove the tube and wax sample from the beaker. Hold the sample up to the light and watch carefully for the first sign of cloudiness. This indicates the beginning of crystallization.

5. At the instant crystallization starts, measure and record the temperature (T_1) of the water in the Styrofoam-cup calorimeter and immediately place the test tube into the calorimeter.

6. Rotate the test tube while the wax solidifies, keeping a constant watch on the temperature of the water. (See Figure 8-2.) Record the maximum temperature (T_2) reached by the water.

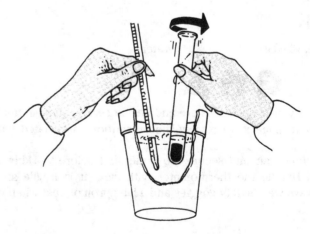

Figure 8-2

8 Calorimetry: Heat of Crystallization of Wax (continued)

Observations and Data

Mass of water (m_1) in the calorimeter: _____ g

Mass of wax sample (m_2):   _____ g

$T_1 =$ _____ $T_2 =$ _____

Specific heat of water (c) = 4.2 J/g-°C

Calculations

1. Find the change in the temperature of the water. ($\Delta T = T_2 - T_1$)

2. Find the heat gained by the water. ($\Delta Q = m_1 \times \Delta T \times c$)

3. Find the heat of crystallization of the wax. $\left(\dfrac{\Delta Q}{m_2} \right)$

Conclusions and Questions

1. Define the term heat of crystallization. What units could be used to express this property?

_____

_____

_____

_____

_____

2. How does the heat of fusion of a substance compare with the heat of crystallization of the same substance?

_____

_____

_____

_____

_____

3. Explain why this experiment could not be conducted using a mixture.

_____

_____

_____

_____

_____

Conservation of Mass

Lab 9

Text reference: **Chapter 6,** pp. 113–118

Pre-Lab Discussion

Matter cannot be created or destroyed by a chemical change. This very important principle is known as the law of conservation of mass. This law applies to ordinary chemical reactions (as opposed to nuclear reactions, in which matter can be changed to energy). During a chemical change (reaction), the atoms of one or more substances (reactants) simply undergo some "rearrangements." The result of these rearrangements is the formation of new, different substances (products). All of the original atoms are still present. It is because of the law of conservation of mass that we are able to write balanced chemical equations. Such equations make it possible to predict the masses of reactants and products that will be involved in a chemical reaction.

In this experiment, aqueous solutions of three different compounds will be used to produce two separate and distinct chemical reactions. The fact that change occurs during each reaction will be readily observable. Balanced chemical equations for the two reactions are:

$$Na_2CO_3(aq) + CaCl_2(aq) \rightarrow 2NaCl(aq) + CaCO_3(s) \qquad \textbf{(Eq. 1)}$$

$$CaCO_3(s) + H_2SO_4(aq) \rightarrow CaSO_4(s) + H_2O + CO_2(g) \qquad \textbf{(Eq. 2)}$$

The combined masses of the three solutions (and their containers) will be measured before and after each reaction has occurred.

This experiment should give you a better understanding of the law of conservation of mass and its importance in chemistry.

Purpose

Determine experimentally whether mass is conserved in a particular set of chemical reactions.

Equipment

laboratory balance
Erlenmeyer flask, 125-mL
rubber stopper (for flask)
graduated cylinder, 10-mL
test tubes, 13×100-mm (2)

corks (to fit test tubes) (2)
labels
safety goggles
lab apron or coat

Materials

1 M aqueous solutions of:
Na_2CO_3 $CaCl_2$ H_2SO_4

Safety

Note the caution alert symbols here and beside certain steps in the "Procedure." Refer to page xi to review the special precautions associated with each symbol.

Handle sulfuric acid with *extra caution*. Always wear safety goggles when handling acids. Report all acid spills to your teacher, and flush with cold water and a dilute solution of sodium bicarbonate ($NaHCO_3$).

Wear a lab apron or coat and safety goggles at all times when working in the lab.

Procedure

1. In a graduated cylinder, measure exactly 10.0 mL of sodium carbonate (Na_2CO_3) solution. Pour into a clean, *dry* 125-mL Erlenmeyer flask. Stopper the flask. Rinse and dry the graduated cylinder.

2. Measure exactly 3.0 mL of 1 *M* calcium chloride ($CaCl_2$) solution and pour into a clean, dry test tube. Cork and label the tube. Rinse and dry the graduated cylinder.

 3. Repeat step 2 with 3.0 mL of 1 *M* sulfuric acid (H_2SO_4) solution. **CAUTION:** *Handle this acid with care.*

4. Place the stoppered flask and the corked test tubes together on the pan of the laboratory balance. TILT THE TEST TUBES to prevent liquids from touching the corks (Figure 9-1). Measure the combined mass of these containers, stoppers, and solutions. This will be mass a in your data table.

5. Remove the flask and the test tube containing the $CaCl_2$ solution from the balance pan. Pour the $CaCl_2$ solution into the Na_2CO_3 solution in the flask. Swirl the flask to thoroughly mix the two solutions. Record your observations.

6. Replace the stopper and cork in their proper containers. Once again, measure the combined mass of the three containers, stoppers, and contents (mass b in data table).

 7. Remove the flask and the test tube containing H_2SO_4 from the balance. *Carefully* pour the H_2SO_4 solution into the flask. WITH THE STOPPER OFF, swirl the flask until all bubbling stops. Record your observations. Allow the flask to cool to room temperature.

8. Replace the stopper and cork. Remeasure the mass of the three containers, stoppers, and contents (mass c in data table).

Figure 9-1

9 Conservation of Mass (continued)

Observations and Data

Qualitative observations

    Step 5:

_____

_____

_____

_____

    Step 7:

_____

_____

_____

_____

_____

Quantitative data

    Mass a (before mixing)   _____ g

    Mass b (after mixing Na_2CO_3 and $CaCl_2$)   _____ g

    Mass c (after mixing H_2SO_4 with contents from
           step 5)   _____ g

Conclusions and Questions

1. What indications that a chemical reaction was taking place did you observe in step 5? In step 7?

_____

_____

_____

_____

2. Why were you instructed to leave the flask unstoppered after the H_2SO_4 solution was added? What might have happened if this were not done?

_____

_____

_____

_____

_____

_____

3. Compare masses *a*, *b*, and *c*. Account for any differences.

_____

_____

_____

_____

4. In your opinion, does this experiment verify the law of conservation of mass? How might the experiment be improved to bring its results more in line with that law?

_____

_____

_____

_____

_____

_____

5. Discuss how the law of conservation of mass relates to the balancing of chemical equations.

_____

_____

_____

_____

_____

6. When you burn a log in the fireplace, the resulting ashes have a mass less than that of the original log. Account for the difference in mass.

_____

_____

_____

_____

Emission Spectra and Energy Levels

Lab 10

Text reference: **Chapter 6,** pp. 127–129

Pre-Lab Discussion

One convenient method of exciting the atoms of an element is to pass an electric current through a sample of the element in the vapor (gaseous) phase. This is the principle behind the spectrum tubes you will use in this investigation (see Figure 10-1). A spectrum tube contains a small sample of an element in the gaseous phase. An electric discharge through the tube will cause the vapor to glow brightly. The glow is produced when excited electrons emit radiant energy as they return to their original levels.

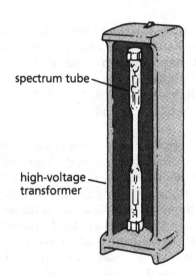

spectrum tube

high-voltage transformer

Figure 10-1

When visible radiant energy from a spectrum tube is passed through a diffraction grating, an emission spectrum (or bright-line spectrum) is produced. Each element has its own unique emission spectrum by which it can be identified. Such a spectrum consists of a series of bright lines of definite wavelength. Each wavelength can be mathematically related to a definite quantity of energy produced by the movement of an electron from one discrete energy level to another. Thus, emission spectra are experimental proof that electrons exist at definite, distinctive energy levels in an atom.

In this experiment, you will study the emission spectra of two elements: hydrogen and mercury. You will calculate the wavelengths of some of the spectral lines of these elements and compare your experimental values with known wavelengths of hydrogen and mercury spectra.

Purpose

Determine the wavelengths associated with specific spectral lines of hydrogen and mercury.

Equipment

spectrum tubes, hydrogen and
  mercury
transformer, high-voltage
diffraction grating
cardboard screen (with vertical slit)
pencils, colored (red, blue, green, violet)

meter stick supports (2)
meter sticks (2)
screen supports (2)
safety goggles
lab apron or coat

Safety

Note the caution alert symbols here and beside certain steps in the "Procedure." Refer to page xi to review the special precautions associated with each symbol.

Handle the high-voltage transformer with care. Be sure it is turned off and disconnected when you change the spectrum tubes. Always wear safety goggles and a lab coat or apron when working in the lab. Take care when handling the spectrum tubes. They are easily broken.

Procedure

1. Set up the apparatus as shown in Figure 10-2. The cardboard screen should be placed on the 50-cm mark of one meter stick. The transformer (with the hydrogen spectrum tube in place) should be placed directly behind the screen so that the glow from the tube is clearly visible through the slit. The diffraction grating should be placed on the second meter stick 100 cm from the tube.

2. One lab partner will view the emission spectrum of hydrogen by looking through the diffraction grating at the slit in the cardboard screen. The other partner will stand behind the transformer and move a pencil slowly along the meter stick. The student viewing the spectrum should indicate when the pencil is at the point where the image of the spectral line closest to the spectrum tube appears to be. Measure the distance, in centimeters, between the tube and the image of the spectral line. Record this distance (x) in your data table.

3. Repeat step 2 for two more spectral lines of hydrogen.

4. *Disconnect the transformer. Carefully* remove the hydrogen spectrum tube from the transformer and insert the mercury spectrum tube. **CAUTION:** *Handle the spectrum tubes with care. They are easily broken.* Reconnect the transformer.

5. Following the procedure outlined in step 2, locate and measure two spectral lines of mercury.

6. Disconnect the transformer. Return the transformer and spectrum tubes to your teacher.

7. Using colored pencils, make qualitative sketches of the spectra of hydrogen and mercury in the space provided under "Observations and Data."

10 Emission Spectra and Energy Levels (continued)

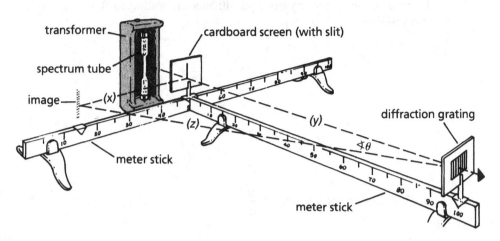

Figure 10-2

Observations and Data

Qualitative drawings of spectra:

hydrogen   *mercury*

DATA TABLE

Element	Color of Line	x (cm)	y (cm)
hydrogen	red		100
	blue-green		100
	blue		100
	violet		100
mercury	green		100
	violet		100

Calculations

Calculate the following and fill in the table on page 55:

1. Find the distance (z) from the diffraction grating to the image of the spectral line: $z = \sqrt{x^2 + y^2}$

2. Find the sine of $\angle\,\theta$: $\sin\theta = \dfrac{x}{z}$

3. Find the wavelength (λ) in cm: $\lambda = d \times \sin\theta$, where $d = 1.9 \times 10^{-4}$ cm.

Name _____

10 Emission Spectra and Energy Levels (continued)

				Wavelength (λ)
Element	Color of Line	z	sin θ	cm
hydrogen	red		_____	
	blue-green			
	blue			
	violet			
mercury	green			
	violet			

Conclusions and Questions

1. Compare your experimental results with the known wavelengths listed:

hydrogen

red 0.6563×10^{-4} cm
blue-green 0.4861×10^{-4} cm
blue 0.4342×10^{-4} cm
violet 0.4359×10^{-4} cm

mercury

green 0.5460×10^{-4} cm
violet 0.4359×10^{-4} cm

_____

_____

_____

_____

_____

_____

_____

_____

_____

2. How might emission spectra be used in studying stars?

_____

_____

_____

_____

_____

_____

3. Relate spectral lines to energy levels in an atom and to the term quanta.

_____

_____

_____

_____

_____

_____

_____

_____

4. Look up and discuss the relationship between the wavelength of a spectral line and the quantity of energy (E) it represents.

_____

_____

_____

_____

_____

_____

_____

_____

_____

Composition of Hydrates

Lab 11

Pre-Lab Discussion

Hydrates are ionic compounds (salts) that have a definite amount of water (water of hydration) as part of their structure. The water is chemically combined with the salt in a definite ratio. Ratios vary in different hydrates but are specific for any given hydrate.

The formula of a hydrate is represented in a special manner. The hydrate of copper sulfate in this experiment has the formula $CuSO_4 \cdot xH_2O$. The unit formula for the salt appears first, and the water formula is last. The raised dot means that the water is loosely bonded to the salt. The coefficient x stands for the number of molecules of water bonded to one unit of salt. This special formula, like all other formulas, illustrates the law of definite composition.

When hydrates are heated, the "water of hydration" is released as vapor. The remaining solid is known as the *anhydrous* salt. The general reaction for heating a hydrate is:

$$\text{hydrate} \xrightarrow{\Delta} \text{anhydrous salt} + \text{water}$$

The percent of water in a hydrate can be found experimentally by accurately determining the mass of the hydrate and the mass of the anhydrous salt. The difference in mass is due to the water lost by the hydrate. The percentage of water in the original hydrate can easily be calculated:

$$\text{percent } H_2O = \frac{\text{mass } H_2O}{\text{mass hydrate}} \times 100$$

In this experiment, as was mentioned, a hydrate of copper sulfate will be studied ($CuSO_4 \cdot xH_2O$). The change from hydrate to anhydrous salt is accompanied by a change in color:

$$\underset{\text{blue}}{CuSO_4 \cdot xH_2O} \xrightarrow{\Delta} \underset{\text{white}}{CuSO_4} + xH_2O$$

This investigation should aid in the understanding of the formulas and composition of hydrates and the law of definite composition.

Purpose

Determine the percentage of water in a hydrate.

Equipment

evaporating dish, porcelain	iron ring
crucible tongs	wire gauze
microspatula	laboratory burner
laboratory balance	safety goggles
ring stand	lab apron or coat

Materials

copper sulfate hydrate, $CuSO_4 \cdot xH_2O$

Safety

Do not touch a hot evaporating dish with your hands. Tie back long hair and secure loose clothing when working around an open flame. Note the caution alert symbols here and beside certain steps in the "Procedure." Refer to page xi to review the special precautions associated with each symbol.

Be sure to wear a lab apron or coat and safety goggles when working in the lab.

Procedure

1. Prepare the setup shown in Figure 11-1.

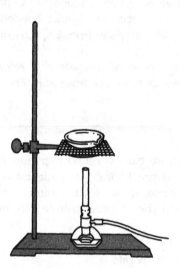

Figure 11-1

2. Heat the dish with the hottest part of the flame for 3 minutes.

3. Using crucible tongs, remove the evaporating dish from the apparatus. Place it on an insulated pad and allow it to cool for several minutes.

4. Find the mass of the evaporating dish to ± 0.01 g. Record the mass in the Observations and Data section.

5. With the evaporating dish on the balance, measure into it exactly 2.00 g of copper sulfate hydrate. Record the data below.

6. Place the evaporating dish + hydrate on the wire gauze. *Gently* heat the dish by moving the burner back and forth around the base. Increase the heat gradually. Avoid any popping and spattering.

7. Heat strongly for 5 minutes or until the blue color has disappeared. During heating, a microspatula may be used to "spread" the solid and break up any "caked" portions of the hydrate. Be careful not to pick up any of the solid on the microspatula. If the edges of the solid appear to be turning brown, remove the heat momentarily and resume heating at a gentler rate.

11 Composition of Hydrates (continued)

8. Allow the evaporating dish to cool for about a minute. *Immediately* find the mass of the dish + anhydrous salt, and record the data below.

Observations and Data

a. Mass of evaporating dish _____ g

b. Mass of evaporating dish + hydrate _____ g

c. Mass of evaporating dish + anhydrous salt _____ g

Calculations

1. Find the mass of the hydrate used (b − a).

2. Find the mass of the water lost (b − c).

3. Find the percentage of water in the hydrate:

$$\text{percent } H_2O = \frac{\text{mass water}}{\text{mass hydrate}} \times 100$$

Conclusions and Questions

1. The true value for the percentage of water in this hydrate is 36.0%. What is your experimental error?

2. Why must you allow the evaporating dish to cool before measuring its mass?

_____

_____

_____

_____

_____

3. Why must you measure the mass of the anhydrous salt immediately upon cooling?

_____

_____

4. Explain how your class's results in this experiment support the law of definite composition.

_____

_____

_____

_____

5. Given the true mole masses of $CuSO_4$ (160 g) and H_2O (18 g), how could you find the exact formula of the hydrate from your experimental data? That is, how could you find the value of x in the formula $CuSO_4 \cdot xH_2O$?

_____

_____

_____

_____

_____

_____

_____

_____

Determining the Gram Atomic Mass of an Element

Lab 12

Text reference: **Chapter 8,** pp. 178–179

Pre-Lab Discussion

The atomic mass (or atomic weight) of an element is the *average* value of the masses of the isotopes in a natural sample of that element. Atomic masses of all the elements are based on the mass of an atom of carbon-12, which has been assigned the value of 12 atomic mass units. An atomic mass unit (represented by the symbol u) is defined as 1/12 the mass of a carbon-12 atom.

In their work, chemists do not deal with individual atoms or molecules. Rather, they deal with relatively large numbers of atoms and molecules. To make their calculations easier, chemists often use units of measure that are made up of large numbers of atoms or molecules. One such quantity is called the **gram atomic mass**, or **gram-atom**. A gram-atom is the mass in grams of 1 mole of atoms. A gram-atom of an element is, therefore, the mass of 6.02×10^{23} atoms of that element. The mass in grams of 1 gram-atom of an element is numerically equal to the atomic mass of that element. For example, 1 gram-atom of carbon-12 has a mass of 12 grams.

There are several methods for determining the gram atomic mass of an element. In this experiment, the gram atomic mass of silver will be calculated using a compound (silver oxide) of known composition (Ag_2O).

Purpose

From measurements of a binary compound of known composition, determine the gram atomic mass of one of the elements in the compound when the atomic mass of the other element is known.

Equipment

crucible and cover   microspatula
ring stand   burner
iron ring   balance
clay triangle   safety goggles
crucible tongs   lab apron or coat

Materials

silver oxide (Ag_2O)

Safety

Tie back long hair and secure loose clothing when working with an open flame. Do not touch the hot crucible or its cover with your fingers. Note the caution alert symbol under "Procedure," and take the precautions indicated. Be sure to wear safety goggles and a lab apron or coat when working in the lab.

Procedure

1. Clean a crucible and cover. Place the crucible in the clay triangle as shown in Figure 12-1. Heat the crucible and cover in the hottest part of the burner flame for about 5 minutes. Be sure to tilt the cover as illustrated. Balance it carefully to avoid breakage. Put out the flame and allow the crucible and cover to cool.

Figure 12-1

2. Measure the mass of the crucible + cover. Record this mass as (a) in your data table.

3. Measure out exactly 1.75 g of dry silver oxide (Ag_2O). Add this compound to the crucible. With the cover on the crucible, measure the mass of the crucible and its contents. Record this mass as (b).

4. To remove oxygen gas from the silver oxide, tilt the cover as before and strongly heat the crucible, cover, and contents in the hottest part of the flame for 15 minutes. Allow the crucible to cool. Measure and record the mass of the crucible, cover, and contents (c).

5. If time permits, reheat strongly for 5 minutes. After cooling, again measure the mass of the crucible, cover, and contents to check for constancy of mass (d).

Observations and Data

a. Mass of crucible + cover   _____ g

b. Mass of crucible + cover + Ag_2O _____ g

c. Mass of crucible + cover + Ag   _____ g

d. Mass after reheating   _____ g

12 Determining the Gram Atomic Mass of an Element (continued)

Calculations

1. Find the mass of the Ag: c − a   _____ g

2. Find the mass of the O: b − c   _____ g

3. Find the number of g-atoms of O:

$$\text{g-atoms O} = \frac{\text{mass of O in g}}{16\ \text{g O/g-atom O}}$$ _____

4. Find the number of g-atoms of Ag:

$$\text{g-atoms Ag} = \frac{2\ \text{g-atoms Ag}}{1\ \text{g-atom O}} \times \text{no. of g-atoms O}$$ _____

5. Find g-atom mass of Ag:

$$\text{g-atomic mass Ag} = \frac{\text{mass of Ag in g}}{\text{no. of g-atoms of Ag}}$$ _____

Conclusions and Questions

1. Write a balanced equation for the decomposition of Ag_2O by heating.

2. What are the most likely sources of error in this experiment?

_____

_____

_____

3. Define a mole. What is the relationship between the mole and the gram-atom?

_____

_____

_____

Use a table of atomic masses in answering questions 4 through 6.

4. To the nearest whole number, how many gram-atoms are in a 120-gram sample of calcium metal? How many atoms is this?

5. What is the gram atomic mass of sodium? What is the mass of 4.5 gram-atoms of this element?

6. What is the gram atomic mass of oxygen (O)? What is the mass of 1 mole of oxygen gas (O_2)? Explain the difference.

_____

_____

_____

_____

_____

Determining an Empirical Formula

Lab 13

Text reference: **Chapter 8,** pp. 192–194

Pre-Lab Discussion

In a sample of a compound, regardless of the size of the sample, the number of gram-atoms of one element in the sample divided by the number of gram-atoms of another element in the sample will form a small whole-number ratio. These small whole-number ratios can be used to determine the subscripts in the empirical formula of the compound. For example, suppose that in a 24-gram sample of a compound, there are 1.5 gram-atoms of carbon (18 g of carbon) and 6 gram-atoms of hydrogen (6 g of hydrogen). These numbers form the small whole-number ratio of 1 to 4:

$$\frac{1.5 \text{ gram-atoms carbon}}{6 \text{ gram-atoms hydrogen}} = \frac{1}{4}$$

The 1-to-4 ratio means that for every 1 atom of carbon in the compound, there are 4 atoms of hydrogen. The empirical formula of the compound is CH_4. (The compound's name is methane.)

In this experiment, the number of gram-atoms of each of two elements in a binary compound will be experimentally determined. From this information, the empirical formula of the compound will be determined.

This experiment will help you understand better the concepts of gram atomic masses and empirical formulas.

Purpose

Using mass relationships, show that magnesium and oxygen combine in a definite whole-number ratio by mass.

Equipment

crucible and cover
ring stand
iron ring
clay triangle
crucible tongs
dropper pipet

scissors
burner
balance
safety goggles
lab apron or coat

Materials

magnesium ribbon (Mg), 35cm

Safety

Do not touch a hot crucible with your fingers, and be sure you use tongs to shift the position of the hot crucible cover in step 3. Use a hand to waft the gas given off in step 6 to your nose. Avoid directly inhaling reaction product gases. Do not place any magnesium ribbon in an open flame.

Observe the caution alert symbols under "Procedure," and follow the precautions indicated. Tie back long hair and secure loose clothing when working with an open flame. Always wear safety goggles and a lab apron or coat when working in the lab.

Procedure

1. Clean a crucible and cover. Dry them by heating them in the hottest part of a burner flame for 3 minutes. Allow them to cool. Measure the mass of just the crucible and record this as (a) under "Observations and Data."

2. Cut a 35-cm length of magnesium ribbon into 1-cm pieces. Place the pieces in the crucible and measure the mass of the crucible and its contents (b).

3. Cover the crucible and place it in a clay triangle (Figure 13-1). Heat *gently* for 2 minutes. Using crucible tongs, carefully tilt the cover to provide an opening for air to enter the crucible. Heat the partially covered crucible *strongly* for 10 minutes.

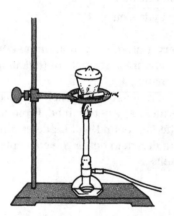

Figure 13-1

4. Turn off the burner, cover the crucible, and allow the contents to cool. When the crucible is cool enough to touch, remove the cover and examine the contents. If any unreacted magnesium remains, replace the cover at a slight tilt, and reheat the crucible strongly for several minutes.

5. Put the cover all the way on and allow to cool. After making sure that all the magnesium has reacted, use a dropper pipet to add enough water to the crucible to just cover the contents. Wash any material that may have spattered onto the inside of the cover into the crucible.

6. Holding the burner in your hand, *gently* heat the contents of the uncovered crucible by moving the burner slowly back and forth. Avoid spattering. Observe the odor of the vapor given off by wafting it toward your nose. Record your observation as (d).

7. When all the liquid has boiled off, repeat steps 5 and 6.

8. When all the liquid has boiled off a second time, *strongly* heat the uncovered crucible for 5 minutes.

9. Turn off the burner and allow the crucible and contents to cool. Measure the combined mass of the crucible + contents (c).

Name _____

13 Determining an Empirical Formula (continued)

Observations and Data

a. Mass of empty crucible   _____ g

b. Mass of crucible + Mg   _____ g

c. Mass of crucible + oxide   _____ g

d. Odor of vapor in step 6:

Calculations

1. Find the mass of magnesium used: b − a   _____ g

2. Find the mass of oxygen that reacted: c − b   _____ g

3. Find the number of g-atoms of Mg used:

$$\text{g-atoms Mg} = \frac{\text{mass of Mg in g}}{24 \text{ g Mg/g-atom Mg}}$$ _____

4. Find the number of g-atoms of O that reacted:

$$\text{g-atoms O} = \frac{\text{mass of O in g}}{16 \text{ g O/g-atom O}}$$ _____

5. Find the ratio of g-atoms of Mg to g-atoms of O: _____

Conclusions and Questions

1. Write the empirical formula of the oxide of magnesium based on your calculations from this experiment.

2. What is the ratio of the mass in grams of magnesium used to the mass in grams of oxygen that reacted? Relate this ratio to the law of definite proportions.

67

3. Why is the ratio found in question 2 different from the ratio found in calculation 5 above?

_____

_____

_____

4. In a chemical formula, explain the significance of subscripts in terms of atoms and molecules. In terms of gram-atoms and moles.

_____

_____

_____

_____

_____

5. The molecular formula of hydrogen peroxide is H_2O_2. What is its empirical formula?

_____

_____

6. How is the chemical composition of carbon monoxide, CO, similar to that of carbon dioxide, CO_2? How is it different?

_____

_____

_____

_____

_____

7. A sample of sulfur having a mass of 1.28 g combines with oxygen to form a compound with a mass of 3.20 g. What is the empirical formula of the compound?

Types of Chemical Reactions   Lab **14**

Text reference: **Chapter 9,** pp. 215–217

Pre-Lab Discussion

There are many kinds of chemical reactions and several ways to classify them. One useful method classifies reactions into four major types. These are: (1) direct combination, or synthesis; (2) decomposition, or analysis; (3) single replacement; and (4) exchange of ions, or double replacement. Not all reactions can be put into one of these categories. Many, however, can.

In a synthesis reaction, two or more substances (elements or compounds) combine to form a more complex substance. Equations for synthesis reactions have the general form $A + B \rightarrow AB$. For example, the formation of water from hydrogen and oxygen is written $2H_2 + O_2 \rightarrow 2H_2O$.

A decomposition reaction is the opposite of a synthesis reaction. In decomposition, a compound breaks down into two or more simpler substances (elements or compounds). Equations for decomposition reactions have the form $AB \rightarrow A + B$. The breakdown of water into its elements is an example of such a reaction: $2H_2O \rightarrow 2H_2 + O_2$.

In a single replacement reaction, one substance in a compound is replaced by another, more active, substance (an element). Equations for single replacement reactions have two general forms. In reactions in which one metal replaces another metal, the general equation is $X + YB \rightarrow XB + Y$. In those in which one nonmetal replaces another nonmetal, the general form is $X + AY \rightarrow AX + Y$. The following equations illustrate these types of reactions:

Zinc metal replaces copper(II) ion:

$$Zn(s) + CuSO_4(aq) \rightarrow ZnSO_4(aq) + Cu(s)$$

Chlorine (a nonmetal) replaces bromide ions:

$$Cl_2(g) + 2KBr(aq) \rightarrow 2KCl(aq) + Br_2(l)$$

In a double replacement reaction, the metal ions of two different ionic compounds can be thought of as "replacing one another." Equations for this type of reaction have the general form $AB + CD \rightarrow AD + CB$. Most replacement reactions, both single and double, take place in aqueous solutions containing free ions. In a double replacement reaction, one of the products is a precipitate, an insoluble gas, or water. An example is the reaction between silver nitrate and sodium chloride in which the precipitate silver chloride is formed:

$$AgNO_3(aq) + NaCl(aq) \rightarrow AgCl(s) + NaNO_3(aq)$$

All of the types of reactions discussed here may be represented by balanced molecular equations. Reactions involving ion exchanges may be represented by ionic equations also. In this investigation you will be concerned only with molecular formulas and equations. In a balanced equation, the number of atoms of any given element must be the same on both sides of the equation. Multiplying the coefficient and the subscript of an element must yield the same result on both sides of the balanced equation.

In this investigation you will observe examples of the four types of reactions described above. You will be expected to balance the equations representing the observed reactions.

Purpose

Observe some chemical reactions and identify reactants and products of those reactions. Classify the reactions and write balanced equations.

Equipment

burner
crucible tongs
microspatula
test tubes, 15×180-mm (7)
test tube holder
test tube rack

wood splints
sandpaper, fine
evaporating dish
safety goggles
lab apron or coat

Materials

zinc, mossy (Zn)
copper wire, 10 cm (Cu)
magnesium ribbon, 5 cm (Mg)
copper(II) carbonate ($CuCO_3$)
6 M hydrochloric acid (HCl)

1 M copper(II) sulfate ($CuSO_4$)
0.1 M zinc acetate ($Zn(C_2H_3O_2)_2$)
0.1 M sodium phosphate (Na_3PO_4)
1 M sodium sulfite (Na_2SO_3)

Safety

In this investigation you will be working with open flames, heating chemicals, handling acids, and producing gaseous products. You should review the safety procedures for these activities given on pages ix–x.

Burning magnesium produces a very bright, hot flame. Make sure you hold the burning metal at arm's length and do not look directly at it.

Remember never to smell a chemical directly. Review the accepted method of wafting gases toward your nose as illustrated on page xi.

Pay special attention to the safety symbols beside certain steps in the procedure. Refer to page xi to review the special precautions associated with each symbol.

Wear safety goggles and protective clothing at all times when working in the lab.

Procedure

PART A SYNTHESIS

1. Use fine sandpaper to clean a piece of copper wire until the wire is shiny. Note the appearance of the wire.

 2. Using crucible tongs, hold the wire in the hottest part of a burner flame for 1–2 minutes. Examine the wire and note any change in its appearance caused by heating.

3. Place an evaporating dish near the base of the burner. Examine a piece of magnesium ribbon. Using crucible tongs,

14 Types of Chemical Reactions (continued)

hold the sample in the burner flame until the magnesium starts to burn. DO NOT LOOK DIRECTLY AT THE FLAME. HOLD THE BURNING MAGNESIUM AWAY FROM YOU AND DIRECTLY OVER THE EVAPORATING DISH. When the ribbon stops burning, put the remains in the evaporating dish. Examine this product carefully.

PART B DECOMPOSITION

4. Place 2 heaping microspatulas of copper(II) carbonate ($CuCO_3$) in a clean, dry test tube. Note the appearance of the sample.

5. Using a test tube holder, heat the $CuCO_3$ strongly for about 3 minutes. Extinguish the flame and then insert a *burning* wood splint into the test tube. If carbon dioxide gas (CO_2) is present, it will put the flame out. Note any change in the appearance of the residue in the test tube.

PART C SINGLE REPLACEMENT

6. Stand a clean, dry test tube in the test tube rack. Add about 5 mL of 6 M hydrochloric acid (HCl) to the tube. **CAUTION.** *Handle acids with care. They can cause painful burns. Do not inhale any HCl fumes.* Now carefully drop a small piece of zinc metal (Zn) into the acid in the test tube. Observe and record what happens.

7. Using a test tube holder, invert a second test tube over the mouth of the test tube in which the reaction is taking place. See Figure 14-1. Remove the inverted tube after about 30 seconds and quickly insert a burning wood splint into the mouth of the tube. (A "pop" indicates the presence of hydrogen gas.) Note the appearance of the substance in the reaction test tube.

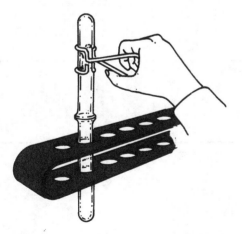

Figure 14-1

8. Add about 5 mL of 1 M copper(II) sulfate ($CuSO_4$) solution to a clean, dry test tube. Place a small amount of zinc metal in the solution. Note the appearance of the solution and the zinc before and after the reaction.

PART D DOUBLE REPLACEMENT

9. Add about 2 mL of 0.1 M zinc acetate ($Zn(C_2H_3O_2)_2$) to a clean, dry test tube. Next, add about 2 mL of 0.1 M sodium phosphate tribasic (Na_3PO_4) solution to the test tube. Observe what happens and note any changes in the mixture.

10. Add about 5 mL of 1 M sodium sulfite (Na_2SO_3) solution to a clean, dry test tube. To this solution, add about 1 mL of 6 M HCl. Note the odor given off by *wafting some of the gas toward your nose.* DO NOT SMELL THE GAS DIRECTLY.

Observations and Data

DATA TABLE

Sample	Before reaction	After reaction
A. Synthesis		
1. Cu		
2. Mg		
B. Decomposition		
3. $CuCO_3$		
C. Single Replacement		
4. Zn + HCl		
5. Zn + $CuSO_4$		
D. Double Replacement		
6. $Zn(C_2H_3O_2)_2$ + Na_3PO_4		
7. Na_2SO_3 + HCl		

14 Types of Chemical Reactions (continued)

Equations

Balance each of the equations by inserting the proper coefficients where needed. Write the names of the reactant(s) and product(s) below the molecular equation for each reaction.

PART A   SYNTHESIS

1. $Cu(s)$ + $O_2(g)$ → $CuO(s)$

2. $Mg(s)$ + $O_2(g)$ → $MgO(s)$

PART B   DECOMPOSITION

3. $CuCO_3(s)$ → $CuO(s)$ + $CO_2(g)$

PART C   SINGLE REPLACEMENT

4. $Zn(s)$ + $HCl(aq)$ → $ZnCl_2(aq)$ + $H_2(g) \uparrow$

5. $Zn(s)$ + $CuSO_4(aq)$ → $ZnSO_4(aq)$ + $Cu(s)$

PART D   DOUBLE REPLACEMENT

6. $Zn(C_2H_3O_2)_2(aq)$ + $Na_3PO_4(aq)$ → $NaC_2H_3O_2(aq)$ + $Zn_3(PO_4)_2(s)$

7. $Na_2SO_3(aq)$ + $HCl(aq)$ → $NaCl(aq)$ + $H_2O(l)$ + $SO_2(g) \uparrow$

Conclusions and Questions

1. In this experiment, what method was used to test for the presence of CO_2 gas? What is another test for CO_2 gas? Write a balanced equation for this test.

_____

_____

_____

_____

_____

_____

_____

_____

2. What test was used to identify hydrogen gas? Write a balanced equation to represent this test.

_____

_____

_____

_____

3. Balance the equations below and identify the type of reaction represented by each equation.

a. $AgNO_3(aq)$ + $Cu(s)$ $\rightarrow$ $Cu(NO_3)_2(aq)$ + $Ag(s)\downarrow$

b. $BaCl_2(aq)$ + $Na_2SO_4(aq)$ $\rightarrow$ $BaSO_4(s)\downarrow$ + $NaCl(aq)$

c. $Cl_2(g)$ + $NaBr(aq)$ $\rightarrow$ $NaCl(aq)$ + $Br_2(l)$

d. $KClO_3(s)$ $\rightarrow$ $KCl(s)$ + $O_2(g)\uparrow$

e. $AlCl_3(aq)$ + $NH_4OH(aq)$ $\rightarrow$ $NH_4Cl(aq)$ + $Al(OH)_3(s)\downarrow$

f. $H_2(g)$ + $O_2(g)$ $\rightarrow$ $H_2O(g)$

_____

_____

_____

_____

_____

_____

Relating Moles to Coefficients of a Chemical Equation

Lab 15

Text reference: **Chapter 10,** pp. 233–238

Pre-Lab Discussion

The mole is defined as Avogadro's number (6.02×10^{23}) of particles. These particles may be atoms, molecules, formula units, ions, electrons, etc. The concept of the mole is very important, especially when dealing with quantitative studies of chemical reactions. When calculating quantities of solids or liquids, molar masses are used. The molar mass of a substance is the mass, in grams, of 1 mole of particles of that substance. When calculating quantities of gases, molar volumes are used. The molar volume is the volume occupied by 1 mole of a gas at STP.

Chemical reactions are represented by balanced chemical equations. Proper interpretation of an equation provides a great deal of information about the reaction it represents and about the substances involved in the reaction. For example, the coefficients in a balanced equation indicate the number of moles of each substance. Thus, the ratio of moles of a substance to moles of any other substance in the reaction can be determined at a glance.

In this experiment, iron filings will be added to an aqueous solution of copper(II) sulfate. A single replacement reaction will take place, the products being iron(II) sulfate and copper metal. The balanced equation for this reaction is:

$$\text{Fe}(s) + \text{CuSO}_4(aq) \rightarrow \text{FeSO}_4(aq) + \text{Cu}(s).$$

The quantities of iron and copper sulfate used as reactants will be such that the copper sulfate will be in excess. Thus, the iron will be the limiting factor in determining the number of moles (gram-atoms) of products that will be formed. As the equation shows, the number of moles of copper produced should be equal to the number of moles of iron reacted.

This experiment should aid in the understanding of balanced equations and single replacement reactions.

Purpose

Find the ratio of moles of a reactant to moles of a product of a chemical reaction. Relate this ratio to the coefficients of these substances in the balanced equation for the reaction.

Equipment

balance	iron ring
burner	wire gauze
beaker, 100-mL	glass stirring rod
beaker, 250-mL	safety goggles
graduated cylinder, 100-mL	lab apron or coat
ring stand	

Materials

copper sulfate crystals ($CuSO_4$)
iron filings (Fe)

Safety

Tie back long hair and secure loose clothing when working with an open flame. Note the caution alert symbol under "Procedure" and follow the precautions indicated. Always wear safety goggles and a lab apron or coat when working in the lab.

Procedure

1. Find the mass of a clean, dry 100-mL beaker. Record this as (a) in your data table.

2. Measure out 8.0 grams of copper sulfate crystals ($CuSO_4$) and add these to the beaker.

3. Measure 50.0 mL of water in a graduated cylinder and add it to the crystals in the beaker.

While one lab partner continues with steps 4 and 5, the other partner should carry out the instructons in step 6.

 4. Set up the apparatus as shown in Figure 15-1. Heat the mixture in the beaker to just *below* boiling. DO NOT ALLOW THE LIQUID TO BOIL.

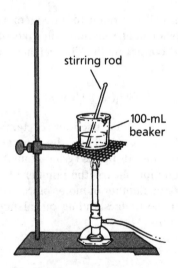

stirring rod

100-mL beaker

Figure 15-1

5. Continue heating and stir the mixture until the crystals are completely dissolved. Turn off the gas and remove the burner.

6. Using the balance, measure precisely 2.24 grams of iron filings. (Remember: do not place any reagent directly on the balance pan.) Record this mass as (b) in the data table.

7. Add the iron filings, *small amounts at a time*, to the hot copper sulfate solution. Stir continuously. After all the iron has been added and the mixture stirred, allow the beaker to sit for 10 minutes while the reaction proceeds. Record your observations as (d) in the data table.

15 Relating Moles to Coefficients of a Chemical Equation (continued)

8. Decant the liquid into a 250-mL beaker as shown in Figure 15-2. Do not disturb the solid at the bottom of the beaker.

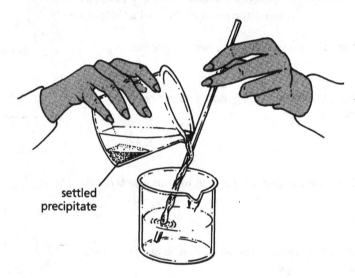

settled
precipitate

Figure 15-2

9. Add about 10 mL of water to the solid in the 100-mL beaker. Stir vigorously in order to wash off the solid. Let the solid settle and decant the liquid. Repeat the washing.

10. Spread the solid out on the bottom of the beaker and place the beaker in a drawer or oven to dry. Complete step 11 and the rest of this experiment at the beginning of the next lab period.

11. Find the mass of the beaker and the *dry* copper metal. Record this as (c) in the data table.

Observations and Data

a. Mass of empty beaker _____ g

b. Mass of iron filings _____ g

c. Mass of beaker + copper _____ g

d. Visual observations:

Calculations

Use the following information, as needed, to carry out the calculations:

$$\text{no. of gram-atoms} = \frac{\text{mass (g)}}{\text{g-atomic mass}}$$

g-atomic mass of Fe = 56 g Fe/g-atom Fe
g-atomic mass of Cu = 64 g Cu/g-atom Cu

1. Find the mass of the copper produced: c − a   _____ g

2. Find the number of g-atoms of copper
produced: _____

3. Find the number of g-atoms of iron reacted: _____

4. Find the whole number ratio of g-atoms of iron to
g-atoms of copper: _____

Conclusions and Questions

1. How does the ratio found in calculation 4 compare with the ratio of
the coefficients of the same two metals in the balanced equation for the
reaction?

_____

_____

2. How many moles (g-atoms) of copper sulfate are used to produce the
solution in this experiment? Why is this amount of copper sulfate said to
be "in excess"?

3. Explain why the iron is the limiting factor in this experiment.

_____

_____

_____

_____

_____

_____

15 Relating Moles to Coefficients of a Chemical Equation (continued)

4. A general description of the single replacement reaction in this experiment is: metal + salt in solution → "new" metal + "new" salt solution. Give a balanced equation for another example of this type of single replacement reaction.

_____

5. Give general descriptions of two other types of single replacement reactions. Using balanced equations, give a specific example of each type.

_____

_____

_____

_____

6. Consider the reaction: $Cu(s) + 2AgNO_3(aq) \rightarrow 2Ag(s) + Cu(NO_3)_2(aq)$. If 3 moles of copper metal reacts, how many moles of silver metal will be produced?

_____

_____

_____

_____

_____

Mole and Mass Relationships

Lab 16

Text reference: **Chapter 10,** pp. 239–243

Pre-Lab Discussion

In a balanced chemical equation, all reactants and products must be represented by symbols or formulas. The total number of atoms of each element must be the same on each side of the equation to satisfy the law of conservation of mass.

A calculation of the formula mass of a reactant or product enables a researcher to convert from grams of a particular substance taking part in a reaction to moles of that substance. The mole relationship given by the coefficients of the balanced equation then allows the researcher to calculate how many moles of every other substance will take part in the reaction.

In this experiment, you will investigate the quantitative relationships in the reaction:

$$NaHCO_3(s) + HCl(aq) \rightarrow NaCl(aq) + CO_2(g) + H_2O(g)$$

A known mass of sodium hydrogen carbonate will be reacted with excess hydrochloric acid. Knowing the mass of $NaHCO_3(s)$ that reacts, you can determine from the balanced equation the mass of NaCl that should be produced. You can compare this theoretical value with the actual experimental mass of NaCl produced.

This experiment should aid in the understanding of the mole-mass relationships that exist in a chemical reaction and in the interpretation of a balanced chemical equation.

Purpose

Compare the experimental mass of a product of a chemical reaction with the mass predicted for that product by calculation.

Equipment

balance	dropper pipet
burner	ring stand
evaporating dish	iron ring
watch glass	wire gauze
microspatula	safety goggles
test tube, 13×100-mm	lab apron or coat

Materials

6 *M* hydrochloric acid (HCl)
sodium hydrogen carbonate ($NaHCO_3$)

Safety

Handle the hydrochloric acid with care. Flush any spills with cold water and a dilute solution of sodium bicarbonate and report them to your teacher. Do not lean over the apparatus when heating it in step 6. Note the caution alert symbols under "Procedure" and follow the precautions indicated. Refer to page xi to review those precautions. Always wear safety goggles and a lab apron or coat when working in the lab.

Procedure

1. Flame dry a clean evaporating dish by heating it in the hot part of a burner flame for about 5 minutes. Allow the dish to cool.

2. Find the combined mass of the evaporating dish plus a watch glass. This is mass (a) in your list of data.

3. Leaving the watch glass and evaporating dish on the balance, move the riders to measure an additional 2.50 g. Using a micro-spatula, add sodium hydrogen carbonate ($NaHCO_3$) to the evaporating dish until the scale balances. Record this mass as (b) in your list of data.

4. Set up the ring stand, ring, and wire gauze as shown in Figure 16-1. Place the watch glass on top of the evaporating dish and place the dish on the wire gauze.

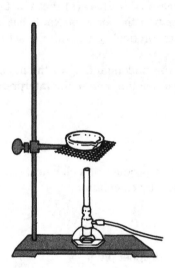

Figure 16-1

 5. Obtain about 5 mL of 6 M hydrochloric acid (HCl) in a clean, dry test tube. **CAUTION:** *Handle this acid carefully. It can cause painful burns if it touches your skin.* Using a dropper pipet, slowly add HCl to the $NaHCO_3$ in the evaporating dish, a few drops at a time. (See Figure 16-2.) Continue adding acid until the reaction (bubbling) stops. Carefully tilt the evaporating dish back and forth a couple of times to make sure that the acid has contacted all the $NaHCO_3$. After making sure that all bubbling has stopped, remove the watch glass and place it *curved side up* on the lab bench.

16 Mole and Mass Relationships (continued)

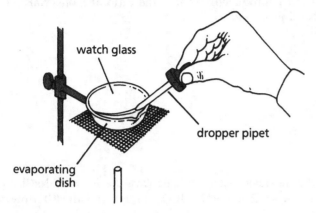

watch glass

dropper pipet

evaporating
dish

Figure 16-2

6. Holding the burner in your hand, *gently* heat the evaporating dish. Use a low flame and move the burner back and forth to avoid spattering. When almost all the liquid is gone, remove the burner and replace the watch glass on the evaporating dish, leaving a small opening for vapor to escape. Heat gently again until no liquid remains. Allow the dish to cool.

7. Find the combined mass of the watch glass, evaporating dish, and contents (NaCl). Record this mass, (c), in your list of data.

Observations and Data

a. evaporating dish + watch glass   _____ g

b. evaporating dish + watch glass + $NaHCO_3$ _____ g

c. evaporating dish + watch glass + NaCl   _____ g

Calculations

1. Find the mass of the $NaHCO_3$ reactant, b − a.   _____ g

2. Find the mass of the NaCl product, c − a.   _____ g

Conclusions and Questions

1. According to the balanced equation for the reaction used in this experiment, what is the ratio of moles of $NaHCO_3$ reacted to moles of NaCl produced?

_____

_____

2. How many moles of $NaHCO_3$ is reacted in this experiment? How many moles of NaCl is produced? What is the ratio of moles $NaHCO_3$ reacted to moles NaCl produced?

3. Using the balanced equation, calculate the mass of NaCl you would expect to get when 2.50 g of $NaHCO_3$ is reacted with HCl. How does this value compare with the mass attained experimentally?

_____

_____

4. If the masses of all but one of the substances that take part in a chemical reaction are known, explain why it is possible to determine the unknown mass by subtraction.

_____

_____

_____

5. In the chemical reaction $CaCO_3 \rightarrow CaO + CO_2$, if 40.0 g of $CaCO_3$ is decomposed:
a. how many grams of CaO is produced?
b. how many grams of CO_2 is produced?

6. In the reaction $N_2 + 3H_2 \rightarrow 2NH_3$, if 20.0 g of hydrogen reacts:
a. how many grams of ammonia is produced?
b. how many grams of nitrogen reacts?

Mass-Mass Relationships in Reactions

Lab 17

Text reference: **Chapter 10,** pp. 239–243

Pre-Lab Discussion

As you have learned, given a balanced chemical equation and the mass of one of the substances in the reaction, the mass of any other substance in the reaction can be calculated. Calculations in which a known mass is used to find an unknown mass in a chemical reaction are called mass-mass calculations.

In this experiment, a double replacement reaction will occur when an aqueous solution of a hydrate of zinc acetate is mixed with an aqueous solution of a hydrate of sodium phosphate tribasic. There are two products of this reaction. One is the insoluble solid (zinc phosphate), which will precipitate out of solution. The other is a soluble salt (sodium acetate), which will remain in solution. The insoluble solid will be separated from the liquid and dried, and its mass determined. The value of the experimentally measured mass of the compound will be compared with the theoretical mass of the compound predicted by a mass-mass calculation.

You may recall that the hydrates of ionic substances have water molecules bound into their crystalline structure. However, they look and feel perfectly dry. When doing mass calculations that involve hydrates, you must be careful to include the mass of the water molecules. For example, the mass of one mole of $CaBr_2 \cdot 6H_2O$ is 308 g/mole:

$$\left.\begin{array}{l} \text{Ca: } 1 \times 40 \text{ g/mole} = 40 \text{ g} \\ 2\text{Br: } 2 \times 80 \text{ g/mole} = 160 \text{ g} \\ 6H_2O: 6 \times 18 \text{ g/mole} = 108 \text{ g} \end{array}\right\} \quad 308 \text{ g/mole } CaBr_2 \cdot 6H_2O$$

This experiment further emphasizes the importance of mass-mass calculations in the chemistry laboratory.

Purpose

To compare the theoretical mass of one of the products of a double replacement reaction with the experimentally determined mass of the same product.

Equipment

balance
graduated cylinder, 100-mL
beakers, 250-mL (2)
beaker, 100-mL
stirring rod

ring stand
iron ring
funnel
safety goggles
lab apron or coat

Materials

zinc acetate hydrate [$Zn(C_2H_3O_2)_2 \cdot 2H_2O$]
sodium phosphate tribasic hydrate ($Na_3PO_4 \cdot 12H_2O$)
filter paper

Safety

Handle glassware with care to avoid breakage. Always wear safety goggles and a lab apron or coat when working in the lab.

Procedure

1. Using the balance, measure out exactly 2.19 g of zinc acetate hydrate [$Zn(C_2H_3O_2)_2 \cdot 2H_2O$]. Record this mass as (a) in your list of data.

2. Place the $Zn(C_2H_3O_2)_2 \cdot 2H_2O$ in a clean 250-mL beaker and add 50 mL of water. Stir thoroughly to make sure *all crystals are dissolved*. Rinse off the stirring rod.

3. Measure out approximately 2.70 g of sodium phosphate tribasic hydrate ($Na_3PO_4 \cdot 12H_2O$). Place it in a clean 100-mL beaker and add 50 mL of water. Stir until all crystals are dissolved.

4. Pour the $Na_3PO_4 \cdot 12H_2O$ solution into the 250-mL beaker containing the solution of $Zn(C_2H_3O_2)_2 \cdot 2H_2O$. Stir. Record your observations as (d) in your list of data.

5. Find the mass of a piece of filter paper. Record this as mass (b). Fold the filter paper and place it in the funnel.

6. Pour the mixture from the 250-mL beaker into the funnel as shown in Figure 17-1. *Pour slowly*. Do not allow the liquid to rise above the edge of the filter paper in the funnel.

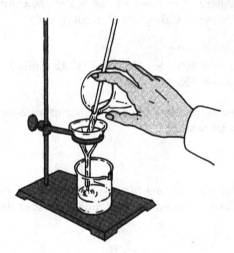

Figure 17-1

7. Rinse the beaker with about 20 mL of water. Pour the rinse water through the filter. Repeat the rinsings and filterings until all the precipitate is out of the beaker.

8. Wash the precipitate by pouring about 10 mL of clean water through the filter.

9. Remove the filter paper and precipitate from the funnel and place overnight in an oven to dry at about 45°C.

10. Find the mass of the *dry* precipitate + filter paper [mass (c) in your list of data].

17 Mass-Mass Relationships in Reactions (continued)

Observations and Data

a. mass of $Zn(C_2H_3O_2)_2 \cdot 2H_2O$ _____ g

b. mass of filter paper   _____ g

c. mass of filter paper + precipitate   _____ g

d. observations

Calculations

1. Write a balanced equation for the double replacement reaction. (The solid formed by the reaction and dried in the oven is zinc phosphate hydrate. Its formula is $Zn_3(PO_4)_2 \cdot 4H_2O$.)

___ $Na_3PO_4 \cdot 12H_2O(aq) +$ ___ $Zn(C_2H_3O_2)_2 \cdot 2H_2O(aq) \rightarrow$

           ___ $Zn_3(PO_4)_2 \cdot 4H_2O(s) +$ ___ $NaC_2H_3O_2(aq) +$ ___ $H_2O(l)$

2. Using mass-mass calculations, find the theoretical mass of the $Zn_3(PO_4)_2 \cdot 4H_2O$ precipitate that should be produced when 2.19 g of $Zn(C_2H_3O_2)_2 \cdot 2H_2O$ reacts completely.   _____ g

3. Find the experimental mass of $Zn_3(PO_4)_2 \cdot 4H_2O$ formed, c − b: _____ g

4. Find your experimental error using the formula: _____ %

$$\text{percent error} = \frac{(\text{observed value} - \text{true value})}{\text{true value}} \times 100$$

Conclusions and Questions

1. What is another name for a double replacement reaction?

_____

2. Give a brief general description of a double replacement reaction. What must one of the products of such a reaction be?

_____

_____

_____

_____

_____

_____

3. Suggest some possible sources of error in this experiment.

_____

_____

_____

_____

_____

_____

4. Define the terms filtrate and precipitate.

_____

_____

_____

_____

Heating and Cooling Curves Lab 18

Text reference: **Chapter 11**, pp. 267–270

Pre-Lab Discussion

Experiments 7 and 8 were concerned with the exchange of heat between a substance and its surroundings when the substance undergoes a change in phase. This transfer of heat was indicated by measuring its effect on the temperature of the surroundings (the water in a calorimeter). No direct measurements of the substance undergoing change were made. In this experiment, you will observe by direct measurement the effects of cooling and heating a pure substance.

In Part A, a pure substance will be cooled (heat removed) at a constant rate. Starting with the substance in its liquid phase at a temperature well above its freezing point, temperature readings will be made at regular intervals until the substance changes to its solid phase and cools to a temperature well below its freezing point. The temperature readings will thus show the effects of removing heat from a pure substance in the liquid phase, during a phase change (liquid to solid), and in the solid phase.

In Part B, the procedure will be reversed, starting with the same substance in its solid phase at a temperature well below its melting point. While heat is added at a constant rate, temperature readings will be made until the substance is in its liquid phase at a temperature well above its melting point.

The data collected in Parts A and B will be used to construct a graph, which will consist of two curved lines: a cooling curve and a heating curve. When completed, the graph will show pictorially what happens to a pure substance as its temperature is raised and lowered over a temperature interval that includes its freezing and melting points. The graph also will show how the freezing and melting points of a pure substance are related.

Purpose

Study the effects of heating and cooling a pure substance through a change of phase. Construct heating and cooling curves of a pure substance using experimental data. Determine the freezing and melting point temperatures of the pure substance.

Equipment

test tube, 18×150-mm	test tube clamp
cork (to fit test tube)	lab burner
beaker, 250-mL	stop watch (or timer with second hand)
thermometer	blue pencil
ring stand	red pencil
iron ring	safety goggles
test tube rack	lab apron or coat
wire gauze	

Materials

lauric acid ($C_{12}H_{24}O_2$)
water

Safety

Heat the lauric acid slowly and carefully to avoid "popping," and avoid inhaling any vapors that may be released during heating. Be careful when using the thermometer to stir the sample. The thermometer is fragile, and the mercury inside it is poisonous. Immediately report any breakage to your teacher.

Tie back long hair and secure loose clothing when working with an open flame.

Note the safety alert symbols here and with certain steps in the "Procedure." Refer to page xi to review the specific precautions associated with each symbol.

Always wear safety goggles and a lab apron or coat when working in the lab.

Procedure

PART A COOLING CURVE

1. Fill a 250-mL beaker three-quarters full of cold tap water.

 2. Obtain a corked test tube containing a sample of the substance (lauric acid) to be studied. Clamp the test tube to a ring stand as shown in Figure 18-1.

Figure 18-1

 3. Remove the cork. Heat the sample CAREFULLY by moving the burner gently back and forth as shown in Figure 18-1. CAUTION: *Before heating, check to see that the mouth of the test tube is pointing away from yourself and others.*

 4. As soon as the sample *begins* to melt, remove the heat and place a thermometer in the sample. Using the thermometer to stir the sample, resume heating gently until the sample is com-

Name _____

18 Heating and Cooling Curves (continued)

pletely melted. DO NOT OVERHEAT. The final temperature of the sample should be about 60°C. If it is higher, wait until it drops to this temperature before proceeding with step 5.

At this point in the experiment, one partner will call out the time every ½ minute and will record temperature data in the Data Table. The other partner will read off the temperature of the sample at each half-minute interval.

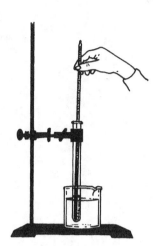

5. When the temperature of the sample is 60°C, set the time at 0 minutes. Immediately immerse the test tube into the cold water bath, making sure the entire sample, but not the entire test tube, is below the surface of the water (Figure 18-2).

6. The recording partner will call out the time every ½ minute. The second partner will use the thermometer to *stir the sample constantly* as long as some liquid remains. At each half-minute interval, this partner will read the temperature to the recording partner.

Figure 18-2

7. Continue this procedure until the temperature of the sample reaches 25°C. Remove the test tube from the water and stand it in a test tube rack.

PART B HEATING CURVE

8. Using a setup like that shown in Figure 18-3 (but without the test tube in the beaker), heat the water in the beaker to a temperature of about 70°C. Remove the heat.

9. While the water was being heated, the sample in the test tube was cooling to approximately room temperature. Set the time at 0 minutes when you record the exact temperature of the sample and immerse it below the water level in the hot water bath. Read and record the temperature of the sample every ½ minute as in Part A.

10. As soon as the thermometer is free to move, it should be used to stir the solid-liquid mixture. Continue stirring and recording the temperature at half-minute intervals until the temperature of the sample reaches 50°C.

11. Remove the thermometer and clean it. Remove the test tube from the water bath and allow it to cool. Replace the cork in the test tube and return the sample to your teacher.

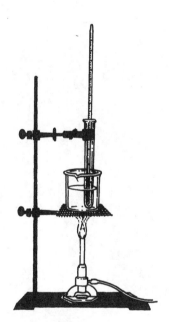

Figure 18-3

Observations and Data

DATA TABLE

Time (min.)	Temp. (°C) Cooling (PART A)	Temp. (°C) Heating (PART B)	Time (min.)	Temp. (°C) Cooling (PART A)	Temp. (°C) Heating (PART B)
0			7		
½			7½		
1			8		
1½			8½		
2			9		
2½			9½		
3			10		
3½			10½		
4			11		
4½			11½		
5			12		
5½			12½		
6			13		
6½			13½		

18 Heating and Cooling Curves (continued)

Calculations

Plot your data from this experiment on the set of axes in Figure 18-4. Use a blue pencil to plot cooling data and a red pencil to plot heating data.

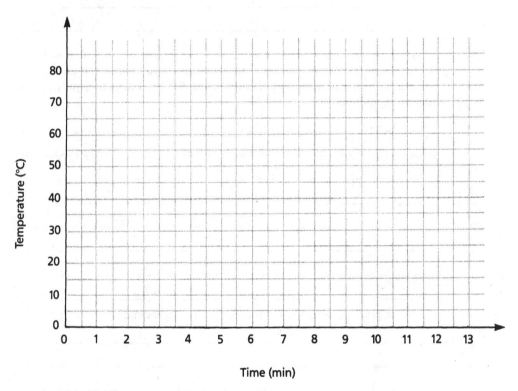

Figure 18-4

Conclusions and Questions

1. Referring to your graph, determine the freezing point of lauric acid. How does this temperature compare with the melting point temperature of the same substance as indicated on the graph?

_____

_____

_____

_____

2. Explain the diagonal parts of the cooling curve in terms of changes in kinetic and potential energy. Do the same for the horizontal portions of the cooling curve.

_____

_____

_____

_____

_____

_____

_____

3. What phase changes are exothermic? Endothermic?

_____

_____

_____

_____

4. In which phase of a substance do its particles have the greatest average kinetic energy?

_____

_____

_____

Boyle's Law

Lab 19

Text reference: **Chapter 12**, pp. 297–303

Pre-Lab Discussion

The apparatus you will use in this experiment is shown in Figure 19-1. It consists of a plunger that fits into a cylinder. Fitted to the bottom of the plunger is a gasket made of rubber or plastic that has been lubricated with a liquid silicone. This gasket provides an airtight seal against the walls of the cylinder. In this experiment, you will trap a sample of air in the cylinder beneath the plunger. You will then add four books, one by one, to the platform on top of the plunger. After adding each book, you will measure the volume of the air trapped beneath the plunger to see what effect the increase in pressure is having on the volume of the air sample.

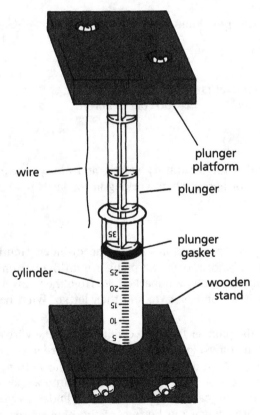

wire

plunger platform

plunger

plunger gasket

cylinder

wooden stand

Figure 19-1

Weight and pressure are not the same physical quantities. However, in this experiment you can use the weight of your chemistry book as a unit of pressure because the weight of two books exerts twice as much pressure as the weight of one book, provided the weights are always applied to the same area. In this experiment, the weights are applied to the same area, namely, the area of the gasket that is in contact with the sample of air.

When you measure the volume of gas trapped below the piston, your measurements will be slightly off because of the existence of friction between the gasket on the plunger and the walls of the cylinder. Every time you place a book on the platform, friction will prevent the plunger from falling as far as it would in the absence of friction. Therefore, every measurement of volume will be slightly larger than it should be. However, there is a way of minimizing the effect of friction. This can be done by making a second series of volume measurements. During the first series, already described above, you gradually add weight, which, because of friction, produces volume readings that are slightly larger than they should be. During the second series, you remove the books that were added during the first series. Each time you remove a book, friction will prevent the plunger from rising as far as it would in the absence of friction. As a result, all the volume readings made during the second series will be slightly smaller than they should be. This effect is just opposite to the effect during the first series, when the values were too large. By averaging the two series of readings, the distortions produced by friction will tend to cancel each other out.

Purpose

To investigate the pressure/volume relationship of a gas.

Equipment

plunger and cylinder apparatus   safety goggles
   (Boyle's law apparatus)   lab coat or apron

Safety

Follow all general rules for laboratory safety, and always wear safety goggles and a lab coat or apron when working in the lab.

Procedure

1. Carefully insert the plunger into the cylinder. Gently push down on the platform over the plunger until the bottom of the plunger is at the graduation marked *30*. Hold the plunger in that position for a second or two, and then let go. What happens? Why?

2. Remove the plunger from the cylinder. With the wire running straight down alongside the plunger, put the wire into the top of the cylinder first, and then begin pushing the bottom of the plunger into the cylinder. The wire will open up a space in the gasket so that air can escape from the cylinder as you push downward. Stop when the bottom of the plunger reaches the 30-mL mark. While holding the plunger at the 30-mL mark, pull the wire out of the cylinder. When you remove your hand, the bottom of the plunger should remain at the 30-mL mark.

3. You are now going to apply larger and larger pressures to the sample of air by resting more and more weight on the platform above the plunger. A convenient weight to use in this experiment is the weight of your chemistry textbook. Gently lower one book onto the platform so that the center of the book is over the center of the platform. Record in Column 2 of Data Table 1 the

19 Boyle's Law (continued)

volume occupied by the sample of air when one book is resting on the platform.

4. Following the step described above, gently rest a second book on top of the first book. Record the new volume in Table 1.

5. Repeat the step for a third book, then a fourth book.

6. As mentioned in the pre-lab discussion, all the measurements you just made are slightly too large because of friction. You will now make a second series of the measurements while books are being removed from the platform. With four books still on the platform, begin the second series by gently pushing down on the top book until the piston falls about 1 cm. Gradually lift your hand off the top book. Record the volume in Column 3 of Table 1.

7. Gradually lift the top book from the platform, leaving three books on the platform, and record the new volume.

8. Gradually lift one book at a time and each time record the new volume, including the volume when no books are on the platform.

DATA TABLE 1   Volume of a Sample of Gas at Different Pressures

	Column 1	Column 2	Column 3	Column 4	Column 5
Trial	Pressure (Number of Books on Platform)	Volume (Series 1)	Volume (Series 2)	Av. Volume (Average of Series 1 & Series 2)	$P \times V$ Product (Col. 1 × Col. 4)
0	0 books	30.0 mL			
1	1.00				
2	2.00				
3	3.00				
4	4.00				

Calculations

1. Record in Column 4 the average of the volumes in Columns 2 and 3.

2. For each trial, multiply the pressure (the number of books) by the average volume and record your results in Column 5 of Data Table 1. Do you get the same product for $P \times V$ for each trial, in accordance with Boyle's law?

3. Assume that only some of the pressure exerted on the sample of air comes from the weight of the books and that there is some additional pressure (some extra pressure) from some other source. Use the symbol x to stand for this extra pressure. Assume also that this extra pressure is the same for all trials of the experiment. Then the total pressure on the sample of air during any of the trials is the sum of these two pressures:

$$\text{Total pressure} = \text{pressure from books} + \text{extra pressure}$$
$$P_{\text{total}} = P_{\text{books}} + x$$

When 2 books are resting on the platform:

$$P_{\text{total}} = 2\text{ books} + x$$

4. Under the assumption given directly above, find the "extra pressure." Because, by Boyle's law, *Pressure × Volume* is supposed to equal a constant, *Pressure × Volume* for one trial should equal *Pressure × Volume* for any and all other trials.

$$P_{\text{a}} \times V_{\text{a}} = P_{\text{b}} \times V_{\text{b}} \qquad \text{(Eq. 1)}$$
where P_{a} and V_{a} = pressure and volume for one trial,
and P_{b} and V_{b} = pressure and volume for another trial.

Using the data for Trials 1 and 2, the math for Equation 1 looks like this:

Trial 1		Trial 2	
(1 book on platform)		(2 books on the platform)	
P_1 × V_1	=	P_2 × V_2	
(1 book + x) × (Volume)	=	(2 books + x) × (Volume)	**(Eq. 2)**

Your calculation of average
volume for Trial 1

Your calculation of average
volume for Trial 2

Using the data you recorded in Data Table 1, solve Equation 2 for x. Show your work below. Use a clean sheet of paper if you need more space. Because the unit of pressure is the *book*, x will have as its unit the *book*.

5. Put the value you obtain for x in Table 2. Because it is assumed that this extra pressure is the same for all trials, put your value of x on all five lines of Column 2. Then fill out Columns 3, 4, and 5 in Table 2.

19 Boyle's Law (continued)

DATA TABLE 2   The *PV* Product Using the Extra Pressure

	Column 1	Column 2	Column 3	Column 4	Column 5
Trial	Pressure (Number of Books on Platform)	The Extra Pressure (x)	The Total Pressure (Columns 1 + 2)	Av. Volume (Average of Series 1 & Series 2)	$P \times V$ Product (Columns 3 × 4)
0	0 books				
1	1.00				
2	2.00				
3	3.00				
4	4.00				

Conclusions and Questions

1. For which trial would the data in Data Table 1 lead you to believe there must be some pressure being exerted on the sample of air in addition to the weight of the books? Explain.

_____

_____

_____

_____

2. When you used the total pressure (pressure from the weight of the books + extra pressure) to obtain the *PV* product in Table 2, did you obtain the same *PV* product for all five trials in accordance with Boyle's law? Explain.

_____

_____

_____

_____

_____

3. Formulate a hypothesis to explain what causes the extra pressure referred to in question 1.

_____

_____

Optional (Your teacher may ask you to answer one or all of the questions that follow.)

4. Design an experiment to test the hypothesis you formulated as your answer to question 3.

_____

_____

_____

_____

_____

_____

_____

_____

_____

_____

_____

_____

_____

_____

_____

_____

_____

5. How would you go about testing to see whether the cylinder, with the plunger inserted, is really airtight?

_____

_____

_____

6. Devise an experimental procedure to determine how much inaccuracy there might be in the measurements of volume in this experiment.

_____

_____

_____

_____

_____

_____

_____

_____

Charles's Law

(Demonstration)

Lab 20

Text reference: **Chapter 12**, pp. 303–309

Pre-Lab Discussion

In this experiment, you will observe the relationship between the volume of a confined gas and its temperature. Charles's law states that at constant pressure, the volume of a fixed mass of a gas varies directly with the Kelvin (or absolute) temperature. This law may be represented as

$$\frac{V}{T} = k$$

The effects of varying the temperature of a fixed mass of gas at constant pressure will be observed and measured. In order for the experimental data to agree with Charles's law, the Celsius temperatures will be converted to Kelvin temperatures. Data then will be plotted and a graph constructed.

Students will be expected to record data, make calculations, and construct graphs independently.

Purpose

Verify experimentally the relationship between Kelvin temperature and the volume of a gas at constant pressure.

Equipment

capillary tube, 1-mm internal diameter, with mercury plug in place	test tube clamp
	rubber stopper, 1-hole
metric ruler, wood	wire gauze
thermometer	400-mL beaker
stirrer	laboratory burner
ring stand	safety goggles
iron ring	lab apron or coat

Materials

ice
water

Safety

Note the safety symbols here and in certain steps in the "Procedure." Refer to page xi to review the specific precautions associated with each symbol. Handle the capillary tube used in this experiment with care. It is fragile and easily broken. Also, the mercury in the plug at the end of the capillary tube is poisonous. Be careful not to spill the mercury or bring it in contact with your skin. Always wear safety goggles and a lab coat or apron while working in the lab.

Procedure

Each step of this procedure will be conducted by the teacher. Students are expected to observe these steps carefully and to record all data.

1. Tape the capillary tube to the metric ruler. The sealed end of the tube should be at the 0 mark of the ruler, as shown in Figure 20-1.

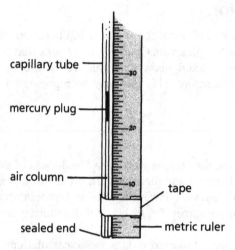

Figure 20-1

2. At room temperature, measure the length (in cm) of the column of air trapped between the bottom of the mercury plug and the sealed end of the tube. Record this measurement and the exact temperature in your data table.

3. Set up the apparatus as shown in Figure 20-2. Fill the 400-mL beaker with an ice-water mixture. Stir until the mixture reaches its lowest temperature (about 0°C). Add ice if needed.

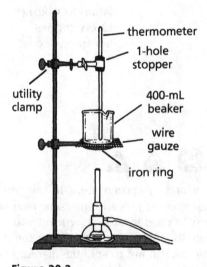

Figure 20-2

20 Charles's Law (continued)

4. Immerse the ruler and tube, making sure that the entire column of trapped air is below water level. Wait several minutes. Record the length of the air column and the exact temperature of the ice-water mixture.

5. Empty the beaker. Refill with tap water. With the tube, ruler, and thermometer immersed, heat the water to about 50°C. Discontinue heating and record the length of the column of air and the exact temperature.

6. Resume heating until the temperature reaches 75°C. Stop heating and record the length of the column of air and the exact temperature.

7. Resume heating and repeat step 6 at 100°C.

8. Repeat all trials if time permits.

Observations and Data

Temperature (°C)	Length of air column (cm)		Average
	Trial 1	Trial 2	of 2 trials
_____	_____	_____	_____
_____	_____	_____	_____
_____	_____	_____	_____
_____	_____	_____	_____
_____	_____	_____	_____

Calculations

1. Convert Celsius temperatures to kelvins (K = °C + 273).

0°C = _____ K

23°C = _____

50°C = _____

75°C = _____

100°C = _____

2. Plot the data on the grid provided in Figure 20-3. Kelvin temperatures (x-axis) should range from 0 K (origin) to 400 K. The length of the column of air (y-axis) should range from 0 to 10 cm.

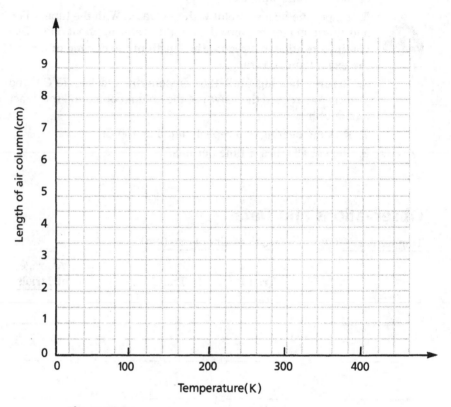

Figure 20-3

3. Once your data are plotted and the curve drawn, extend the curve (extrapolate) to the origin using a dotted line.

Conclusions and Questions

1. According to your graph, how are volume and Kelvin temperature related?

_____

_____

_____

2. Explain why, in terms of graph extrapolation, 0 kelvin is called absolute zero.

_____

_____

_____

_____

_____

20 Charles's Law (continued)

3. If the volume of a gas at STP is 300.0 mL, what is its volume at 25°C (pressure constant)?

4. Explain why the Kelvin scale is very convenient to use in scientific calculations.

_____

_____

5. A temperature change of 1 K is equivalent to a change of how many degrees Celsius?

_____

_____

Molar Volume of a Gas   Lab 21

Text reference: **Chapter 12**, pp. 311–313

Pre-Lab Discussion

Avogadro's hypothesis states that equal volumes of all gases contain equal numbers of molecules under the same conditions of temperature and pressure. It follows from this hypothesis that all gas samples containing the same number of molecules will occupy the same volume under the same conditions of temperature and pressure. A special name is given to the volume occupied by 1-mole samples of gases at STP. This volume is called the *molar volume*. In this experiment, you will make an experimental determination of the molar volume.

The basis of this experiment is the following reaction, in which you will react a known mass of magnesium with excess hydrochloric acid to produce the substances shown:

$$Mg(s) + 2HCl(aq) \rightarrow MgCl_2(aq) + H_2(g)$$

The hydrogen gas is the product that is of interest to you in this experiment. You will make an experimental determination of the number of moles of hydrogen molecules produced and the volume occupied by these molecules. The number of moles of hydrogen will be determined indirectly. The balanced equation for this reaction shows that the molar ratio of magnesium reacted to hydrogen gas produced is 1:1. Therefore, by determining the mass of magnesium that reacts and the number of moles that this mass is equal to, you will also determine the number of moles of hydrogen gas produced. The volume of hydrogen gas produced will be measured directly on the scale of a gas-measuring tube. The gas laws of Boyle and Charles will be used to correct this volume, measured *under laboratory conditions*, to the volume the sample of gas would occupy *at STP*. The collected data (number of moles and volume at STP) will be used to calculate the molar volume of the hydrogen gas.

This experiment should aid in the understanding of the mole concept and the concept of molar volume of a gas.

Purpose

Determine the volume of 1 mole of hydrogen gas at STP using experimental data, known mathematical relationships, and a balanced chemical equation.

Equipment

gas-measuring tube	battery jar (or 1000-mL beaker)
one-hole stopper (for gas tube)	graduated cylinder, 10-mL
ring stand	metric ruler
utility clamp	safety goggles
thermometer	lab apron or coat
beaker, 400-mL	

Materials

magnesium ribbon (Mg)   cotton thread
3 M hydrochloric acid (HCl)

Safety

Handle the 3 M HCl with care; always wear safety goggles when working with strong acids. Note the caution alert symbol under "Procedure" and follow the precautions indicated. Be sure to always wear safety goggles and a lab coat or apron when working in the lab. Handle the gas-measuring tubes and other glassware very carefully to avoid breakage.

Procedure

1. Obtain a piece of magnesium ribbon from your teacher. Measure the length of the piece of ribbon (±0.1 cm). Record the length as (a) in your data table. Also record the mass of 1 meter of magnesium ribbon. These data will be provided by the teacher. Record as (b).

2. Obtain a piece of cotton thread about 15 cm long. Tie one end of the thread around the piece of magnesium ribbon, leaving about 10 cm of thread free. Bend the piece of magnesium so that it will fit easily into the gas-measuring tube.

 3. Obtain about 10 mL of 3 M hydrochloric acid (HCl). **CAUTION:** *Handle this acid with care.* Carefully pour the HCl into a gas-measuring tube.

4. Tilt the gas-measuring tube slightly. Using a beaker, slowly fill the gas-measuring tube with water at room temperature. Try to avoid mixing the acid and water as much as possible.

5. Lower the piece of magnesium ribbon 4 or 5 cm into the gas-measuring tube. Drape the thread over the edge of the tube and insert the one-hole rubber stopper into the tube as shown in Figure 21-1.

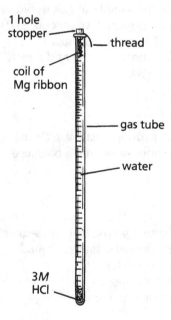

1 hole
stopper — thread
coil of
Mg ribbon
— gas tube
— water
3M
HCl

Figure 21-1

Name _____

21 Molar Volume of a Gas (continued)

6. Add about 300 mL of water at room temperature to a 400-mL beaker. Set up a ring stand and utility clamp, and place the beaker of water in the position shown in Figure 21-2.

7. Place your finger over the hole in the rubber stopper and invert the gas-measuring tube. Lower the stoppered end of the tube into the beaker of water. Clamp the tube in place so that the stoppered end is a few centimeters above the bottom of the beaker (Figure 21-2). Record your visual observations as (g) in the data table.

8. Let the apparatus stand about 5 minutes after the magnesium has completely reacted. Then, tap the sides of the gas-measuring tube to dislodge any gas bubbles that may have become attached to the sides of the tube. Place your finger over the hole in the stopper and transfer the tube to a battery jar filled with water. Lower the end of the tube into the water and remove your finger from the hole.

9. Move the tube up or down (to equalize pressure) until the water level in the tube is the same as that in the battery jar. On the scale of the gas-measuring tube, read the volume of the gases in the tube. Record this volume as (c) in your data table.

10. In the data table, record the room temperature, (d), and the barometric pressure, (e).

11. If time permits and your teacher so indicates, repeat the experiment.

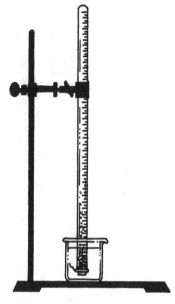

Figure 21-2

Observations and Data

	Trial 1	Trial 2	Avg. of 2 trials
a. length of Mg ribbon	_____ cm	_____ cm	_____ cm
b. mass of 1 meter of Mg	_____ g	_____ g	_____ g
c. volume of H_2 gas in tube	_____ mL	_____ mL	_____ mL
d. room temperature	_____ °C	_____ °C	_____ °C
e. barometric pressure	_____ mm Hg	_____ mm Hg	_____ mm Hg
f. water vapor pressure at room temperature, P_{H_2O} (from Appendix B).	_____ mm Hg	_____ mm Hg	_____ mm Hg

g. visual observations:

_____

_____

_____

_____

_____

Calculations

1. Find the mass of the Mg strip:

$$\frac{0.050 \text{ meter}}{1.00 \text{ meter}} = \frac{x \text{ grams}}{\text{mass of 1-meter length}}$$

2. Calculate the number of moles of Mg reacted (which is equal to the number of moles of H_2 gas produced):

$$\text{no. of moles Mg} = \frac{\text{mass of Mg reacted (g)}}{24 \text{ g Mg/mole Mg}}$$

3. Find the pressure exerted by the H_2 gas in the tube:

$$P_{H_2} = P_{\text{barometric}} - P_{H_2O}$$

4. Convert room temperature from °C to kelvin: $k = °C + 273$

5. Find the volume of the H_2 gas at STP:

$$\frac{P_1 V_1}{T_1} = \frac{P_2 V_2}{T_2} \quad \text{OR} \quad V_2 = V_1 \times \frac{P_1}{T_1} \times \frac{T_2}{P_2}, \text{ where:}$$

$P_1 = P_{H_2}$ (from calculation 3)
V_1 = experimental value of H_2 (c)
T_1 = room temperature (K)
$T_2 = 273$ K
$P_2 = 760$ mm Hg
V_2 = volume of H_2 at STP

6. Find the volume of 1 mole of H_2 gas at STP:

$$\frac{\text{moles of } H_2 \text{ gas (from calculation 2)}}{\text{volume of } H_2 \text{ gas } (V_2)} = \frac{1 \text{ mole}}{x \text{ mL}}$$

$x =$ _____ mL/mole = _____ L/mole

Name _____

21 Molar Volume of a Gas (continued)

Conclusions and Questions

1. The accepted value for the molar volume of a gas is 22.4 liters (22 400 mL). How does your experimentally determined value compare with this accepted value? Calculate your percentage error.

2. What are some possible sources of error in this experiment?

_____

_____

_____

_____

3. Find the volume of the following masses of gases at STP:
a. 80 g O_2 **b.** 10 g H_2 **c.** 14 g N_2 **d.** 66 g CO_2

4. How many liters would the following number of moles of any gas occupy at STP?
a. 0.25 mole   **b.** 0.5 mole   **c.** 1 mole   **d.** 2 moles   **e.** 2.5 moles

5. What happens to the other product of the reaction used in this experiment?

_____

_____

Determining the Molecular Mass of a Gas

Lab 22

Text reference: **Chapter 12**, pp. 314–317

Pre-Lab Discussion

In this lab, you will make an experimental determination of the molecular mass of an unidentified gas. This determination will be based on the following relationship:

$$\frac{m}{V_{STP}} = \frac{m_m}{22.4 \text{ L}}$$

where m = the mass in grams of a sample of a gas

V_{STP} = the volume of the gas sample at STP

m_m = the molar mass of the gas (mass of 1 mole of the gas)

The ratio on the left side of the equation represents the density of the gas at STP, because density equals mass divided by volume. The ratio on the right side of the equation is another mass: volume ratio. This ratio also gives the density of the gas at STP, because 1 mole of any gas occupies 22.4 L at STP. Thus, both ratios represent the same quantity, that is, the density of a given gas at STP. The two ratios therefore can be set equal to each other, producing the equation shown.

If the mass and volume of a sample of a gas at STP are known, m_m can be calculated using the equation above. This mass in grams is numerically equal to the molecular mass of the gas. This method for determining the molecular mass of a gas also can be used for liquids. In such cases, the liquid must be heated until it boils. A sample of the vapor is collected, and the mass and volume of the sample are measured.

When using this method in the laboratory, the gas sample is collected and its volume measured under laboratory conditions of temperature and pressure. The gas laws of Boyle and Charles are used to correct this volume to what it would be at STP. The computed volume is used to calculate m_m.

This experiment will give you a better understanding of molar volume, molar mass, and molecular mass.

Purpose

Determine the molecular mass of a substance from measurements of the density of its vapor.

Equipment

flask, Erlenmeyer (125-mL)	straight pin
beaker, 400-mL	graduated cylinder, 100-mL
ring stand	thermometer
iron ring	burner
wire gauze	balance
utility clamp	safety goggles
crucible tongs	lab apron or coat

Materials

unidentified liquid   aluminum foil (5-cm square)

Safety

Tie back long hair and secure loose clothing when working with an open flame. Note that the vapor produced in the experiment (steps 7 and 8) is flammable. Do not bring the burner flame close to the escaping vapor. Always wear safety goggles and a lab coat or apron when working in the lab. Note the caution alert symbols here and with certain steps in the "Procedure" and follow the precautions indicated. You can review these precautions on page xi.

Procedure

1. Set up a ring stand, ring, and wire gauze. Place a 400-mL beaker about two-thirds full of cold tap water on the ring. Heat the water to boiling. While the water is heating, complete procedural steps 2, 3, and 4.

2. Using a 5-cm square of aluminum foil, make an air-tight cap over the mouth of a 125-mL Erlenmeyer flask. With a pin, make a *tiny* hole (as small as possible) in the center of the cap.

3. Find the mass of the flask + cap. Record this mass as (a) in your data list.

4. Remove the cap and add about 3 mL of the unidentified liquid to the flask. Replace the aluminum cap securely.

5. When the water in the beaker is boiling vigorously, measure the temperature of the water and record as (d) in your data list.

6. Measure and record the barometric pressure (e).

7. *Carefully* lower the flask into the boiling water in the beaker and clamp in place as shown in Figure 22-1. Adjust the flame to keep the water boiling gently.

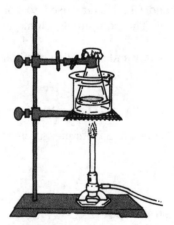

Figure 22-1

8. Continue heating the water until all the liquid in the flask has evaporated and hot vapor no longer comes out of the pinhole in the aluminum cap.

KEEP THE FLAME AWAY FROM THE ESCAPING VAPOR

Name _____

9. Loosen the clamp and, using crucible tongs, remove the flask and set it on the lab bench to cool. During cooling, the vapor inside the flask will condense to a liquid.

10. After all the vapor in the flask has condensed, wipe the flask and cap dry with a piece of toweling. Find the combined mass of the flask + cap + condensate. Record as (b). Dispose of the liquid as instructed by your teacher.

11. Fill the flask to the top with tap water. Using a 100-mL graduated cylinder, measure the exact volume of the water in the flask. This represents the volume of the vapor (V_1), before it condensed. Record this volume as (c) in your data list.

Observations and Data

a. mass of flask + cap _____ g

b. mass of flask + cap + condensate _____ g

c. volume of flask (V_1) _____ mL

d. temperature of water, (T_1) _____ °C

_____ K

e. barometric pressure _____ mm Hg

Calculations

1. Find the mass of the condensed vapor:

$$m = b - a$$

2. Find the volume of the vapor at STP:

$$V_2 = V_1 \times \frac{P_1}{P_2} \times \frac{T_2}{T_1} \quad \text{(Note: } P_2 \text{ and } T_2 \text{ are STP)}$$

3. Find the molecular mass of the gas sample:

$$\text{molecular mass} = \frac{m \text{ (g)} \times 22.4 \text{ (L/mole)}}{V_2 \text{ (L)}} \quad \text{(Note: } V_2 \text{ is converted to liters)}$$

Conclusions and Questions

1. Using the molecular formula supplied by the teacher, calculate the actual molecular mass of the unidentified substance.

2. Compare the true molecular mass of the substance with the experimentally determined value. Find your percent error.

3. What are some likely sources of error in this experiment?

_____

_____

_____

_____

4. A gas has a density of 1.25 g/L at STP. What is its molecular mass?

5. At STP, 10 liters of a gas has a mass of 1.34 grams. What is the mass of 1 mole of this gas?

Mass-Volume Relationships in Reactions

Lab 23

Text reference: **Chapter 12**, pp. 318–321

Pre-Lab Discussion

Many chemical reactions involve the production of a gas from a solid reactant. Given a balanced equation for such a reaction and the mass of any of the substances involved, you can use the molar relationship between mass and volume to find the volume of the gas produced. Such calculations are known as mass-volume problems.

This experiment is based on the decomposition of copper(II) carbonate basic. The balanced equation for the reaction is:

$$CuCO_3 \cdot Cu(OH)_2(s) \xrightarrow{\Delta} 2CuO(s) + CO_2(g) + H_2O(g)$$

The CO_2 gas is collected by the water-displacement method. This CO_2 is saturated with water vapor and is collected at room conditions. Thus, certain corrections must be made in order to determine its *dry* volume at STP. These corrections involve the use of Dalton's law of partial pressures and the combined gas laws of Boyle and Charles.

This experiment should help you understand the molar relationship between mass and volume and solve mass-volume problems.

Purpose

Compare the volume of CO_2 gas (corrected to STP) attained experimentally with the theoretical volume predicted by mass-volume calculations.

Equipment

balance
burner
test tube, 18×150-mm
rubber stopper, one-hole
  (for test tube)
glass tube
tubing, delivery
pneumatic trough
collecting bottles, 250-mL (2)

ring stand
utility clamp
microspatula
glass squares (2)
graduated cylinder, 100-mL
thermometer
safety goggles
lab apron or coat

Materials

copper(II) carbonate basic [$CuCO_3 \cdot Cu(OH)_2$]

Safety

Tie back long hair and secure loose clothing when working with an open flame. Note the safety alert symbols here and with certain steps in the "Procedure" and take the precautions indicated. You can review those precautions on page xi. Always wear safety goggles and a lab coat or apron when working in the lab.

Procedure

1. Measure out exactly 2.21 g of copper(II) carbonate basic [$CuCO_3 \cdot Cu(OH)_2$] and add it to a clean, dry test tube. Record this mass as (a) in your data list.

2. Clamp the test tube to a ring stand as illustrated in Figure 23-1. The test tube should be set at an angle, as shown, and the $CuCO_3 \cdot Cu(OH)_2$ should be spread along the lower half of the tube.

Figure 23-1

3. Find the total volume of two collecting bottles by filling them with tap water and carefully measuring the water in a graduated cylinder. Record this volume as (b) in your data list.

4. Half fill a pneumatic trough with water. *Completely fill* the two collecting bottles with water and place a glass square over the mouth of each. Invert each bottle and place it in the pneumatic trough, as illustrated in Figure 23-2. *Do not allow any water to leak out of these bottles.*

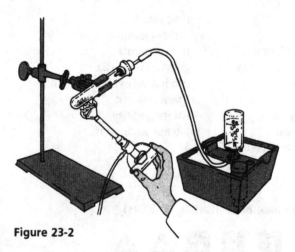

Figure 23-2

5. Assemble the glass tube, stopper, and delivery tube. Set up apparatus as shown in Figure 23-2.

6. Holding the burner in your hand, heat the $CuCO_3 \cdot Cu(OH)_2$ *gently* at first, moving the burner up and down the test tube.

23 Mass-Volume Relationships in Reactions (continued)

7. When one collecting bottle is filled with gas, *immediately* place the second bottle over the delivery tube. Once the bubbling slows down, heat the tube strongly until no more gas is produced. *Stop heating and take the delivery tube out of the trough at once.* Cover the mouth of the second collecting bottle with a glass square and remove it from the trough.

8. Using a graduated cylinder, measure the volume of water remaining in the second collecting bottle. Record this volume as (c) in your data list.

9. Measure the temperature of the water in the second bottle and record as (d) in your data list. (This is the same as the temperature of the gas.)

10. Record the barometric pressure as (e) in your data list.

Observations and Data

a. mass of $CuCO_3 \cdot Cu(OH)_2$ _____ g

b. total volume of collecting bottles   _____ mL

c. volume of water remaining in bottle   _____ mL

d. temperature of water, T_1 _____ °C

         _____ K

e. barometric pressure   _____ mm Hg

Calculations

1. Using the balanced equation for this reaction, calculate the volume of CO_2 that should be produced by the decomposition of 2.21 g of $CuCO_3 \cdot Cu(OH)_2$ at STP: _____ mL

2. Find the volume of CO_2 gas (V_1) collected in this experiment:

$$V_1 = b - c$$ _____ mL

3. Find the pressure exerted by *dry* CO_2 gas. (Refer to the table of water vapor pressures in Appendix B.)

$$P_1 = P_{barometric} - P_{H_2O}$$ _____ mm Hg

4. Calculate the volume (V_2) of the CO_2 gas at STP:

$$V_2 = \frac{P_1 V_1 T_2}{P_2 T_1} \qquad \text{where:} \quad \begin{aligned} T_1 &= \text{water temp (K)} \\ P_2 &= 760 \text{ mm Hg} \\ T_2 &= 273 \text{ K} \end{aligned}$$

5. Calculate your percentage error:

$$\text{percent} = \frac{\text{observed value} - \text{true value}}{\text{true value}} \times 100$$

Conclusions and Questions

1. Calculate the mass of H_2O produced by the decomposition of 2.21 g of $CuCO_3 \cdot Cu(OH)_2$. What happens to this water?

2. Suggest some possible sources of error in this experiment.

_____

_____

_____

_____

_____

_____

_____

_____

_____

_____

_____

_____

23 Mass-Volume Relationships in Reactions (continued)

3. In the decomposition reaction $2KClO_3(s) \rightarrow 2KCl(s) + 3O_2(g)$, what volume of O_2 gas at STP would be produced from 3.66 g of $KClO_3$?

4. In the reaction $N_2(g) + 3H_2(g) \rightarrow 2NH_3(g)$, how many grams of NH_3 gas would be formed when H_2 gas, having a volume of 11.2 liters at STP, reacts with excess N_2 gas?

Graham's Law of Diffusion

Lab 24

Text reference: **Chapter 12,** pp. 318–321

Pre-Lab Discussion

Gases have no definite volume. They spread out, or diffuse, and occupy all the space available to them. This spreading of gases is called diffusion. A gas will diffuse even if another gas is present in the same space. The molecules of gases are far enough apart to allow other gas molecules to fit in between.

Gases diffuse at different rates. Graham's law states that, under equal conditions of temperature and pressure, gases diffuse at rates inversely proportional to the square roots of their molecular masses. Mathematically this may be stated as

$$\frac{R_1}{R_2} = \frac{\sqrt{M_2}}{\sqrt{M_1}}$$

The term *rate* implies that something happens in a given period of time. The rate of diffusion of a gas is the distance its molecules travel per unit time. In an equal period of time, the distances traveled by molecules of two different gases are related by:

$$\frac{D_1}{D_2} = \frac{\sqrt{M_2}}{\sqrt{M_1}}$$

This inverse relationship indicates that the distance traveled by the heavier gas (gas with greater molecular mass) will be less than that traveled by the lighter gas in the same period of time.

In this experiment, two gases—HCl and NH_3—will be introduced simultaneously into opposite ends of a glass tube. At the point where the two gases meet inside the tube, a chemical reaction will occur that produces a white powder. The equation for the reaction is: $HCl(g) + NH_3(g) \rightarrow NH_4Cl(s)$. Using the point where the powder forms as a reference point, the distance traveled by each gas can be measured. By comparing the ratio of these distances with the ratio of the square roots of the known molecular masses of the two gases, Graham's law can be verified.

Purpose

Verify Graham's law by measuring the distances traveled during the same period of time by two different gases of known molecular mass.

Equipment

glass tubing, 10 mm × 60 cm
dropper pipets (2)
cotton swabs
wax marking pencil

metric ruler
safety goggles
lab apron or coat

Materials

HCl (conc)
$NH_3 \cdot H_2O$ (ammonia water, conc)
acetone (for drying test tubes)

Safety

Note the caution alert symbols here and under certain steps in the "Procedure." Refer to page xi to review the specific precautions associated with each symbol. Be sure there are no open flames in the lab when the acetone is in use. Handle both the concentrated HCl and the concentrated $NH_3 \cdot H_2O$ solutions with great care. Avoid getting any of either of these chemicals on your skin. Always wear safety goggles and a lab apron or coat when working in the lab.

Procedure

 1. Obtain a 50-cm length of glass tubing (10 mm internal diameter). Make sure it is completely dry. Lay the tubing on your bench.

2. Place one cotton swab in each end of the tubing. Using a marking pencil, mark the glass to indicate the position of the end of each swab as illustrated in Figure 24-1.

Figure 24-1

 3. Remove the cotton swabs from the tubing. Mark the stem of one of the swabs with the marker for purposes of identification. Using dropper pipets, place about five drops of concentrated HCl on the unmarked cotton swab and five drops of concentrated $NH_3 \cdot H_2O$ solution on the marked cotton swab. **CAUTION:** *Handle these chemicals with care. They can cause painful burns if they come in contact with the skin.*

4. Immediately and *simultaneously* insert the moistened ends of the cotton swabs into opposite ends of the tube, to the lines previously marked.

 5. After several minutes, a white ring will form where the gases HCi and NH_3 meet inside the tube to form the white compound NH_4Cl (ammonium chloride). Mark the point on the tube where the white ring is formed.

6. Remove the cotton swabs, rinse them with water, and dispose of them as instructed by your teacher.

7. Measure the distance traveled by each gas.

8. Rinse the tubing with water. It may be dried by rinsing it with acetone. **CAUTION:** *Acetone is highly flammable.*

9. The procedure can be repeated if time permits.

24 Graham's Law of Diffusion (continued)

Observations and Data

	Trial 1	Trial 2	Average of 2 trials
Distance traveled by NH_3	_____	_____	_____
Distance traveled by HCl	_____	_____	_____

Molecular masses are: $NH_3 = 17$
                        $HCl = 36.5$

Calculations

1. Calculate the ratio: $\dfrac{\text{Distance } NH_3}{\text{Distance HCl}}$

2. Calculate the ratio: $\dfrac{\sqrt{M_{HCl}}}{\sqrt{M_{NH_3}}}$

Conclusions and Questions

1. How well did the two ratios compare? Taking the experimental error into consideration, was Graham's law verified by this experiment?

_____

_____

_____

2. Compare gases with liquids and solids according to the kinetic molecular theory.

_____

_____

_____

_____

_____

_____

_____

3. How could this experiment be used to find the molecular mass of an unknown gas?

_____

_____

_____

_____

_____

_____

4. It is known that the density of a gas at STP is its molecular mass divided by 22.4 L. Based on this information, state Graham's law in an alternative form.

_____

_____

_____

Flame Tests

Pre-Lab Discussion

The normal electron configuration of atoms or ions of an element is known as the "ground state." In this most stable energy state, all electrons are in the lowest energy levels available. When atoms or ions in the ground state are heated to high temperatures, some electrons may absorb enough energy to allow them to "jump" to higher energy levels. The element is then said to be in the "excited state." This excited configuration is unstable, and the electrons "fall" back to their normal positions of lower energy. As the electrons return to their normal levels, the energy that was absorbed is emitted in the form of electromagnetic energy. Some of this energy may be in the form of visible light. The color of this light can be used as a means of identifying the elements involved. Such crude analyses are known as flame tests.

Only metals, with their loosely held electrons, are excited in the flame of a laboratory burner. Thus, flame tests are useful in the identification of metallic ions. Many metallic ions exhibit characteristic colors when vaporized in the burner flame. In this experiment, characteristic colors of several different metallic ions will be observed, and an unidentified ion will be identified by means of its flame test.

Purpose

Observe the characteristic colors produced by certain metallic ions when vaporized in a flame. Identify an unknown metallic ion by means of its flame test.

Equipment

graduated cylinder, 10-mL	wire loop, platinum (or nichrome)
laboratory burner	glass-marking pencil
test tubes, 13×100-mm (8)	safety goggles
test tube rack	lab apron or coat

Materials

hydrochloric acid, HCl (conc)   Unidentified solutions
0.5 M solutions of nitrates of:
    Na^+, K^+, Li^+, Ca^{2+}, Sr^{2+}, Ba^{2+}, Cu^{2+}

Safety

Handle concentrated HCl with great care. Report spills at once to your teacher and flush them with cool water and $NaHCO_3$ solution. Note the caution alert symbols here and with certain steps in the "Procedure." Refer to page xi for the specific precautions associated with each symbol. Always wear safety goggles and a lab coat or apron when working in the lab.

Procedure

1. Measure 5 mL of tap water in a graduated cylinder and pour the water into a 13×100 test tube. Using a marking pencil, mark the outside of the tube to indicate the level of the water. Discard the water. Using the marked tube as a guide, mark seven *clean* test tubes at approximately the same level. Place the clean tubes in a test tube rack. Set the other test tube aside.

2. Into each of the *clean* test tubes, pour 5 mL of a different nitrate solution. Mark each test tube to indicate the metallic ion it contains.

3. Pour about 10 mL of concentrated hydrochloric acid into a 50-mL beaker. **CAUTION:** *Use extreme care in handling this acid.* To clean the wire loop, dip the loop in the acid and then heat the loop in the outer edge of the burner flame. Continue to clean the loop in this manner until no color is observed in the flame.

4. Dip the clean wire loop into one of the nitrate solutions. Place the loop in the outer edge of the burner flame and move the loop up and down (Figure 25-1). Note the color in the flame. Record your observations in the data list provided.

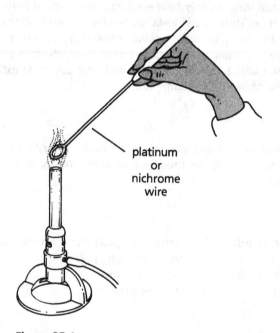

platinum
or
nichrome
wire

Figure 25-1

5. Clean the wire loop as described in step 3. Repeat step 4 using a different nitrate solution.

6. Test each nitrate solution in the same manner, cleaning the loop thoroughly between tests. Record all your observations in the data list.

7. Obtain a sample of an unknown solution. Perform a flame test and identify the metallic ion present by the color of the flame.

25 Flame Tests (continued)

Observations and Data

Metallic Ion	Color in Flame
Na^+	_____
K^+	_____
Li^+	_____
Ca^{2+}	_____
Sr^{2+}	_____
Ba^{2+}	_____
Cu^{2+}	_____
Unknown_____	_____

Conclusions and Questions

1. What inaccuracies may be involved in using flame tests for identification purposes?

_____

_____

_____

_____

_____

2. Which pairs of ions produce similar colors in the flame tests?

_____

_____

_____

_____

3. Explain how the colors observed in the flame tests are produced.

_____

_____

_____

_____

_____

_____

4. Define these terms:
  a. quanta   **b.** ground state   **c.** excited state

_____

_____

_____

_____

_____

5. What is a spectroscope? What is observed if the flame tests are viewed through a spectroscope?

_____

_____

_____

_____

_____

_____

Group 2: The Alkaline Earth Metals

Lab 26

Text reference: **Chapter 14**, pp. 364–368

Pre-Lab Discussion

The elements in Group 2 of the periodic table are called the alkaline earth elements. Like the elements in Group 1 (the alkali metals), the elements in Group 2 are chemically active and are never found in nature in the elemental state. Like all members of a group, or family, the elements in Group 2 share certain common characteristics.

The metallic character—the tendency to donate electrons during chemical reaction—of the Group 2 elements increases as you go down the group. The more metallic of these elements typically react with water to form hydroxides and hydrogen gas. An example of such a reaction would be:

$$Ca(s) + 2HOH \rightarrow Ca(OH)_2(aq) + H_2(g)$$

As metallic character increases (as you go down the group), the tendency for these elements to form ions increases. Also as you go down the group, the solubilities of the hydroxides formed by the elements of this group increase. The more active the metal, the more basic its saturated hydroxide solution.

The solubilities of alkaline earth compounds also show some interesting and useful tendencies. For example, the sulfate compounds of alkaline earth metals show decreasing solubilities as you go down the group. This characteristic is used as a means of separating and identifying metallic ions of this group. Carbonates of all alkaline earth metals are quite insoluble.

In this experiment, you will observe some of the characteristics of the alkaline earth metals discussed here and will write balanced equations for all reactions.

Purpose

Investigate some reactions of some Group 2 elements and gain some insights into the properties of these alkaline earth elements.

Equipment

balance
burner
test tubes, 13×100-mm (3)
test tube holder
test tube rack
wood splints

pH paper
stirrer
flame tester
filter paper
safety goggles
lab apron or coat

Materials

calcium turnings (Ca)
magnesium ribbon (Mg)
magnesium sulfate crystals
   (MgSO$_4$)
calcium sulfate crystals
   (CaSO$_4$)
barium sulfate crystals (BaSO$_4$)
distilled water
phenolphthalein solution

saturated solutions of:
   calcium hydroxide (Ca(OH)$_2$)
   magnesium hydroxide (Mg(OH)$_2$)
   barium hydroxide (Ba(OH)$_2$)
0.1 M solutions of:
   sodium carbonate (Na$_2$CO$_3$)
   magnesium chloride (MgCl$_2$)
   calcium chloride (CaCl$_2$)
   barium chloride (BaCl$_2$)

Safety

Handle all chemicals with care; avoid spills and contact with your skin. Heat chemicals exactly as instructed. When heating a substance in a test tube, point the tube away from yourself and others. Tie back long hair and secure loose clothing when working with an open flame. Note the caution alert symbols here and with certain steps of the "Procedure." Refer to page xi for the specific precautions associated with each symbol. Always wear safety goggles and a lab coat or apron when working in the lab.

Procedure

Record all observations and results in the "Observations and Data" section.

PART A

1. Pour about 5 mL of distilled water into a clean, dry test tube and place the tube in the test tube rack. Add a calcium turning to the water in the tube. To collect the gas being released, invert a clean, dry test tube over the reactant tube, holding the inverted tube with a test tube holder (Figure 26-1).

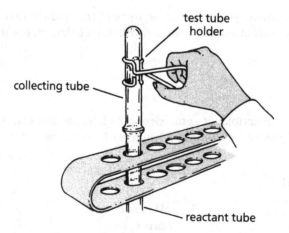

Figure 26-1

2. Test for hydrogen gas by inserting a burning wood splint into the upper part of the inverted tube. (See Figure 26-2.)

26 Group 2: The Alkaline Earth Metals (continued)

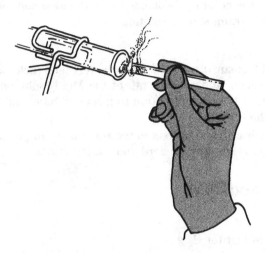

Figure 26-2

3. Add a few drops of phenolphthalein solution to the reactant tube. After making your observations, discard the contents of the tube and clean and dry the tube.

4. Repeat step 1, using a 10-cm piece of magnesium ribbon in place of the calcium. If no visible reaction occurs, heat the water to boiling, using a test tube holder to hold the tube over the burner flame. **CAUTION:** *Point the tube away from yourself and others while heating.*

5. Once the water is boiling, stand the tube in a test tube rack and, using a test tube holder, invert a collecting tube over the reactant tube. After a few seconds, test for hydrogen gas.

6. Turn off the burner and add a few drops of phenolphthalein to the reactant tube. Record your observations. Discard the contents of the tube, and clean and dry the tube.

PART B

7. Obtain 5-mL samples of saturated solutions of calcium hydroxide, magnesium hydroxide, and barium hydroxide. Test each solution with pH paper. Record the pH of each solution.

PART C

8. Using the laboratory balance, measure out a 1-g sample of magnesium sulfate. Place it in a clean, dry test tube.

9. Repeat step 8 for calcium sulfate and barium sulfate.

10. Add 5 mL of distilled water to each tube. Using a glass stirring rod, stir each mixture thoroughly, getting as much of each solid to dissolve as possible. Record your observations of the relative solubilities of each of these compounds.

11. Conduct a flame test for calcium ions (Ca^{2+}) and for barium ions (Ba^{2+}). Dip the wire loop of a flame tester into the solution of calcium sulfate. Place the loop in the burner flame. Observe and record the color of the flame. Clean the loop and repeat the test on the barium sulfate solution.

PART D

12. Stand 3 clean, dry test tubes in the test tube rack. Using the 0.1 M solutions, add about 5 mL of the $MgCl_2$ solution to one tube, 5 mL of the $CaCl_2$ solution to a second tube, and 5 mL of $BaCl_2$ to the third tube.

13. To each of the solutions in the test tubes, add about 1 mL of the Na_2CO_3 solution. Record your observations.

Observations and Data

PART A

Ca + HOH: Result of test for H_2 gas

_____

Result of adding phenolphthalein

_____

Mg + HOH: Result of test for H_2 gas (before heating)

_____

Result of test for H_2 gas (after heating)

_____

Result of adding phenolphthalein

_____

PART B

pH readings:

$Mg(OH)_2$

$Ca(OH)_2$

$Ba(OH)_2$

PART C

Apparent solubility:

$MgSO_4$

$CaSO_4$

$BaSO_4$

Flame test results:

Ca^{2+}

Ba^{2+}

26 Group 2: The Alkaline Earth Metals (continued)

PART D

Observations:

_____

_____

_____

Conclusions and Questions

1. Write balanced equations for each change that occurred as part of this experiment in steps 1, 4, 10, and 13.

_____

_____

_____

_____

_____

_____

_____

_____

2. Describe the reactivity of the metals in Group 2 in terms of their location in the group.

_____

_____

_____

3. How does the reactivity of an alkaline earth metal compare with that of an alkali metal (Group 1) in the same period?

_____

_____

4. What oxidation states can the alkaline earth metals exhibit?

_____

_____

5. Why does the metallic character of the alkaline earth metals increase as you go down the group?

_____

_____

_____

_____

Group 17: The Halogens

Lab 27

Text reference: **Chapter 14,** pp. 364–368

Pre-Lab Discussion

The elements in Group 17 of the periodic table are called the halogen family. Like the elements in Groups 1 and 2, members of the halogen family are too reactive to be found in nature as free elements to any great extent. In the elemental form, halogens exist as covalently bonded diatomic (two-atom) molecules. During chemical reaction, halogens ionize to form ions. These ions are known as halide ions, or simply halides.

Unlike the elements in Groups 1 and 2, the halogens are active *non-metals*. That is, they show a strong tendency to accept electrons during chemical reaction. This chemical activity decreases as you move down the group. This trend may be seen in reactions between halogens and halides. A more active halogen will "take away" electrons from the halide of a less active member of the group, as illustrated in the following "equation":

$$Cl_2(g) + 2I^-(aq) \rightarrow 2Cl^-(aq) + I_2(s)$$

In this reaction, elemental chlorine forms halide (chloride) ions by taking electrons away from the ions of the less active halogen iodine. The iodine atoms thus produced combine to form diatomic iodine molecules. The general formula for such reactions is $A_2 + 2B^- \rightarrow 2A^- + B_2$, where A is always a more active halogen than B.

Halides in solution can be separated by differences in solubility of certain of their metallic salts. If the ions F^-, Cl^-, Br^-, and I^- are all present in an aqueous solution, they can be separated by adding metallic ions with which they form insoluble salts. For example, F^- will react with Ca^{2+} ions to form an insoluble salt (CaF_2) that will precipitate out of solution. The other three halides will not. However, Cl^-, Br^-, and I^- will all react with Ag^+ ions to form salts that are insoluble in water. These salts may be distinguished from one another by differences in their solubilities in ammonia water, $NH_3(aq)$.

In this experiment, you will observe some reactions of the halogens and will verify some of the properties of these substances discussed above.

Purpose

Learn about the relative activity of the halogens and the methods of separating halides in solution.

Equipment

test tubes, 13×100-mm (4)   pipet dropper
test tube rack   safety goggles
stoppers, cork (for test tubes)   lab apron or coat

Materials

0.1 *M* solutions of:
    NaF
    NaCl
    NaBr
    NaI
    Ca(NO$_3$)$_2$
    AgNO$_3$

1,1,2-trichloro-1,2,2-trifluoroethane
    (FCCl$_2$CClF$_2$)
3.0 *M* NH$_3$(*aq*)
chlorine water

Safety

Be sure you do not inhale any 1,1,2-trichloro-1,2,2-trifluoroethane or allow the chemical to come in contact with your skin (step 5). It is an irritant. Also, avoid spilling chlorine water on clothing or your skin. Chlorine water and ammonia gas are strong irritants to the eyes. Note the safety alert symbols here and with certain steps in the "Procedure." Refer to page xi for specific precautions associated with each symbol. Always wear safety goggles and a lab coat or apron when working in the lab.

Procedure

Record all observations and results in the "Observations and Data" section.

PART A

1. Stand four clean, dry test tubes in a test tube rack. To each test tube, add about 5 mL of one of the following solutions, adding a different solution to each tube: 0.1 *M* NaF, 0.1 *M* NaCl, 0.1 *M* NaBr, and 0.1 *M* NaI.

2. Add five drops of 0.1 *M* Ca(NO$_3$)$_2$ to each solution. Record your observations. Discard the mixtures as instructed. Clean and dry the test tubes.

3. Add about 1 mL each of 0.1 *M* solutions of NaF, NaCl, NaBr, and NaI, respectively, to four clean, dry test tubes. Add five drops of 0.1 *M* AgNO$_3$ to each solution. Note the formation of precipitates.

4. To each solution in which precipitates form, add about 10 drops of 3.0 *M* NH$_3$(*aq*). Record your observations. Discard the mixtures. Clean and dry the test tubes.

PART B

5. Add about 1 mL each of 0.1 *M* solutions of NaF, NaBr, and NaI, respectively, to three clean, dry test tubes. To each solution, add 1 mL of 1,1,2-trichloro-1,2,2-trifluoroethane and record your observations. **CAUTION:** *Do not inhale 1,1,2-trichloro-1,2,2-trifluoroethane vapors and do not allow this chemical to come in contact with the skin.*

6. Add five drops of chlorine water to each test tube of step 5. Stopper and shake each tube. Record your observations.

PART C

7. Obtain a letter-coded "unknown" solution. Note the letter of your "unknown" in your "Observations and Data," Part C.

27 Group 17: The Halogens (continued)

8. The "unknown" solution contains the sodium salt of *one* of the halide ions (F^-, Cl^-, Br^-, I^-). Using what you learned in Parts A and B, write out a sequence of steps needed to identify your "unknown" halide. Use quantities indicated in previous parts of this experiment. *Check your proposed sequence with your teacher before proceeding. Make all suggested corrections.*

9. Using your corrected sequence of steps, identify the "unknown" halide ion. Remember to follow the **CAUTION** instruction listed in Part B. Write the ion in "Observations and Data," Part C. Repeat your sequence to be sure you have identified the ion correctly.

Observations and Data

Record your visual observations in the spaces provided. Do *not* write chemical equations.

PART A

2. $NaF + Ca(NO_3)_2$:

_____

$NaCl + Ca(NO_3)_2$:

_____

$NaBr + Ca(NO_3)_2$:

_____

$NaI + Ca(NO_3)_2$:

_____

3. $NaF + AgNO_3$:

_____

$NaCl + AgNO_3$:

_____

$NaBr + AgNO_3$:

_____

$NaI + AgNO_3$:

_____

4.

_____

_____

_____

PART B

5.

_____

_____

6. NaF + Cl_2:

_____

NaBr + Cl_2:

_____

NaI + Cl_2:

_____

PART C

7. Coded letter of "unknown":

_____

8. Sequence of steps:

_____

_____

_____

_____

_____

_____

_____

_____

_____

9. "Unknown" halide ion:

_____

Conclusions and Questions

1. Complete and balance the following equations:

   a. $NaF(aq) + Ca(NO_3)_2(aq) \rightarrow$

   b. $NaCl(aq) + AgNO_3(aq) \rightarrow$

   c. $NaBr(aq) + AgNO_3(aq) \rightarrow$

   d. $NaI(aq) + AgNO_3(aq) \rightarrow$

   e. $NaBr(aq) + Cl_2(g) \rightarrow$

   f. $NaI(ag) + Cl_2(g) \rightarrow$

2. Which halides will be replaced by F_2? by Cl_2? by Br_2? by I_2?

_____

_____

_____

_____

_____

27 Group 17: The Halogens (continued)

3. Explain why fluorine has only one oxidation state $(1-)$ when combined with other elements.

_____

_____

_____

4. How can F^- be distinguished from the other three halides?

_____

_____

_____

5. How can Cl^- be distinguished from Br^- and I^-?

_____

_____

_____

_____

6. How can you distinguish between a solution of Br^- and one of I^-?

_____

_____

_____

_____

7. Explain the formation of two distinct liquid layers when 1,1,2-trichloro-1,2,2,-trifluoroethane is added to aqueous solutions.

_____

_____

8. What is the purpose of the 1,1,2-trichloro-1,2,2-trifluoroethane that is used in Part B of the procedure?

_____

_____

_____

_____

_____

_____

Three-Dimensional Models of Covalent Molecules

Lab 28

Text reference: **Chapter 15**, pp. 412–416

Pre-Lab Discussion

A *single covalent bond* is formed when two atoms share a pair of electrons. Each atom provides one of the electrons of the pair. If the two atoms are alike, the bond is said to be *nonpolar covalent*. If the atoms are unlike, one exerts a greater attractive force on the electrons, and the bond is *polar covalent*. More than one pair of electrons can be shared. This results in a double or triple bond.

A group of atoms held together by covalent bonds is called a *molecule*. Molecules can be either polar or nonpolar. If bonds are nonpolar, the molecule is nonpolar. If bonds are polar, molecules can still be nonpolar if the charge distribution throughout the molecule is symmetrical. A molecule's symmetry depends on its shape, that is, the positions in space of the atoms making up the molecule. Some possible shapes are linear, angular (bent), pyramidal, and tetrahedral.

Although we represent molecules on paper as being two-dimensional for convenience, they are actually three-dimensional. By building molecular models, chemists come to understand the bonding, shapes, and polarity of even the most complex molecules.

Purpose

Build three-dimensional models of some simple covalent molecules. Predict their shapes and polarities from knowledge of bonds and molecule polarity rules.

Equipment

molecular model building set

Safety

All general lab safety rules should be followed. Always wear safety goggles and a lab apron or coat when working in the lab.

Procedure

1. Obtain a molecular model building set. Study the color code identifying the different kinds of atoms.

2. Observe that the following atoms have one hole (bonding site): hydrogen, fluorine, chlorine, bromine, and iodine. The atoms with two holes are oxygen and sulfur. A nitrogen atom has three holes, and a carbon atom has four holes.

3. Construct models of the following molecules:

H_2	HF	CH_3OH
H_2O	C_2H_2	H_2O_2
CH_4	CH_2Cl_2	O_2
Cl_2	N_2	H_2S
NH_3	CO_2	

4. Record your observations below.

Observations and Data

Name	Formula	Structural representation	Shape	Molecule polarity
hydrogen	H_2		_____	_____
water	H_2O		_____	_____
methane	CH_4		_____	_____
chlorine	Cl_2		_____	_____
ammonia	NH_3		_____	_____
hydrogen fluoride	HF		_____	_____
ethyne	C_2H_2		_____	_____
dichloromethane	CH_2Cl_2		_____	_____
nitrogen	N_2		_____	_____
carbon dioxide	CO_2		_____	_____
methanol	CH_3OH		_____	_____
hydrogen peroxide	H_2O_2		_____	_____
oxygen	O_2		_____	_____
hydrogen sulfide	H_2S		_____	_____

28 Three-Dimensional Models of Covalent Molecules
(continued)

Conclusions and Questions

1. Which molecules were nonpolar because all bonds were nonpolar?

_____

_____

_____

2. Which molecules had polar covalent bonds but were nonpolar because of symmetry?

_____

_____

_____

3. Which two shapes appeared to produce polar molecules?

_____

_____

_____

4. Name two types of substances that do not contain molecules with covalent bonds.

_____

_____

_____

Bonds, Polarity, and Solubility

Lab 29

Pre-Lab Discussion

"Like dissolves like" is an expression chemists use when discussing the solubility of substances. It means that, in general, nonpolar substances dissolve in nonpolar solvents and polar substances dissolve in polar solvents. (Ionic substances also dissolve in polar solvents.)

What determines the polarity of a molecule? First, keep in mind that true molecules contain covalent bonds. (Ionic compounds are not molecular.) The polarity of a molecule is determined by the type of covalent bond (polar or nonpolar) and by the arrangement of the bonds. If all the bonds in a molecule are nonpolar, the molecule is definitely nonpolar. If all of the bonds in a molecule are polar, then the arrangement of the bonds determines the polarity of the molecule. If the bonds are arranged symmetrically, the positive and negative charges in the molecule will be evenly distributed and the molecule will be nonpolar. If the bonds are not symmetrically arranged, the charges in the molecule will not be evenly distributed. One "end" of the molecule will be slightly negative, the other "end" will be slightly positive, and the molecule will be polar.

Examples of the three cases just described are illustrated in Figure 29-1. As indicated, water molecules and carbon tetrachloride molecules both contain polar bonds. However, the bonds in the water molecule are not symmetrically arranged. As a result, the oxygen end of the molecule is slightly more negative than the hydrogen end, and the molecule is polar. The symmetrical arrangement of polar bonds in the carbon tetrachloride molecule produces an even distribution of charges, making it nonpolar.

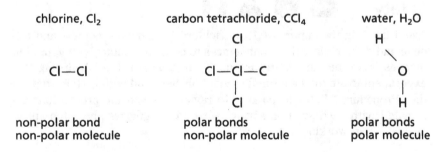

Figure 29-1

Some substances show an "intermediate" polarity because of complex bond arrangements in their molecular structures. Such substances, sometimes described as polar-nonpolar, show some degree of solubility with both polar and nonpolar substances.

When discussing solubility, we usually think in terms of the tendencies of solids to dissolve in liquids. However, liquid-liquid solutions are also important in chemistry. Liquids that dissolve in each other are said to be *miscible*. If two liquids dissolve in each other completely in all proportions, they are said to be completely miscible. If one dissolves in the other to a limited extent, the liquids are said to be partially miscible. If they don't dissolve in each other at all (that is, if one is only very, very slightly soluble in the other), they are said to be immiscible. A mixture of two immiscible liquids forms two distinct layers, with the less dense layer on top. A mixture of two partially soluble liquids will form two layers only if enough of each liquid is present.

In this experiment, you will investigate the solubilities of an ionic solid and a nonpolar solid in liquids of varying polarities. You also will investigate the miscibilities of liquids of varying polarities in each other. This experiment should lead to a better understanding of molecular polarities and the effects of polarity on solubility.

Purpose

Relate solubilities of various combinations of substances to their molecular polarities.

Equipment

test tubes, 13×100-mm (5)   graduated cylinder, 10-mL
test tube rack   marking pencil
microspatula   safety goggles
stoppers or corks (for test tubes) lab apron or coat

Materials

Solids: sodium chloride crystals (NaCl)—ionic
         iodine crystals (I_2)—nonpolar
Liquids: distilled water (H_2O)—polar
         1,1,2-trichloro-1,2,2-trifluoroethane ($FCCl_2CClF_2$)—effectively
             nonpolar
         toluene (C_7H_8)—nonpolar
         ethanol (C_2H_5OH)—intermediate

Safety

Avoid inhaling the vapors of 1,1,2-trichloro-1,2,2-trifluoroethane and toluene and do not allow these substances to come in contact with your skin or eyes. Also, be sure there are no open flames in the lab during this experiment. Note the caution alert symbols here and with certain steps in the "Procedure." Refer to page xi to review the specific precautions associated with each symbol. Always wear safety goggles and a lab apron or coat when working in the lab.

Procedure

PART A SOLUBILITY OF SOLIDS IN LIQUIDS

1. Place four clean, dry test tubes in a test tube rack. Using a marking pencil, number the test tubes 1 through 4.

 2. Measure 5 mL of distilled water in a graduated cylinder and pour it into test tube #1. Using the level of the water in test tube #1 as a guide, add the same amount of liquid to each of the

29 Bonds, Polarity, and Solubility (continued)

numbered test tubes as follows: #2—1,1,2-trichloro-1,2,2-trifluoroethane; #3—toluene; #4— ethanol. **CAUTION:** *Handle these chemicals with care. Do not breathe their vapors or allow them to come in contact with your skin or eyes.*

3. To each of the test tubes, add two crystals of iodine. Stopper and shake each tube. Record your observations in Data Table 1. Clean and dry the test tubes.

4. Repeat steps 1 through 3, substituting sodium chloride crystals for iodine.

PART B   MISCIBILITY OF LIQUIDS

5. Measure 5 mL of distilled water and pour it into a clean, dry test tube. Add 5 mL of 1,1,2-trichloro-1,2,2-trifluoroethane to the distilled water. Stopper and shake the tube. Record your observations in Data Table 2.

6. Repeat step 5, substituting 5 mL of toluene for the 1,1,2-trichloro-1,2,2-trifluoroethane.

7. Measure 5 mL of 1,1,2-trichloro-1,2,2-trifluoroethane and pour it into a clean, dry test tube. Add 5 mL of toluene to the 1,1,2-trichloro-1,2,2-trifluoroethane. Stopper and shake the tube. Record your observations in Data Table 2.

8. Place three clean, dry test tubes in the test tube rack and number them 1 through 3. Add 5 mL of ethanol to each of the tubes.

9. Add 5 mL of each of the following liquids to the numbered tubes as follows: #1—distilled water; #2—1,1,2-trichloro-1,2,2-trifluoroethane; #3—toluene. Stopper and shake each tube. Record your observations.

Observations and Data

PART A

Describe the degree of solubility by indicating soluble, slightly soluble, or insoluble.

DATA TABLE 1

liquid	I₂ crystals	NaCl crystals
water		
1,1,2-trichloro-1,2,2-trifluoroethane		
toluene		
ethanol		

PART B

Describe the degree of mixing by indicating miscible or immiscible.

DATA TABLE 2

liquid	water	FCCl$_2$CClF$_2$	toluene
1,1,2-trichloro- 1,2,2-trifluoroethane			
toluene			
ethanol			

Conclusions and Questions

1. What type of bonding is present in iodine molecules?

_____

_____

2. In which liquids used in this experiment was iodine soluble? Describe the type of bonding and the polarity of each of these liquids. Relate the solubility of the iodine in these liquids to the expression "like dissolves like."

_____

_____

_____

_____

_____

_____

3. Explain why iodine is not soluble in water.

_____

_____

_____

_____

4. What type of bonding is present in sodium chloride crystals?

_____

_____

5. In which liquids was sodium chloride insoluble? Explain why it was insoluble in these liquids.

_____

_____

_____

_____

29 Bonds, Polarity, and Solubility (continued)

6. Explain why sodium chloride dissolves in water.

_____

_____

_____

_____

_____

7. Discuss the bond types, arrangements, and molecular polarities in the four liquids used in this experiment. Explain your miscibility results in Part B in terms of "like is miscible with like."

_____

_____

_____

_____

_____

_____

_____

_____

_____

_____

_____

Solubility of a Salt

Lab 30

Text reference: **Chapter 16,** pp. 440–444

Pre-Lab Discussion

The solubility of a pure substance in a particular solvent is the quantity of that substance that will dissolve in a given amount of the solvent. Solubility varies with the temperature of the solvent. Thus, solubility must be expressed as quantity of solute per quantity of solvent at a specific temperature. For most ionic solids, especially salts, in water, solubility varies directly with temperature. That is, the higher the temperature of the solvent (water), the more solute (salt) that will dissolve in it.

In this experiment, you will study the solubility of potassium nitrate (KNO_3) in water. You will dissolve different quantities of this salt in a given amount of water at a temperature close to the water's boiling point. Each solution will be observed as it cools, and the temperature at which crystallization of the salt occurs will be noted and recorded. The start of crystallization indicates that the solution has become saturated. At this temperature, the solution contains the maximum quantity of solute that can be dissolved in that amount of solvent.

After solubility data for several different quantities of solute have been collected, the data will be plotted on a graph. A solubility curve for KNO_3 will be constructed by connecting the plotted points.

Purpose

Collect the experimental data necessary to construct a solubility curve for potassium nitrate (KNO_3) in water.

Equipment

balance	stirring rod
burner	ring stand
microspatula	iron ring
test tubes, 18×150-mm (4)	utility clamp
test tube holder	wire gauze
test tube rack	marking pencil
beaker, 400-mL	safety goggles
thermometer	lab apron or coat
graduated cylinder, 10-mL	

Materials

potassium nitrate (KNO_3)   distilled water

Safety

Tie back long hair and secure loose clothing when working with an open flame. Be sure you use a test tube holder when removing tubes from the hot water bath. Note the caution alert symbols here and with certain steps in the "Procedure." Refer to page xi for the specific precautions associated with each symbol. Always wear safety goggles and a lab apron or coat when working in the lab.

Procedure

While one lab partner carries out the instructions in steps 1 through 4, the other partner should go on to step 5.

1. Using a marking pencil, number four test tubes 1 through 4. Place the tubes in a test tube rack.

2. On the balance, measure out exactly 2.0 g of potassium nitrate (KNO_3). Pour the salt into test tube #1.

3. Repeat step 2 for the following masses of KNO_3. Add each quantity to the test tube indicated:

    4.0 g to test tube #2
    6.0 g to test tube #3
    8.0 g to test tube #4

4. Add exactly 5.0 mL distilled water to each test tube.

5. Fill a 400-mL beaker about three-fourths full of tap water. This will be used as a water bath. Using the water bath and test tube #1, prepare the setup shown in Figure 30-1. Heat the water to 90°C and adjust the flame to maintain the water at about this temperature.

6. Stir the KNO_3-water mixture with a glass stirring rod until the KNO_3 is completely dissolved. Remove the stirrer and rinse it off. Loosen the clamp and, using a test tube holder, remove the tube.

7. While lab partner number one repeats step 6 for test tube #2, lab partner number two should place a *warm* thermometer (dipped into the hot-water bath) into the solution in test tube #1. Hold the test tube up to the light and watch for the first sign of crystallization in the solution. At the *instant* crystallization starts, observe and record the temperature. Should crystallization start too quickly (because of a cold thermometer), redissolve the solid in the hot-water bath and repeat this step.

8. Steps 6 and 7 should be followed for all four test tubes. One lab partner should stir the KNO_3 until it dissolves, and the other partner should record the temperatures of crystallization. Record all temperatures in "Observations and Data."

9. If any doubtful results are obtained, the procedure can be repeated by redissolving the salt in the hot-water bath and allowing it to recrystallize.

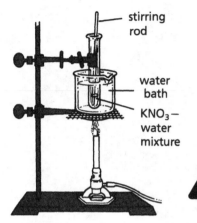

stirring rod

water bath

KNO_3— water mixture

Figure 30-1

Observations and Data

test tube #	grams of KNO_3/5.0 mL H_2O	crystallization temperature (°C)
1	2.0 g/5.0 mL	_____
2	4.0 g/5.0 mL	_____
3	6.0 g/5.0 mL	_____
4	8.0 g/5.0 mL	_____

30 Solubility of a Salt (continued)

Calculations

1. Using proportions, convert the experimental mass/volume ratios to equivalent mass/100-mL ratios.

2.0 g/5.0 mL = _____ g/100 mL

4.0 g/5.0 mL = _____ g/100 mL

6.0 g/5.0 mL = _____ g/100 mL

8.0 g/5.0 mL = _____ g/100 mL

2. Plot your experimental data on the grid provided. Plot mass of solute per 100 mL of water on the y-axis and temperature on the x-axis.

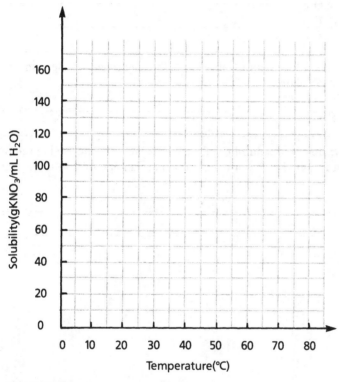

Figure 30-2

3. Construct a solubility curve by connecting the plotted points on your graph.

Conclusions and Questions

1. How many grams of KNO_3 can be dissolved in 100 mL of H_2O at the following temperatures?
   a. 30°C   **b.** 60°C   **c.** 70°C

_____

_____

_____

2. Define the terms saturated, unsaturated, and supersaturated.

_____

_____

_____

_____

_____

3. Classify the following KNO_3 solutions as saturated, unsaturated, or supersaturated. Explain your answer.
    a. 75 g KNO_3/100 mL H_2O at 40°C
    b. 60 g KNO_3/100 mL H_2O at 50°C

_____

_____

_____

_____

4. Do the solubilities of all ionic solids increase as the temperature increases? Explain.

_____

_____

5. How does the solubility of a gas change with increasing temperature? Draw a rough sketch showing the general shape of a solubility curve of a gas.

_____

_____

6. The graph in Appendix E in the back of this lab manual shows solubility curves for several compounds. Which of the compounds represented on this graph become _less_ soluble as temperature increases?

_____

_____

Precipitates and Solubility Rules

Pre-Lab Discussion

In a general sense, solubility can be thought of as the tendency of a substance (the solute) to dissolve in another substance (the solvent). For qualitative purposes, such terms as "soluble," "insoluble," and "slightly soluble" can be used to describe these tendencies.

Ionic compounds (salts and bases) dissolve in water by a process known as **dissociation**. In this process, the crystal lattice of the solid breaks down, and free ions move throughout the solution. The total number of positive charges is equal to the total number of negative charges in an ionic solution.

If aqueous (water) solutions of two different ionic compounds are mixed, one of two things will occur. If all of the ions remain free, "nothing" will happen. That is, the mixture will remain clear, or transparent. However, if two oppositely charged ions are attracted to each other strongly enough, they will bond together to form an ionic compound that is insoluble in water. In such a case, a precipitate forms.

In this investigation, aqueous solutions of several different ionic compounds will be used. Different combinations of solutions will be mixed and the reaction results observed. For those mixtures in which precipitates form, equations will be written for the double replacement (exchange of ions) reactions. You then will be able to state a hypothesis about the tendency of various ions to form stable, or insoluble, salts.

Purpose

Observe the formation of various precipitates and, based on your observations, formulate a hypothesis regarding general solubility rules.

Equipment

test tubes,   safety goggles
  18×150-mm (5)   lab apron or coat
test tube rack
dropper pipet

Materials

Solution Set A   *Solution Set B*
  0.1 M AgNO$_3$ 0.1 M Zn(C$_2$H$_3$O$_2$)$_2$
  0.1 M BaCl$_2$ · 2H$_2$O   0.1 M FeCl$_3$
  0.1 M Na$_2$CO$_3$ 0.1 M NaOH
  0.1 M (NH$_4$)$_2$SO$_4$ 0.1 M MgBr$_2$
  0.1 M Ca(NO$_3$)$_2$ 0.1 M K$_2$CO$_3$
  0.1 M K$_3$PO$_4$ 0.1 M NaC$_2$H$_3$O$_2$

Safety

Observe all normal safety precautions. Wear safety goggles and protective clothing at all times when working in the lab.

Procedure

1. Obtain a set of six solutions (Set A or Set B).

2. Place five clean test tubes into a test tube rack. Using a dropper pipet, add several drops of one of the solutions from your set to each of the test tubes. Set the remainder of this solution aside. (You will not be using it again.) Rinse the pipet.

3. Using the pipet, add several drops of one of the other solutions to the solution in one of the test tubes. Observe and record the results. Rinse the pipet.

4. Repeat step 3, adding a different solution to each of the remaining test tubes. After each test, observe and record results. Rinse the pipet after each use.

5. Discard the materials in the test tubes. Wash and dry the tubes.

6. Place four clean test tubes in the test tube rack. Add several drops of one of the solutions (other than the one used in step 2) to each of the tubes. Set the remainder of this solution aside.

7. Mix the solution in the test tubes with the remaining solutions in your set, adding several drops of a different solution to each tube. Record all your observations.

8. Continue this procedure until all possible combinations have been tested.

9. Repeat these steps using the solutions from the other set.

Observations and Data

There are 15 combinations for each solution set. In each rectangular box, write "ppt" if a precipitate forms for that combination. If no precipitate forms, write "NR" (no reaction).

SOLUTION SET A

	$AgNO_3$	$BaCl_2$	Na_2CO_3	$(NH_4)_2SO_4$	$Ca(NO_3)_2$
$BaCl_2$					
Na_2CO_3					
$(NH_4)_2SO_4$					
$Ca(NO_3)_2$					
K_3PO_4					

31 Precipitates and Solubility Rules (continued)

SOLUTION SET B

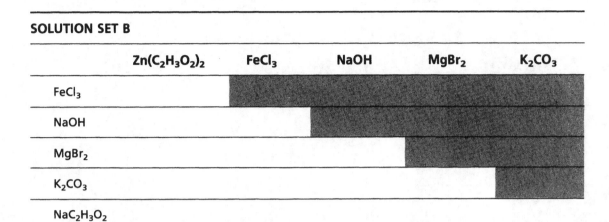

	Zn(C$_2$H$_3$O$_2$)$_2$	FeCl$_3$	NaOH	MgBr$_2$	K$_2$CO$_3$
FeCl$_3$					
NaOH					
MgBr$_2$					
K$_2$CO$_3$					
NaC$_2$H$_3$O$_2$					

Equations

1. Write an equation for the dissociation of each salt in solution.

$AgNO_3 \rightarrow$

$BaCl_2 \rightarrow$

$Na_2CO_3 \rightarrow$

$(NH_4)_2SO_4 \rightarrow$

$Ca(NO_3)_2 \rightarrow$

$K_3PO_4 \rightarrow$

$Zn(C_2H_3O_2)_2 \rightarrow$

$FeCl_3 \rightarrow$

$NaOH \rightarrow$

$MgBr_2 \rightarrow$

$K_2CO_3 \rightarrow$

$NaC_2H_3O_2 \rightarrow$

Refer to the table of solubilities in Appendix D in the back of this lab manual for help in writing the ionic equations in parts 2 and 3 of this section.

2. For each precipitate formed in the experiment, write an ionic equation for the double replacement reaction that occurred.

SET A

SET B

3. Write a net ionic equation for the formation of each precipitate formed in the experiment. (Omit spectator ions.)

SET A

SET B

31 Precipitates and Solubility Rules (continued)

Conclusions and Questions

1. Formulate a hypothesis about the relative tendency of the following ions to form soluble or insoluble salts when in water:

Na^+, K^+, NH_4^+, Ag^+, NO_3^-, Cl^-, CO_3^{2-}, PO_4^{3-}, $C_2H_3O_2^-$

_____

_____

_____

_____

_____

_____

2. Compare your experimental results and conclusions with the solubility data in the table in Appendix D.

_____

_____

_____

Rates of Reaction

Lab 32

Text reference: **Chapter 17**, pp. 471–475

Pre-Lab Discussion

The **rate** of a chemical reaction is the time required for a given quantity of reactant(s) to be changed to product(s). Reaction rate usually is expressed in terms of moles per unit time. This rate is affected by several factors, including the nature of the reactants, concentration of the reactants, temperature, pressure, and the presence of catalysts. In this experiment, you will study the effects of temperature and concentration.

A chemical reaction is the result of effective collisions between particles of reactants. Increasing the temperature of a system raises the average kinetic energy of the particles of the system. This results in more collisions and, of greater importance, more effective collisions per unit time. This affects the rate of the reaction.

At constant temperature, increasing the concentration of one or more of the reactants increases the number of particles present and, hence, the number of collisions. This affects the rate of the reaction.

In this experiment, two solutions will be mixed, and the completion of the reaction will be marked by a color change. One solution contains the iodate ion (IO_3^-). The other contains the hydrogen sulfite ion (HSO_3^-) and soluble starch. The entire reaction takes place in two stages. The ionic equations for these stages are:

1. $IO_3^-(aq) + 3HSO_3^-(aq) \rightarrow I^-(aq) + 3SO_4^{2-}(aq) + 3H^+(aq)$

2. $5I^-(aq) + 6H^+(aq) + IO_3^-(aq) \rightarrow 3I_2(aq) + 3H_2O(l)$

In the presence of starch molecules (not shown), molecular iodine (I_2) produces a characteristic blue color. The rate of the entire reaction can be determined by timing the interval between the time the two solutions are mixed and the appearance of the blue color. By varying the concentration of one of the reactants (at constant temperature) and then varying the temperature alone, you can observe and record the effects of these two factors on reaction rate.

This experiment should provide a better understanding of reaction rates and the factors that affect these rates.

Purpose

Study the effect that changing the concentration of a reactant has on the rate of a chemical reaction. Study the effect that changing the temperature has on the rate of a chemical reaction. Formulate hypotheses about how reaction rates are affected by changes in temperature and in concentration of reactants.

Equipment

beaker, 250-mL
beakers, 100-mL (2)
graduated cylinders, 10-mL (2)
test tubes, 18×150-mm (2)
thermometer

timer (stop watch or clock
    with second hand)
safety goggles
lab apron or coat

Materials

Solution A (with IO_3^- ion)
Solution B (with HSO_3^- ion and
    soluble starch)

distilled water
ice cubes

Safety

Avoid spilling reagent solutions on your skin or clothing. Wash off any spills immediately with cold tap water. Note the caution alert symbols here and with certain steps in the "Procedure." Refer to page xi to review the precautions associated with each symbol. Always wear safety goggles and a lab apron or coat when working in the lab.

Procedure

PART A

1. Using a clean, dry, 10-mL graduated cylinder, measure exactly 10.0 mL of Solution A and pour it into a 100-mL beaker.

2. Using a second 10-mL graduate, measure exactly 10.0 mL of Solution B and pour it into a second 100-mL beaker.

3. Prepare to time the reaction. While one lab partner pours Solution A into Solution B, the second partner should immediately start timing the reaction. Pour the solutions back and forth several times from one beaker to the other to ensure thorough mixing. Then allow the mixture to stand. At the instant a color change occurs, the partner timing the reaction should note the elapsed time. Record this in your data list. Rinse and dry the beakers and graduated cylinders.

4. Measure exactly 10.0 mL of Solution B into one of the beakers. Using a clean graduated cylinder, measure exactly 9.0 mL of Solution A into the other beaker. Dilute this solution by adding exactly 1.0 mL of distilled water. Follow the step 3 instructions for mixing the solutions and timing the reaction. Record the elapsed time in your data list. Rinse and dry the beakers and graduated cylinders.

5. Repeat step 4 four more times, using increasingly dilute samples of Solution A. Use the following ratios of Solution A to distilled water (in mL): 8 to 2; 7 to 3; 6 to 4; and 5 to 5. Rinse and dry the beakers and graduated cylinders after each trial. Record elapsed times in Part A of "Observations and Data."

32 Rates of Reaction (continued)

PART B

6. Measure 10.0 mL of Solution A into one test tube and 10.0 mL of Solution B into a second test tube.

7. Half fill a 250-mL beaker with cold tap water. Add ice cubes to the water and stir *carefully* with the thermometer. Continue stirring (and adding ice as needed) until the temperature of the ice-water mixture is about 5°C.

Figure 32-1

8. Place the two test tubes in the ice-water bath and let them stand until the solutions are at the same temperature as the ice water (Figure 32-1). *Always rinse and wipe the thermometer after removing it from a solution.*

9. When the solutions are at the same temperature as the ice water, prepare to time the reaction. One lab partner should start timing the reaction the instant the second partner pours Solution A into Solution B. Quickly pour the mixture back and forth from test tube to test tube several times and return the mixture to the ice-water bath. At the instant a color change occurs, note the time elapsed. Measure the temperature of the mixture immediately. Record the exact temperature and elapsed time in your data table. Discard the mixture as instructed. Rinse and dry the test tubes.

10. Repeat step 6.

11. Prepare a water bath at a temperature of about 15°C. Repeat steps 8 and 9 at this new temperature. Record your observations in your data table.

12. Repeat these procedures using warm baths at the following temperatures: 25°C; 35°C; 45°C. Use warm tap water to prepare these baths. Rinse and dry the test tubes after each trial.

Observations and Data

Solution B (mL)	Solution A (mL)	H_2O (mL)	Time (sec)
10	10	0	_____
10	9	1	_____
10	8	2	_____
10	7	3	_____
10	6	4	_____
10	5	5	_____

PART B

DATA TABLE

Trial #	Temperature (°C)	Time (sec)
1		
2		
3		
4		
5		

Calculations

1. Plot your data from Part A on the grid provided. Draw a line through the plotted points to produce a curve showing the effect of concentration of reactants on reaction rate.

32 Rates of Reaction (continued)

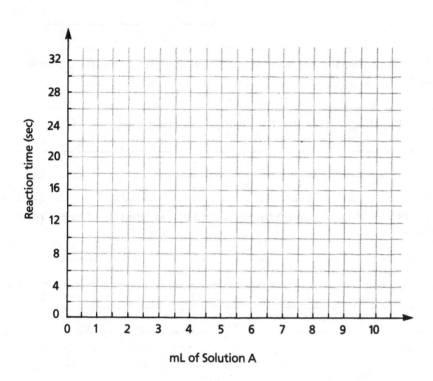

2. Plot your data from Part B on the grid provided. Draw a line through the plotted points to produce a curve showing the effect of temperature on reaction rate.

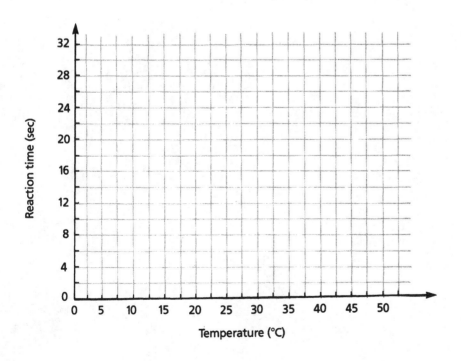

Conclusions and Questions

1. Based on your experimental data, make a general statement (hypothesis) about the effect of concentration of reactants on reaction rate.

_____

_____

2. Make a similar hypothesis about the effect of temperature on reaction rate.

_____

3. What other factors affect the rate of a reaction?

_____

_____

_____

4. How does the "collision theory" relate to the rate of a chemical reaction?

_____

_____

_____

_____

Heats of Reaction

(Demonstration)

Lab 33

Text reference: **Chapter 17**, pp. 482–484

Pre-Lab Discussion

The energy involved in a chemical reaction is expressed in terms of the amount of heat released or absorbed during the course of the reaction. This *heat of reaction* (ΔH) is measured in kilojoules per mole. By convention, when ΔH is included as part of the equation for a reaction, it is placed on the product side of an exothermic reaction and on the reactant side of an endothermic reaction.

To illustrate, consider the equations for the synthesis (exothermic reaction) and decomposition (endothermic reaction) of 1 mole of liquid water:

(synthesis) $H_2(g) + \frac{1}{2}O_2(g) \rightarrow H_2O(l) + 285 \text{ kJ}$

(decomposition) $H_2O(l) + 285 \text{ kJ} \rightarrow H_2(g) + \frac{1}{2}O_2(g)$

Note that when this convention is followed, the value of ΔH in an equation is always positive. However, when heat of reaction is considered separately—that is, when it is not an integral part of an equation—some method must be used to tell whether the heat is released or absorbed. For this purpose, ΔH of an exothermic reaction (heat released) is given a minus sign; ΔH of an endothermic reaction (heat absorbed) is given a plus sign. Thus, the heat of *formation* of 1 mole of water is given as -285 kJ. The heat of decomposition of 1 mole of water is $+285$ kJ.

In this experiment, you will study three related exothermic reactions involving sodium hydroxide (NaOH), a strong base. In the first reaction, solid sodium hydroxide will dissociate into ions as it dissolves in water. The heat produced by this reaction (ΔH_1) is called the *heat of solution* of NaOH. In the second reaction, an aqueous solution of NaOH will be reacted with an aqueous solution of hydrochloric acid (HCl). The heat of this reaction (ΔH_2) is called the *heat of neutralization* of NaOH. In the third reaction, solid NaOH will be reacted with an aqueous solution of HCl. This reaction is actually a combination of the first two reactions. The solid NaOH will dissociate into ions as it dissolves in the acid solution and then is neutralized by the acid. Thus, the heat of this reaction (ΔH_3) should be equal to $\Delta H_1 + \Delta H_2$. Using calculations based on the data collected in this experiment, you will attempt to verify the additive nature of heats of reaction.

This experiment should provide a better understanding of heats of reaction and reinforce your knowledge of calorimetry.

Purpose

Determine heats of reaction of three related exothermic reactions. Show the additive nature of the heats of reaction of these reactions.

Equipment

balance
Styrofoam cup
graduated cylinder, 100-mL
microspatula

thermometer
safety goggles
lab apron or coat

Materials

0.5 M hydrochloric acid (HCl)
1.0 M HCl
distilled water

sodium hydroxide (NaOH) pellets
1.0 M NaOH

Safety

Solid sodium hydroxide and concentrated aqueous solutions of sodium hydroxide are highly corrosive to the skin and eyes. Wear safety goggles and a lab coat or apron, and be sure you have on long sleeves throughout the experiment, even if it is done as a demonstration. Note the caution alert symbols here and with certain steps in the "Procedure." Refer to page xi to review the precautions associated with each symbol.

Procedure

PART A

1. Measure exactly 100.0 mL of distilled water into a graduated cylinder. Pour the water into a clean, dry Styrofoam cup and allow it to stand until it reaches room temperature.

 2. Using a microspatula (or forceps) to handle the pellets, measure out exactly 2.00 g of sodium hydroxide (NaOH) onto the balance. **CAUTION:** *Do not handle NaOH. It is very corrosive.*

3. Measure the temperature of the water in the Styrofoam cup to ±0.5°C. Record this as T_o in Part A of the data table.

4. Add the NaOH pellets to the water in the cup. Use the thermometer to stir the mixture until all the NaOH has dissolved and the temperature stops rising. Record the highest temperature as T_f in Part A of the data table.

5. Discard the solution as instructed by your teacher. Rinse off the thermometer and rinse and dry the Styrofoam cup.

PART B

 6. Measure out exactly 50.0 mL of 1.0 M HCl and pour it into the Styrofoam cup. **CAUTION:** *Handle this acid carefully to avoid burns.* Allow the acid to stand until it reaches room temperature. Record this temperature as T_o in Part B of the data table.

7. Add exactly 50.0 mL of 1.0 M NaOH solution to the HCl solution. Stir with the thermometer. Record the highest temperature as T_f in Part B of the data table.

8. Discard the solution. Rinse off the thermometer and rinse and dry the Styrofoam cup.

33 Heats of Reaction (continued)

PART C

9. Measure out exactly 100.0 mL of 0.5 *M* HCl and pour it into the Styrofoam cup. *Handle this acid carefully.* Allow it to stand until it reaches room temperature.

10. Measure out exactly 2.00 g of NaOH crystals as in step 2. *Remember the caution—do not handle the pellets.*

11. Measure the temperature of the acid in the cup. Record this as T_o in Part C of the data table.

12. Add the NaOH pellets to the acid and stir the mixture with the thermometer. Record the highest temperature as T_f in Part C of the data table.

Observations and Data

DATA TABLE

PART A	
Mass of 100 mL of H_2O	100 g
Mass of NaOH pellets	2.00 g
T_o	_____ °C
T_f	_____ °C

PART B	
Approximate mass of 50 mL NaOH (*aq*) + 50 mL HCl (*aq*)	100 g
T_o	_____ °C
T_f	_____ °C

PART C	
Approximate mass of 100 mL HCl(*aq*)	100 g
Mass of NaOH pellets	2.00 g
T_o	_____ °C
T_f	_____ °C

Calculations

PART A

1. Find ΔT: $\Delta T = T_f - T_o$ _____ °C

2. Find the number of joules absorbed by the H_2O
(released by the NaOH): _____ J

no. of joules = mass (in grams) of $H_2O \times \Delta T \times 4.2$ J/g-°C

3. Find the number of joules released per gram of
NaOH: _____ J/g

$$\text{J/g NaOH} = \frac{\text{joules (from 2)}}{2.00 \text{ g NaOH}}$$

4. Find ΔH_1 in kJ/mole NaOH: _____ kJ/mole

$$\Delta H_1 = \text{J/g NaOH} \times 40 \text{ g NaOH/mole NaOH} \times \frac{1}{1000} \text{ kJ/J}$$

PART B

5. Find ΔT: $\quad \Delta T = T_f - T_o$ _____ °C

6. Find the number of joules produced by the
reaction of NaOH(aq) and HCl(aq): _____ J

no. of J = mass of solutions (in grams) $\times \Delta T \times 4.2$ J/g-°C

7. Find ΔH_2 in kJ/mole NaOH (NOTE: 50 mL of
1.0 M NaOH(aq) contains 0.050 mole NaOH): _____ kJ/mole

$$\Delta H_2 = \frac{\text{joules (from 6)}}{0.050 \text{ mole}} \times \frac{1}{1000} \text{ kJ/J}$$

33 Heats of Reaction (continued)

PART C

8. Find ΔT: $\Delta T = T_f - T_o$ _____ °C

9. Find the number of joules absorbed by the HCl
solution (released by the NaOH):   _____ J

no. of joules = mass (in g) of HCl(aq) $\times$ ΔT $\times$ 4.2 J/g-°C

10. Find the number of joules released per g of NaOH: _____ J/g

$$\text{J/g NaOH} = \frac{\text{joules (from 9)}}{2.00 \text{ g NaOH}}$$

11. Find ΔH_3 in kJ/mole NaOH: _____ kJ/mole

$$\Delta H_3 = \text{J/g NaOH} \times 40 \text{ g/mole NaOH} \times \frac{1}{1000} \text{ kJ/J}$$

Conclusions and Questions

1. Write ionic equations for the three reactions observed in this experiment.

_____

_____

_____

2. In your own words, describe the process (or processes) that produced ΔH_1, ΔH_2, and ΔH_3.

_____

_____

_____

_____

_____

_____

_____

3. Write an algebraic equation, using the symbol ΔH with subscripts, to show the relationship between the heats of reaction of the three reactions in this experiment.

_____

4. Does your experimental data verify the equation in question 3?

_____

_____

5. What are some possible sources of error in this experiment?

_____

_____

_____

6. How does this experiment illustrate the law of conservation of energy?

_____

_____

_____

_____

_____

Chemical Equilibrium and Le Chatelier's Principle

Lab 34

Text reference: **Chapter 18,** pp. 524–527

Pre-Lab Discussion

In most of the chemical reactions you have studied so far, at least one of the reactants has been "used up." The point at which a reactant is used up marks the end of the reaction, and the reaction is said to have "gone to completion." Under ordinary circumstances, the product(s) of such reactions are not able to react to re-form the original reactants. Thus, these are "one way" reactions. They proceed in one direction only.

Many other chemical reactions do not go to completion. Rather, the products of these reactions remain in contact with each other and react to re-form the original reactants. Such reactants are said to be *reversible*. In a reversible reaction, the forward and reverse reactions proceed at the same time. When the *rates* of the two reactions are equal, a state of **chemical equilibrium** is said to exist. Under such conditions, both the forward and reverse reactions continue with *no net change* in the quantities of either products or reactants.

A state of equilibrium is affected by concentration and temperature and, if gases are involved, by pressure. If a system at equilibrium is subjected to a change in one or more of these factors, a stress is placed on the system. According to Le Chatelier's principle, when a stress is placed on a system at equilibrium, the equilibrium will shift in the direction that tends to relieve the stress. Equilibrium will be reestablished at a different point, that is, with different concentrations of reactants and products.

In this experiment, we will study two equilibrium systems. The equilibrium equation for the reversible reaction of the first system is:

$$Fe^{3+} + SCN^- \rightleftarrows Fe(SCN)^{2+}$$
$$\text{(light brown)} \qquad \text{(red)}$$

The addition of any substance to the system that increases the concentration of Fe^{3+} or SCN^- will favor the forward reaction. This will cause the equilibrium to shift to the right. The addition of any substance that decreases the concentration of these ions will have the opposite effect.

The equilibrium equation for the second system is:

$$2CrO_4^{2-} + 2H_3O^+ \rightleftarrows Cr_2O_7^{2-} + 3H_2O$$
$$\text{(yellow)} \qquad \text{(orange)}$$

The addition of an acid to this system increases the H_3O^+ concentration and causes the equilibrium to shift to the right. The addition of any substance that causes a decrease in H_3O^+ concentration will have the opposite effect.

By studying these two systems, you should achieve a better understanding of equilibrium systems and their responses to stress.

Purpose

Study equilibrium systems and their responses to stress as described by Le Chatelier's principle.

Equipment

beaker, 100-mL
graduated cylinder, 10-mL
test tubes, 13×100-mm (5)
test tube rack

dropper pipet
marking pencil
safety goggles
lab apron or coat

Materials

$0.1\ M\ FeCl_3$
$0.1\ M\ KSCN$
$0.1\ M\ KCl$
distilled water

$0.1\ M\ K_2CrO_4$
$0.1\ M\ K_2Cr_2O_7$
$1.0\ M\ HCl$
$1.0\ M\ NaOH$

Safety

Handle the HCl and NaOH solutions with care. They are corrosive substances and can injure the skin or eyes. Flush any spills with cold water and report them to your teacher. Note the caution alert symbols here and with certain steps in the "Procedure." Refer to page xi to review the precautions associated with each symbol. Always wear safety goggles and a lab apron or coat when working in the lab.

Procedure

PART A

1. Using a marking pencil, number four test tubes 1 through 4 and stand the tubes in a test tube rack.

2. Measure out 5 mL of $0.1\ M\ FeCl_3$ and pour it into a 100-mL beaker. Add 5 mL of $0.1\ M\ KSCN$ to the same beaker. Dilute the contents of the beaker with distilled water until the solution is a light reddish-orange color. Divide the solution equally among the four numbered test tubes. Set test tube 1 at one end of the rack to be used for color comparison.

3. Using a dropper pipet, add $0.1\ M\ FeCl_3$ drop by drop to the solution in test tube 2 until a color change occurs. Record your observations in Part A of "Observations and Data." Rinse the pipet.

4. Repeat step 3, but instead of $FeCl_3$, add the following solutions drop by drop to the test tube indicated. Rinse the pipet after each use.

test tube 3 $0.1\ M\ KSCN$
test tube 4 $0.1\ M\ KCl$

Record your observations.

5. Discard the solutions. Wash and rinse the test tubes and invert them in the rack to drain.

PART B

6. Using a marking pencil, number four test tubes 5 through 8. Stand the tubes in a rack.

34 Chemical Equilibrium and Le Chatelier's Principle
(continued)

7. Measure out 10 mL of 0.1 M K_2CrO_4. Pour 5 mL each into test tube 5 and test tube 6. Rinse the graduated cylinder and measure out 10 mL of 0.1 M $K_2Cr_2O_7$. Divide this equally between test tube 7 and test tube 8.

8. Using a dropper pipet, add 1.0 M HCl drop by drop to test tube 5 until the color changes. Record your observations.

9. Repeat step 8 with test tube 6. As soon as the color changes, rinse the pipet and use it to add 1.0 M NaOH drop by drop to the solution until the color changes again. Record your observations for this step.

10. Using the pipet, add 1.0 M NaOH to test tube 7 until the color changes. Record your observations.

11. Repeat step 10 with test tube 8. As soon as the color changes, rinse the pipet and use it to add 1.0 M HCl to the solution until the color changes again. Record your observations.

Observations and Data

PART A

Color

test tube 2 _____

test tube 3 _____

test tube 4 _____

PART B

Color Change

test tube 5 _____

test tube 6 _____

test tube 7 _____

test tube 8 _____

Conclusions and Questions

1. Write equilibrium equations for the reversible reactions that take place in Part A and Part B.

2. Using Le Chatelier's principle, explain how the addition of $FeCl_3$ to the solution in test tube 2 (step 3) affected the equilibrium that existed in the solution. Give similar explanations for the addition of each of the other substances (step 4).

_____

_____

_____

_____

_____

_____

_____

3. Using the equilibrium equation for the reaction and Le Chatelier's principle, explain the color changes noted in Part B.

_____

_____

_____

_____

_____

_____

Solubility Product Constant   Lab 35

Pre-Lab Discussion

There are many ionic compounds considered to be "insoluble" in water. However, no compound is completely insoluble. Every ionic compound dissolves (dissociates into its ions) to some extent when placed in water. Recall that a saturated solution is one that has dissolved in it all the solute it can hold at the given conditions. Thus, only a very small quantity of a slightly soluble ionic compound is needed to produce a saturated solution of that compound.

In a saturated solution of an ionic solid, an equilibrium exists between the ions in the solution and any undissolved solid. For example, the equilibrium equation for a saturated solution of lead chloride (a slightly soluble salt) in contact with the solid phase is:

$$PbCl_2(s) \rightleftarrows Pb^{2+}(aq) + 2Cl^-(aq)$$

Even though no observable change is taking place in the system represented by this equation, a dynamic equilibrium exists. The solid dissociates into ions at the same rate that the ions recombine to form the solid. As long as the temperature remains constant, the concentrations of all components of the system remain constant.

The concentration of ions in a saturated solution of a slightly soluble salt (such as $PbCl_2$) will usually be very small. It has been determined that for such solutions, the product of the molar concentrations (moles/liter) of the ions, each raised to the power represented by its coefficient in the dissociation equation, is a constant. This special equilibrium constant is called the **solubility product constant** (K_{sp}) of that substance. The K_{sp} of a saturated solution of lead chloride can be expressed as:

$$K_{sp} = [Pb^{2+}] \times [Cl^-]^2$$

Note that the Cl^- concentration is raised to the power of 2, which is the coefficient of this ion in the equilibrium equation for a saturated solution of $PbCl_2$.

Because solubilities vary with temperature, the solubility product constant of a substance must apply at a specific temperature. The temperature generally used for this purpose is 25°C (298 K).

In this experiment, you will attempt to determine the solubility product constant for lead iodide, a slightly soluble salt. The equilibrium equation for a saturated solution of this compound is:

$$PbI_2(s) \rightleftarrows Pb^{2+}(aq) + 2I^-(aq)$$

Purpose

Determine experimentally the solubility product constant of a slightly soluble salt.

Equipment

Erlenmeyer flask, 125-mL
graduated cylinder, 10-mL
graduated cylinder, 100-mL
thermometer

rubber stopper (for flask)
safety goggles
lab apron or coat

Materials

0.010 M Pb(NO$_3$)$_2$
0.020 M KI
distilled water

Safety

Follow all general lab safety procedures. Note the caution alert symbols here and with certain steps in the "Procedure." Refer to page xi to review specific precautions associated with each symbol. Always wear safety goggles and a lab coat or apron when working in the lab.

Procedure

1. Using a 10-mL graduated cylinder, measure 5.0 mL of 0.010 M Pb(NO$_3$)$_2$ and add it to a clean, dry 125-mL Erlenmeyer flask. Using a 100-mL graduated cylinder, measure exactly 90.0 mL of distilled water. Add the water to the flask, and swirl the flask to mix the contents. Rinse and dry the 10-mL graduated cylinder.

2. Using the 10-mL graduated cylinder, measure out 5.0 mL of 0.020 M KI and add it to the mixture in the flask. Stopper the flask and shake it vigorously to mix the contents thoroughly. Remove the stopper and measure the temperature of the solution. Record the temperature in "Observations and Data." Assume that this temperature will be the same for all the trials.

3. Allow the flask to stand for 7 to 10 minutes, and then check the solution for a cloudy appearance. Record your observations in "Observations and Data" for Trial 1. Use one of the following to describe the sample: (a) clear, (b) contains sparkling flakes, (c) shows yellow precipitate. Discard the solution as instructed by your teacher. Wash and dry the flask.

4. Repeat steps 1 through 3 using the volumes indicated below. Record your observations, as indicated in step 3.

	Pb(NO$_3$)$_2$	H$_2$O	KI
Trial 2:	10.0 mL	80.0 mL	10.0 mL
Trial 3:	15.0 mL	70.0 mL	15.0 mL
Trial 4:	20.0 mL	60.0 mL	20.0 mL
Trial 5:	25.0 mL	50.0 mL	25.0 mL

5. Repeat the experiment if time permits.

6. Dispose of the solutions and mixtures as instructed by your teacher.

35 Solubility Product Constant (continued)

Observations and Data

Temperature _____ °C

<u>Appearance</u>

Trial 1 _____

Trial 2 _____

Trial 3 _____

Trial 4 _____

Trial 5 _____

Calculations

1. Find the number of moles of Pb^{2+} in the volume of 0.010 M $Pb(NO_3)_2$ in which sparkling flakes first appeared:

moles of Pb^{2+} = molarity (moles/liter) × volume (mL) × 10^{-3} liters/mL

$$= 0.010 \text{ mol } Pb(NO_3)_2/L \times \text{\_\_\_\_ mL } Pb(NO_3)_2 \times \frac{1 \text{ L}}{1000 \text{ mL}}$$

2. For every trial, the volume of the solution of $Pb(NO_3)_2$, H_2O, and KI was 100 mL. Thus, the number of moles of Pb^{2-} from calculation 1 was used to make a solution with a volume of 100 mL. What was the concentration of the Pb^{2+} ion in this solution, as expressed as molarity (moles of Pb^{2+} ion per liter of solution)?

3. Find the number of moles of I^- in the volume of 0.020 M KI.

$$\text{mol of } I^- = 0.020 \text{ mol KI/L} \times \text{\_\_\_\_ mL KI} \times \frac{1 \text{ L}}{1000 \text{ mL}}$$

4. The number of moles of I^- (from calculation 3) was used to make a solution with a volume of 100 mL. What was the concentration of the I^- ion in this solution, expressed as molarity?

5. Write the solubility product expression for the equilibrium:

$$PbI_2 \rightleftarrows Pb^{2+}(aq) + 2I^-(aq)$$

6. Use the solubility product expression you determined in calculation 5 and the molar concentrations you calculated for Pb^{2+} (calculation 2) and I^- (calculation 4) to calculate the solubility product constant for PbI_2.

Conclusions and Questions

Where necessary, refer to the Table of Solubility Product Constants in Appendix C to help you answer these questions.

1. What is the accepted value for the K_{sp} of PbI_2 given in the table? How does this value compare with your experimental result? What may account for any difference between your result and the accepted value?

_____

_____

_____

_____

_____

_____

2. Write the expression for the K_{sp} of the following salts: $Mg(OH)_2$; $Cu(IO_3)_2$; Ag_2CrO_4.

_____

_____

3. What is the accepted value for the K_{sp} of each of the salts in question 2?

_____

_____

4. Using the accepted value for the K_{sp} of AgCl at 25°C, calculate the concentration in moles per liter of Ag^+ in a saturated solution of the salt.

Properties of Acids and Bases

Lab 36

Text reference: **Chapter 18**, pp. 556–560

Pre-Lab Discussion

Acids ionize in aqueous solution to produce hydronium ions (H_3O^+). The strength of an acid depends on the degree to which it ionizes. Strong acids ionize almost completely, while weak acids ionize to a lesser degree. Bases dissociate in aqueous solution to produce hydroxide ions (OH^-). (Ammonia gas, NH_3, actually ionizes in aqueous solution to produce a weak base.) The properties of acids and bases depend on the presence of free H_3O^+ or OH^- as the predominant ion in a solution.

In this experiment, you will observe the following:

1. The effects of acids and a base on various indicators.

2. Reactions of acids and metals. The single replacement can be represented by the general equation:

metal + acid → metallic ion + hydrogen gas + water

$$M(s) + 2H_3O^+(aq) \rightarrow M^{2+}(aq) + H_2(g) + 2H_2O(l)$$

3. Reaction of an acid with a carbonate. The double replacement reaction can be represented by the general equation:

carbonate + acid → carbon dioxide + water

$$CO_3{}^{2-}(aq) + 2H_3O^+(aq) \rightarrow CO_2(g) + 3H_2O(l)$$

4. Neutralization reaction. Acids neutralize bases (and vice versa). For example, when HCl combines with NaOH, the net reaction is $H_3O^+ + OH^- \rightarrow 2H_2O$. In this reaction, 1 mole of HCl neutralizes 1 mole of NaOH.

5. The effects of some common household substances on various indicators.

This experiment should aid in the understanding of the properties and reactions of acids and bases, neutralization reactions, single and double replacement reactions, and the relative activities of metals.

Purpose

Observe and study some typical properties and reactions of acids and bases.

Equipment

test tubes, 18×150-mm (5)	wood splint
test tube rack	rubber stopper, 1-hole (to fit test tube)
dropper pipets (2)	glass tubing, with right-angle bend
microspatula (or scoop)	safety goggles
spot plate	lab apron or coat

Materials

6 M HCl

6 M HC₂H₃O₂

0.5 M NaOH

1.0 M HCl

phenolphthalein solution

litmus paper, red and blue

pH paper

limewater

zinc, mossy

magnesium ribbon

iron filings

copper wire (or sheet)

CaCo₃

vinegar

lemon juice

tomato juice

milk

household ammonia

Safety

Handle acid and base solutions with care, and avoid spills on your clothing or skin. Flush any spills with cool water and NaHCO₃ solution and report them to your teacher. Note the caution alert symbols here and with certain steps in the "Procedure." Refer to page xi to review the precautions associated with each symbol. Always wear safety goggles and a lab apron or coat when working in the lab.

Procedure

Note: All observations should be recorded in the appropriate spaces in the "Observations and Data" section.

PART A   EFFECT OF ACIDS AND BASE ON INDICATORS

1. To separate depressions in your spot plate, add about five drops of each of the following: (1) 6 *M* HCl; (2) 6 *M* HC₂H₃O₂; (3) 0.5 *M* NaOH. **CAUTION:** *Handle these chemicals with care.* Using a different piece of clean, dry red litmus paper for each of the three solutions, dip the end of a piece of red litmus paper into each solution.

2. Next, dip the ends of pieces of blue litmus paper into the same depressions. Finally dip the ends of pieces of pH paper into the same depressions.

3. Add one drop of phenolphthalein to the solution in each depression. Discard the solutions as instructed and rinse the spot plate with water. Then dry it with a paper towel.

PART B   REACTIONS OF ACIDS WITH METALS

4. To separate depressions on one side of your spot plate, add small quantities of each of the following: (1) zinc (2) magnesium (3) iron (4) copper.

5. To each depression, add just enough 6 *M* HCl to cover the metal. Observe the relative reactivities of the metals with this acid.

6. On the other side of your spot plate, repeat steps 4 and 5 using 6 *M* HC₂H₃O₂ in place of the HCl. Contrast each metal's reactivity with HC₂H₃O₂ against each metal's reactivity with HCl. Discard the contents of the spot plate as instructed and rinse and dry the spot plate.

7. Place a small quantity of zinc in a depression in your spot plate. Add enough 6 *M* HCl to just cover the zinc. As the reaction proceeds, hold an inverted test tube over the zinc for about 1

36 Properties of Acids and Bases (continued)

minute. Without turning the test tube upright, quickly insert a *burning* wood splint into the test tube. Discard the contents of the spot plate and clean and dry the plate.

PART C   REACTIONS OF ACIDS WITH CARBONATES

8. *Carefully* insert a right-angle bend of glass tubing into a one-hole rubber stopper.

9. Half fill a clean test tube with limewater solution. Place a small amount of $CaCO_3$ into a second clean test tube. Add enough 6 *M* HCl to just cover the carbonate. Insert the rubber-stopper-glass-tubing assembly into the test tube containing the $CaCO_3$ and HCl.

10. Put the open end of the glass tubing into the limewater solution in the test tube.

11. Discard the solutions and clean and rinse the test tubes.

PART D   NEUTRALIZATION

12. Using a clean dropper pipet, add 10 drops of 1.0 *M* HCl to a clean test tube. Add one drop of phenolphthalein. Test with pH paper.

13. Using a second dropper pipet, add 0.5 *M* NaOH drop by drop to the acid in the test tube. After the addition of each drop, swirl the test tube gently so the drop mixes thoroughly with the acid. Count the total number of drops of NaOH needed to cause a color change. Once a color change is observed, test the mixture with pH paper.

PART E   ACIDITY AND BASICITY OF HOUSEHOLD SUBSTANCES

14. To different depressions in your spot plate, add about five drops of each of the following: vinegar, lemon juice, tomato juice, milk, household ammonia.

15. Test each substance as you did in Part A, using red litmus paper, blue litmus paper, pH paper, and phenophthalein.

Observations and Data

PART A

DATA TABLE

	red litmus	blue litmus	pH paper	phenolphthalein
6 *M* HCl				
6 *M* HC$_2$H$_3$O$_2$				
0.5 *M* NaOH				

PART B

1. Reactivity in decreasing order (fastest to slowest):

1._____ 2._____ 3._____ 4._____

2. Comparative reactivities (very fast, fast, slow, very slow, no apparent reaction):

	with HCl	with $HC_2H_3O_2$
zinc	_____	_____
magnesium	_____	_____
iron	_____	_____
copper	_____	_____

3. Results of burning splint test:

PART C

4. Results of limewater test:

PART D

5. Number of drops of 0.5 M NaOH to neutralize 10 drops of 1.0 M HCl:

_____

pH of neutral solution: _____

PART E

DATA TABLE

	red litmus	blue litmus	pH paper	phenolphthalein
vinegar				
lemon juice				
tomato juice				
milk				
household ammonia				

36 Properties of Acids and Bases (continued)

Equations

Write balanced molecular equations for the reaction of:

1. each metal with 6 M HCl

_____

_____

_____

2. each metal with 6 M $HC_2H_3O_2$

_____

_____

3. $CaCO_3$ with HCl

_____

4. HCl with NaOH

_____

Conclusions and Questions

1. What type of reaction occurs between a metal and an acid? Write a general equation for this type of reaction.

_____

_____

2. Explain the difference in reaction rates of a given metal with two different acids.

_____

_____

_____

_____

_____

_____

3. Write a balanced equation for the reaction between CO_2 gas and lime-water, $Ca(OH)_2$. What is the name of the milky precipitate that forms?

_____

_____

4. Explain the difference in the volumes (number of drops) of HCl and NaOH required to produce a neutral solution in Part D of this experiment.

_____

_____

_____

5. Which household substances were acidic? Which was almost neutral? Which was basic?

_____

_____

_____

Conductivity, Ionization, and Dissociation

Text reference: **Chapter 19,** pp. 547–550

Pre-Lab Discussion

The electrical conductivity of a substance is a measure of its ability to transport an electric current. An electric current consists of moving charged particles. Thus, the ability to conduct an electric current depends on the presence of mobile, or "free," charged particles, either electrons or ions. In solids, only loosely held electrons are free to move. An electric current in a solid (usually an active metal) consists of a flow of electrons. In liquids, the presence of free ions (positive and negative charges) is necessary for conductivity. When two electrodes, one positively charged and the other negatively charged, are introduced into a liquid containing free ions, the positive and negative ions will move in opposite directions (toward oppositely charged electrodes). This movement of charged particles constitutes an electric current through the liquid.

Free ions are produced as a result of dissociation or ionization. Dissociation describes the behavior of ionic compounds. In the solid phase, ions are held rigidly in the crystal structure by ionic bonds. Dissociation occurs when ionic solids (salts and bases) are dissolved in water or melted. In either case, the bonds holding the ions in the crystal lattice are broken and the ions are free to move. Dissociation by solution in water can be illustrated as follows:

$$NaCl(s) \xrightarrow{H_2O} Na^+(aq) + Cl^-(aq)$$

$$NaOH(s) \xrightarrow{H_2O} Na^+(aq) + OH^-(aq)$$

Ionization describes the behavior of polar-molecular substances. These substances do *not* consist of ions in their anhydrous (undissolved) state. Many acids fall into this category. When dissolved in water (also a polar-molecular substance), these polar molecules ionize, or form ions, as illustrated in the following equation:

$$HCl + H_2O \rightarrow H_3O^+(aq) + Cl^-(aq)$$

Most organic compounds (the compounds of carbon) do not conduct an electric current, either when pure or when dissolved in water. This is because all organic compounds have molecular structures. Except for certain compounds that have polar molecules, organic compounds do not dissolve in water. Of those that do dissolve in water, only some are ionized in solution. Organic acids do ionize to varying degrees in solution and, thus, conduct an electric current.

In this investigation, we will test the ability (or lack of ability) of various substances and solutions to conduct an electric current. Among the substances tested will be the following organic compounds: sugar, ethanol, and acetic acid.

Purpose

Compare the conductivities of pure substances and the solutions of those substances. Relate experimental results to the tendencies of the substances to ionize or dissociate.

Equipment

beaker, 50-mL
beaker, 100-mL
conductivity apparatus
microspatula

ring stand
clamp
safety goggles
lab apron or coat

Materials

sodium chloride (NaCl)
sugar, sucrose ($C_{12}H_{22}O_{11}$)
copper strip (Cu)
distilled water
tap water
ethanol (C_2H_5OH)

glacial acetic acid ($HC_2H_3O_2$)
6 M acetic acid
0.1 M acetic acid
6 M hydrochloric acid (HCl)
0.1 M hydrochloric acid
0.1 M sodium hydroxide

Safety

Handle glacial acetic acid and the acid and base solutions with care. Avoid spills on skin or clothing. Flush any spills with cool water and report them to your teacher. Exercise caution, as instructed by your teacher, when working with the conductivity apparatus. Note the caution alert symbols here and with certain steps in the "Procedure." Refer to page xi to review the precautions associated with each symbol. Always wear safety goggles and a lab coat or apron when working in the lab.

Procedure

PART A   SOLIDS

 1. Set up the conductivity apparatus as shown in Figure 37-1. **CAUTION:** *Make sure that your hands and your bench surface are completely DRY whenever you are handling the conductivity apparatus. Apparatus should be UNPLUGGED at all times when not being used to test for conductivity.*

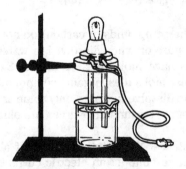

Figure 37-1

37 Conductivity, Ionization and Dissociation (continued)

2. In a 50-mL beaker, place enough NaCl so that the electrodes of the apparatus do not touch the glass bottom of the beaker during testing. Test the dry NaCl for conductivity. Record your observations in the data table. UNPLUG THE APPARATUS. Clean the electrodes by wiping with a paper towel. Rinse and thoroughly dry the beaker.

3. Repeat step 2 for sugar ($C_{12}H_{22}O_{11}$). After testing each sample, unplug the testing apparatus and clean and dry the electrodes and beaker.

4. With the apparatus unplugged, place the copper strip between the electrodes so that it is in contact with each electrode. Plug in the apparatus and test the metal strip for conductivity. Record your observations.

PART B PURE LIQUIDS

5. Half fill a 100-mL beaker with distilled water and set it to one side. This will be used to clean the electrodes of the conductivity apparatus.

6. Test the conductivity of the following liquids: distilled water, tap water, ethanol, and glacial acetic acid. (Note: *glacial* acetic acid is *pure* acetic acid.) For each test, add about 20 mL of liquid to a 50-mL beaker and place the electrodes in the liquid. After each test, UNPLUG THE APPARATUS and dip the electrodes in the beaker of distilled water set aside earlier. Wipe dry with a paper towel. Also rinse and dry the beaker after each test.

PART C SOLUTIONS

7. Dissolve a heaping spatula of NaCl in about 30 mL of distilled water. Test the conductivity of the solution. UNPLUG THE APPARATUS. Clean and dry the electrodes and the beaker.

8. Repeat step 7 for $C_{12}H_{22}O_{11}$.

9. Test 20-mL samples of each of the following solutions for conductivity: 0.1 M NaOH, 6 M HCl, 0.1 M HCl, 6 M HC$_2$H$_3$O$_2$, and 0.1 M HC$_2$H$_3$O$_2$. After each test, unplug the apparatus and clean and dry the electrodes and beaker.

Observations and Data

DATA TABLE

	Conductivity				
Sample	none	poor	fair	good	excellent
PART A Solids					
NaCl					
$C_{12}H_{22}O_{11}$					
Cu					
PART B Pure Liquids					
distilled water					
tap water					
C_2H_5OH					
$HC_2H_3O_2$ (glacial)					
PART C Solutions					
NaCl(aq)					
$C_{12}H_{22}O_{11}$(aq)					
0.1 M NaOH					
6 M HCl					
0.1 M HCl					
6 M $HC_2H_3O_2$					
0.1 M $HC_2H_3O_2$					

37 Conductivity, Ionization and Dissociation (continued)

Conclusions and Questions

1. What class of solids conducts electricity?

_____

2. Explain why ionic compounds (salts and bases) in the solid phase do not conduct an electric current. In the liquid state (molten) and in aqueous solution, these same compounds do conduct an electric current. Explain.

_____

_____

_____

_____

_____

3. Based on your experimental evidence, how do organic solids and liquids rate as electrical conductors?

_____

_____

_____

4. Explain the difference in conductivity of 6 M and 0.1 M HCl.

_____

_____

_____

_____

_____

5. Explain the differences in conductivity of glacial acetic acid, 6 M acetic acid, and 0.1 M acetic acid.

_____

_____

_____

_____

_____

_____

_____

Determining Hydrogen Ion Concentration of Strong and Weak Acids

Lab 38

Text reference: **Chapter 19,** pp. 550–555

Pre-Lab Discussion

When HCl gas dissolves in water, it completely ionizes, as shown by the equation for its ionization:

$$HCl(g) \rightarrow H^+(aq) + Cl^-(aq)$$

The single arrow pointing to the right shows that HCl is a strong acid that completely ionizes. This means that if 1 mole of HCl dissolves in water to form 1 liter of solution, that solution will contain 1 mole of hydrogen ions and 1 mole of chloride ions. That is, the concentration of both the hydrogen ion and the chloride ion will be 1 mole per liter, or 1 molar. Therefore, a 1 molar hydrochloric acid solution is one in which the hydrogen ion concentration is 1 molar.

The behavior of acetic acid contrasts with that of HCl. If 1 mole of acetic acid is added to water to form 1 liter of solution, less than 1 mole of hydrogen ions will be formed because acetic acid, a weak acid, does not ionize completely. This fact is indicated by the double arrow in the equation for its ionization:

$$HC_2H_3O_2(l) \rightleftarrows H^+(aq) + C_2H_3O_2^-(aq)$$

A 1 molar acetic acid solution, therefore, has a hydrogen ion concentration that is less than 1 molar. This difference between hydrochloric acid and acetic acid needs to be clearly understood as you do this experiment.

Weak acids—those that do not ionize completely in water solution—attain an equilibrium between the ions formed and the un-ionized molecules. The equilibrium constant for the system is called the ionization constant, and is represented by the symbol K_a. Ionization constants for acids are used to determine the relative strengths of acids. The ionization of a weak acid, HB, can be represented by the equation

$$HB(aq) \rightleftarrows H^+(aq) + B^-(aq)$$

The expression for the ionization constant of this acid is:

$$K_a = \frac{[H^+][B^-]}{[HB]}$$

In this experiment, you will prepare some acid solutions of known hydrogen ion concentrations, and you will observe the colors of some acid-base indicators in each of these solutions. These same indicators then will be added to some solutions with hydrogen ion concentrations that are not known. You will compare the colors of the indicators in the solutions of unknown concentration to their colors in the solutions of known concentration. This comparison will tell you the hydrogen ion concentrations in the unknowns.

From your determination of the hydrogen ion concentration in an acetic acid solution, you will calculate the ionization constant of acetic acid.

Purpose

Use acid-base indicators to determine the hydrogen ion concentration of a strong acid and a weak acid. Use experimental data to calculate the ionization constant of the weak acid.

Equipment

test tubes, 13×100-mm (12)   marking pencil
test tube rack   safety goggles
graduated cylinder, 10-mL   lab apron or coat
measuring pipet

Materials

distilled water   Indicators:
0.1 M HCl   methyl orange
0.1 M $HC_2H_3O_2$ orange IV
1.0 M $HC_2H_3O_2$
strong acid solution (conc. unknown)

Safety

Handle acid solutions with extreme care. Avoid spills on your skin or clothing. Rinse any spills with cold water and $NaHCO_3$ solution and report them to your teacher. Note the caution alert symbols here and with certain steps in the "Procedure." Refer to page xi to review the precautions associated with each symbol. Always wear safety goggles and a lab coat or apron when working in the lab.

Procedure

 CAUTION: *Use extreme care when handling the acids in this experiment. They can cause painful burns if they come in contact with the skin or get into the eyes.*

PART A   PREPARATION OF SOLUTIONS OF KNOWN HYDROGEN ION CONCENTRATION

In this part of the experiment, you will prepare two identical sets of HCl solution. Each set will consist of 2 mL of solution at four different concentrations. (See Figure 38-1.)

   1. Concentration 1. Obtain 5 mL of 0.1 M HCl stock solution. Using a measuring pipet, put 2 mL of this solution into a clean, dry test tube for concentration 1 of Set 1. Put another 2 mL into a second test tube for concentration 1 of Set 2. Label the tubes 0.1 M HCl and place them in a test tube rack. Save the remaining 1 mL of the stock solution for making concentration 2. Clean your pipet.

Name _____

38 Determining Hydrogen Ion Concentration of Strong and Weak Acids (continued)

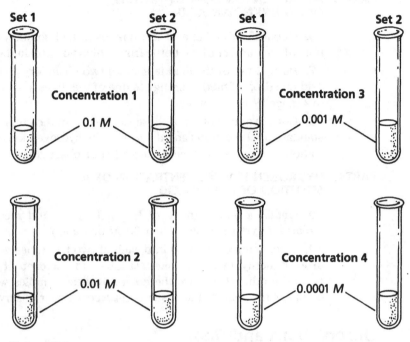

Set 1   Set 2   Set 1   Set 2

Concentration 1

0.1 M

Concentration 3

0.001 M

Concentration 2

0.01 M

Concentration 4

0.0001 M

Figure 38-1

2. Concentration 2. Using a 10-mL graduated cylinder, measure out 4.5 mL of distilled water and pour it into a clean, dry test tube. From the 1 mL of 0.1 M HCl remaining from step 1, carefully pipet 0.5 mL into the 4.5 mL of distilled water. (The 0.5 mL of acid solution left over from step 1 can be discarded.) Gently swirl the test tube to bring about thorough mixing. Put 2 mL of this solution into each of two test tubes for concentration 2 of Sets 1 and 2. Label the tubes 0.01 M HCl and place them in the rack. The 1 mL of 0.01 M HCl that is left over will be used to make concentration 3. Clean the pipet.

3. Concentration 3. Using a 10-mL graduated cylinder, measure out 4.5 mL of distilled water and pour it into a clean, dry test tube. From the 1 mL of 0.01 M HCl left over from the previous step, pipet 0.5 mL into the 4.5 mL of distilled water. (The 0.5 mL of the 0.01 M solution left over from step 2 can be discarded.) Gently swirl the test tube to bring about mixing. Put 2 mL of this solution into each of two test tubes for concentration 3 of Sets 1 and 2. Label the tubes 0.001 M HCl and place them in the rack. The 1 mL of 0.001 M HCl that is left over will be used to make concentration 4. Clean the pipet.

4. Concentration 4. Following the same general procedure as in step 3, prepare 5 mL of 0.0001 M HCl solution by adding 0.5 mL of the 0.001 M HCl (left over from step 3) to 4.5 mL of distilled water. Put 2 mL of this 0.0001 M solution into each of two test tubes for concentration 4 of Sets 1 and 2. Label the tubes 0.0001 M HCl and place them in the rack. The 1 mL of 0.0001 M HCl that remains can be discarded.

197

5. Add one drop of methyl orange indicator to each test tube of Set 1 and one drop of orange IV indicator to each test tube in Set 2. These two sets of test tubes are your standard acid solutions. Note their colors in the data table.

PART B   HYDROGEN ION CONCENTRATION OF AN UNKNOWN ACID

6. Obtain 5 mL of one of the unknown acid solutions. Make note of the number of the bottle from which you obtain the acid.

7. Place 2 mL of the acid in each of two clean, dry test tubes. Add one drop of methyl orange to one of the tubes and one drop of orange IV to the other.

8. Compare the colors of these samples with the colors of the standard acid solutions and determine the hydrogen ion concentration of the unknown acid. Record your observations.

PART C   HYDROGEN ION CONCENTRATION OF A SOLUTION OF ACETIC ACID

9. Obtain a 5-mL sample of $HC_2H_3O_2$. Note and record the molarity of your sample (either 0.1 M or 1.0 M).

10. Place 2 mL of the acid into each of two test tubes. Add one drop of methyl orange to one test tube and one drop of orange IV to the other. Compare the colors of these samples with the colors of the standard acid solutions. Record your observations.

Observations and Data

PART A

DATA TABLE

Indicator	HCl concentration			
	0.1 M	0.01 M	0.001 M	0.0001 M
methyl orange				
orange IV				

PART B

Unknown acid: Label #_____

Concentration _____ M

PART C

Acetic acid: Molarity_____ M

H^+ concentration _____

38 Determining Hydrogen Ion Concentration of Strong and Weak Acids (continued)

Conclusions and Questions

1. Write the equilibrium equation for the ionization of acetic acid.

_____

2. Using the notations

$$[H^+] \quad [C_2H_3O_2{}^-] \quad \text{and} \quad [HC_2H_3O_2]$$

for the molar concentrations of the particles that take part in the ionization of acetic acid, write the expression for the ionization constant of that acid.

3. If 1 mole of acetic acid is diluted with water to make 1 liter of acid solution, you might think that the concentration of acetic acid molecules in this solution is 1 molar.
   a. Why is this not exactly true?
   b. Why is "1 molar" a very close approximation for the concentration of these molecules?

_____

_____

_____

_____

_____

4. Use the expression for K_a from question 2 and the information you obtained in Part C of the "Procedure" to calculate the numerical value of the ionization constant of acetic acid.

5. How does your calculated numerical value for the ionization constant of acetic acid differ from that given in the literature? How would you explain this difference?

_____

_____

_____

_____

_____

6. Explain why a 0.1 M HCl solution has a hydrogen ion concentration of 0.1 M while a 0.1 M HC$_2$H$_3$O$_2$ solution has a hydrogen ion concentration of about 0.001 M.

_____

_____

_____

_____

_____

_____

Acid-Base Titration

Lab 39

Text reference: **Chapter 20,** pp. 584–586

Pre-Lab Discussion

In the chemistry laboratory, it is sometimes necessary to experimentally determine the concentration of an acid solution or a base solution. A procedure for making this kind of determination is called an **acid-base titration**. In this procedure, a solution of known concentration, called the *standard solution*, is used to neutralize a precisely measured volume of the solution of unknown concentration to which one or two drops of an appropriate acid-base indicator have been added. If the solution of unknown concentration is acidic, a standard base solution is added to the acid solution until it is neutralized. If the solution of unknown concentration is basic, a standard acid solution is added to the base solution until it is neutralized.

When carrying out an acid-base titration, you must be able to recognize when to stop adding the standard solution, that is, when neutralization is reached. This is the purpose of the acid-base indicator mentioned above. A sudden change in color of the indicator signals that neutralization has occurred. At this point, the number of hydronium ions from the acid is equal to the number of hydroxide ions from the base. The point at which this occurs is called the *end point* of the titration. When the end point is reached, the volume of the standard solution used is carefully determined. Then, the measured volumes of the two solutions and the known concentration of the standard solution can be used to calculate the concentration of the other solution. The following steps tell how to calculate the unknown concentration:

1. Write the balanced equation for the reaction. From the coefficients, determine how many moles of acid reacts with 1 mole of base (or vice versa). Use the coefficients to form a mole ratio.

2. *If the mole ratio is 1:1,* the following relationship can be used to calculate the unknown concentration:

$$M_a \times V_a = M_b \times V_b$$

where M_a = molarity of the acid solution
M_b = molarity of the base solution
V_a = volume of the acid solution
V_b = volume of the base solution

The equation for this relationship can be rewritten to find the solution of unknown concentration. For example, if the molarity of the base were unknown, the equation would be

$$M_b = \frac{M_a \times V_a}{V_b}$$

3. *If the mole ratio is not 1:1,* the calculation of the unknown molarity is slightly more complicated. For example, if 2 moles of standard acid solution is needed to neutralize 1 mole of base of unknown concentration, the following relationship exists:

$$M_a \times V_a = 2(M_b \times V_b)$$

The 2 in this equation is known as the *mole factor*.

In Part A of this experiment, you will determine the molarity of a solution of NaOH by titrating it with a standard solution of HCl. The equation for this reaction is

$$HCl + NaOH \rightarrow NaCl + H_2O$$

Because the mole relationship of H^+ to OH^- is 1:1, no mole factor will be needed in your calculations.

In Part B of the experiment, you will titrate household white vinegar. Most commercial vinegars contain at least 4% acetic acid by weight. You will use the NaOH solution whose molarity you determined in Part A for the titration of the vinegar.

Up to this point in your laboratory work, most of your quantitative experiments have required you to calculate mass relationships. This is known as *gravimetric analysis*. Titration requires you to use volume relationships, a technique known as *volumetric analysis*.

This experiment should lead to a better understanding of the properties of acids and bases, neutralization reactions, and titration techniques.

Purpose

Determine the molarity of a NaOH solution by titrating it with a standard HCl solution. Determine the molarity of a sample of white vinegar.

Equipment

burets, 50-mL (2)   dropper pipet
buret stand   pipet, 10-mL
double buret clamp   suction bulb
graduated cylinder, 10-mL   safety goggles
Erlenmeyer flask, 250-mL   lab apron or coat
beakers, 250-mL (2)

Materials

0.100 *M* HCl (standard solution)   distilled water
NaOH (concentration unknown)   detergent solution
phenolphthalein   white vinegar

Safety

Follow all precautions for working with acids and bases. Note the caution alert symbols here and with certain steps in the "Procedure." Refer to page xi to review the precautions associated with each symbol. Always wear safety goggles and a lab coat or apron when working in the lab.

39 Acid-Base Titration (continued)

Procedure

PART A TITRATION OF BASE OF UNKNOWN CONCENTRATION

1. Wash two burets with detergent solution. Rinse them thoroughly, first with tap water, then with distilled water.

2. Obtain about 100 mL of standard acid solution in a clean, dry 250-mL beaker. Obtain about the same amount of the base of unknown concentration in a second 250-mL beaker. **CAUTION:** *Handle these solutions with care. They can cause painful burns if they come in contact with the skin.*

3. Pour about 10 mL of acid into one buret and rinse the inside surface of the buret thoroughly. Allow the acid to run out the buret tip. Fill the buret to slightly above the 0.0-mL mark with acid. Then allow the acid to flow out the buret tip until the bottom of the meniscus is at the 0.0-mL mark (see Figure 39-1). Be sure there are no bubbles in the tip. If bubbles are present, add a little more acid to the buret and allow it to drain through the tip until it is free of bubbles and the meniscus is at 0.0 mL.

4. Repeat step 3 using the base solution in the second buret.

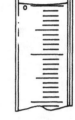

Figure 39-1

Starting with step 5 of the "Procedure," one lab partner should carry out the instructions while the second partner records the data.

5. Place a 125-mL Erlenmeyer flask under the acid buret as in Figure 39-2. Holding a sheet of white paper behind the buret to make the scale easier to read, allow exactly 10.0 mL of acid to flow into the flask.

6. Add exactly 10.0 mL of distilled water to the flask. Then, using a clean dropper pipet, add three drops of phenolphthalein. Swirl the flask to mix all the ingredients.

7. Place the flask on a sheet of white paper under the buret containing the base solution. To avoid splashing, be sure the tip of the buret is in the flask (See Figure 39-2).

8. Swirling the flask gently, begin the titration by adding NaOH to the flask drop by drop. Continue until a faint pink color remains for about 30 seconds. If "overtitration" occurs (the pink color is too deep), follow your teacher's instructions for correcting this condition.

9. Note and record the exact final volume reading on the scale of the base buret. Discard the solution in the flask as instructed. Wash and rinse the flask.

10. Repeat the titration (steps 5 through 9). It is not necessary to refill the burets. Simply read and record the initial volumes of the solutions in the burets carefully.

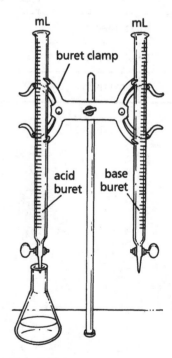

Figure 39-2

After one lab partner has completed two titrations of the NaOH, the lab partners should switch roles. The recording partner should complete two trials (steps 5 through 9) while the other partner takes over the recording duties. **NOTE:** *Be sure to read and record the initial volumes of the solutions in the burets at the beginning of each trial.*

PART B TITRATION OF WHITE VINEGAR

11. Using a pipet and suction bulb, measure 10 mL of white vinegar into a 250-mL Erlenmeyer flask. Add 100 mL of distilled water.

12. Add three drops of phenolphthalein and *carefully* titrate, using the same NaOH solution used in Part A.

13. If overtitration occurs, add a measured amount of vinegar to the flask (using the pipet) until the solution is colorless. This time, reach the end point carefully by titrating drop by drop with the NaOH solution.

Observations and Data

PART A

DATA TABLE

	Trial 1		Trial 2		Trial 3		Trial 4	
	HCl	NaOH	HCl	NaOH	HCl	NaOH	HCl	NaOH
Initial reading								
Final reading								
Volume used								

PART B

Total volume: white vinegar = _____

Total volume: NaOH solution = _____

Calculations

PART A

For each trial, calculate the molarity of the NaOH solution using the relationship $M_b = \dfrac{M_a \times V_a}{V_b}$

Trial 1 _____

Trial 2 _____

Trial 3 _____

Trial 4 _____

Name _____

39 Acid-Base Titration (continued)

PART B

To determine the molarity of the NaOH solution used, average the results calculated in Part A. Then use the relationship

$$V_a \times M_a = V_b \times M_b$$

to calculate the molarity of the white vinegar. The volumes of acid and base are those in Part B of "Observations and Data."

Conclusions and Questions

1. How reproducible were the results of your two trials? How did your results compare with those of your partner?

_____

_____

_____

_____

2. Define these terms: standard solution; titration; end point; volumetric analysis; gravimetric analysis.

_____

_____

_____

_____

_____

_____

_____

_____

_____

_____

3. If 30.0 mL of 0.500 M KOH is needed to neutralize 10.0 mL of HCl of unknown concentration, what is the molarity of the HCl?

4. How many mL of 0.100 M NaOH is needed to titrate 20.0 mL of 0.100 M H_2SO_4? Use a balanced equation for the neutralization reaction and explain your calculations.

5. Explain why people can use white vinegar in preparing foods and in cooking without danger to the skin or the internal organs.

_____

_____

_____

_____

_____

_____

_____

Hydrolysis of a Salt

Lab 40

Text reference: **Chapter 20,** pp. 586–589

Pre-Lab Discussion

A **salt** is an ionic compound containing positive ions other than H^+ and negative ions other than OH^-. Most salts will dissociate to some degree when placed in water. In many cases, ions from the salt will react with water to produce hydronium ions or hydroxide ions. Any chemical reaction in which water is one of the reactants is called a **hydrolysis** reaction.

Salts can be thought of as being derived from the neutralization of an acid and a base. A salt formed from a strong acid and a strong base* will not hydrolyze (react with water). When placed in water, these salts dissociate completely, and their ions remain uncombined in solution. An example of such a salt is NaCl, formed from a strong acid (HCl) and a strong base (NaOH).

Salts formed from a strong acid and a weak base hydrolyze to form a solution that is slightly acidic. In this kind of hydrolysis, the water molecules actually react with the cation of the weak base. For example, when ammonium chloride, NH_4Cl, hydrolyzes, water molecules react with the NH_4^+ ion:

$$NH_4^+ + 2H_2O \rightarrow NH_4OH + H_3O^+$$

The formation of the H_3O^+ ion from this reaction makes the solution acidic.

Salts formed from a weak acid and a strong base hydrolyze to form a solution that is slightly basic. In this kind of hydrolysis, it is the anion of the weak acid that actually reacts with the water. For example, when sodium acetate, $NaC_2H_3O_2$, hydrolyzes, water molecules react with the acetate ion:

$$C_2H_3O_2^- + H_2O \rightarrow HC_2H_3O_2 + OH^-$$

The formation of the OH^- ion from this reaction makes the solution basic.

Salts formed from a weak acid and a weak base produce solutions that may be slightly acidic, slightly basic, or neutral, depending on how strongly the ions of the salt are hydrolyzed.

In this experiment, you will test several different salt solutions with pH paper and phenolphthalein solution to determine their acidity or basicity.

Purpose

Determine the relative acidity or basicity of various salt solutions. Determine the pH of these solutions.

---

*Some strong acids: HI, HBr, HCl, HNO_3, H_2SO_4. Strong bases: Most hydroxides, especially those of the Group 1 and 2 metals.

Equipment

test tubes, 13×100-mm (7)

test tube rack

marking pencil

dropper pipet

safety goggles

lab apron or coat

Materials

pH paper, universal
(range 0–14)

phenolphthalein

0.1 M solutions of:

KBr	$SrCl_2$
Na_2S	$NH_4C_2H_3O_2$
Na_2CO_3	$Fe(NO_3)_3$

Safety

Handle reagent solutions with care and avoid spills. Always wear safety goggles and a lab apron or coat when working in the lab.

Procedure

1. Number six clean, dry test tubes 1 through 6. Stand the test tubes in a test tube rack.

2. To the test tube indicated, add 5 mL of the following salt solutions:

test tube 1	KBr	test tube 4	$SrCl_2$
test tube 2	Na_2S	test tube 5	$NH_4C_2H_3O_2$
test tube 3	Na_2CO_3	test tube 6	$Fe(NO_3)_3$

3. Using a dropper pipet, add two drops of phenolphthalein to each tube. Record your observations in the data table.

4. Test each solution with pH paper and record your results.

5. Fill in the rest of the data table.

Observations and Data

DATA TABLE

Test tube	Salt	Effect on indicator	pH	Parent acid	Strength of acid	Parent base	Strength of base
1	KBr						
2	Na_2S						
3	Na_2CO_3						
4	$SrCl_2$						
5	$NH_4C_2H_3O_2$						
6	$Fe(NO_3)_3$						

40 Hydrolysis of a Salt (continued)

Equations

1. Complete the equations for the dissociation of each salt:

a. $KBr \rightarrow$

b. $Na_2S \rightarrow$

c. $Na_2CO_3 \rightarrow$

d. $SrCl_2 \rightarrow$

e. $NH_4C_2H_3O_2 \rightarrow$

f. $Fe(NO_3)_3 \rightarrow$

2. Complete each ionic equation. Beneath it, write the equation that results when all spectator ions have been eliminated.

a. $K^+ + Br^- + H_2O \rightarrow$

b. $2Na^+ + S^{2-} + 2H_2O \rightarrow$

c. $2Na^+ + CO_3^{2-} + 2H_2O \rightarrow$

d. $Sr^{2+} + 2Cl^- + 4H_2O \rightarrow$

e. $NH_4^+ + C_2H_3O_2^- + H_2O \rightarrow$

f. $Fe^{3+} + 3NO_3^- + 6H_2O \rightarrow$

Conclusions and Questions

1. How do your observations and pH readings compare with the expected results based on the equations for the hydrolysis reactions?

_____

_____

_____

_____

_____

_____

2. What is a spectator ion? Name the spectator ions present in each hydrolysis reaction in this experiment.

_____

_____

_____

_____

3. A salt formed from a strong acid and a strong base produces a neutral solution. A salt of a weak acid and a weak base may or may not produce a neutral solution. Explain.

_____

_____

_____

_____

_____

_____

_____

_____

4. Commercial baking soda is $NaHCO_3$. It often is used to counteract excess acidity in the stomach. Explain why baking soda is an effective antacid using what you have learned in this lab on hydrolysis.

_____

_____

_____

_____

_____

_____

Redox: Oxidation-Reduction Reactions

Lab 41

Text reference: **Chapter 21,** pp. 613–616

Pre-Lab Discussion

Oxidation is broadly defined as the loss, or apparent loss, of electrons by an atom or ion. Similarly, *reduction* is the gain, or apparent gain, of electrons by an atom or ion. Neither oxidation nor reduction can ever occur alone. Whenever electrons are lost by one substance, they must be gained by another. Reactions involving the exchange or transfer of electrons from atoms or ions of one substance to those of another substance are called **oxidation-reduction reactions,** or **redox reactions,** for short. In such reactions, the substance that is oxidized (loses electrons) is called the *reducing agent.* The substance that is reduced (gains electrons) is called the *oxidizing agent.*

Because they are made up of two distinct processes—oxidation and reduction—redox reactions can be represented by two *half-reactions.* For example, the balanced equation for the reaction of sodium with chlorine is

$$2Na + Cl_2 \rightarrow 2NaCl$$

In half-reaction form, the equation for this reaction is

$$2Na \rightarrow 2Na^+ + 2e^- \quad \text{(oxidation)}$$
$$Cl_2 + 2e^- \rightarrow 2Cl^- \quad \text{(reduction)}$$

As the equations for these half-reactions show, the two electrons lost by the sodium atoms are gained by the chlorine atoms. For any redox reaction, the number of electrons gained in the reduction half-reaction must equal the number of electrons lost in the oxidation half-reaction.

In theory, every half-reaction is reversible. In one direction, it is an oxidation half-reaction. In the reverse direction, it is a reduction half-reaction. The Table of Standard Electrode Potentials in Appendix A of this lab manual lists *reduction* half-reactions. Thus, it is a table of reduction potentials. However, each reaction can be reversed and written as an oxidation half-reaction, in which case the *sign* of the electrode potential ($E°$) is reversed. For example, the reduction half-reaction $F_2(g) + 2e^- \rightarrow 2F^-$ heads the list in this table. In this half-reaction, F_2 is reduced and is thus the oxidizing agent. The electrode potential for this half-reaction is +2.87 volts. By reversing this half-reaction, you get $2F^- \rightarrow F_2(g) + 2e^-$, which is an oxidation half-reaction. F^- is oxidized and is thus the reducing agent. The electrode potential for this half-reaction is −2.87 volts.

The Table of Standard Electrode Potentials can be used to predict whether or not a redox reaction will occur spontaneously. For a redox reaction to occur, the reduction half-reaction must appear higher in the table than the oxidation half-reaction. Consider the *possible* redox reaction:

$$Fe(s) + Pb(NO_3)_2(aq) \rightarrow Pb(s) + Fe(NO_3)_2(aq)$$

If this reaction does occur, the half-reactions will be:

$$Fe(s) \rightarrow Fe^{2+} + 2e^- \quad \text{(oxidation)}$$
$$Pb^{2+} + 2e^- \rightarrow Pb(s) \quad \text{(reduction)}$$

In the table, the half-reaction for the reduction of Pb^{2+} does appear higher on the list than that for the oxidation of $Fe(s)$ (the reverse of the half-reaction for the reduction of Fe^{2+}). Thus, the redox reaction will occur. As another check, the algebraic sum of the $E°$ values of two half-reactions must be positive for the reaction to occur. In this case, $E°$ of the reduction reaction is -0.13, while that of the oxidation reaction is $+0.44$. The algebraic sum is $+0.31$.

In this experiment, you will prepare several different combinations of substances and observe whether or not any visible redox reactions occur. This lab should help provide a better understanding of redox reactions and the use of the Table of Standard Electrode Potentials.

Purpose

Study some simple redox reactions. Determine the relative strengths of some oxidizing agents and reducing agents.

Equipment

test tubes, 18×100-mm (8)	dropper pipet
test tube rack	burner
test tube holder	safety goggles
graduated cylinder, 10-mL	lab apron or coat
microspatula	

Materials

0.1 M solutions of:
   $AgNO_3$
   $Pb(NO_3)_2$
   $Zn(NO_3)_2$
   $Cu(NO_3)_2$
   $FeCl_3$
   $SnCl_2$

6 M HCl
silver foil
iron filings
1-cm strips of:
   zinc
   lead
   copper

Safety

Handle the hydrochloric acid with extreme care. Avoid spills on your skin or clothing. Flush any spills with cool water and $NaHCO_3$ solution and report them to your teacher. Note the caution alert symbols here and with certain steps of the "Procedure." Refer to page xi for the precautions associated with each symbol. Always wear safety goggles and a lab coat or apron when working in the lab.

Procedure

PART A RELATIVE ACTIVITY OF SOME METALS

1. Add 5 mL of 0.1 M $AgNO_3$ to a clean, dry test tube. Add a piece of copper metal to this solution. Add 5 mL of 0.1 M $Cu(NO_3)_2$ to a second test tube and add a piece of silver foil to

41 Redox: Oxidation-Reduction Reactions (continued)

the solution. Allow both test tubes to stand for several minutes. Record your observations.

2. Stand two test tubes in a test tube rack. Add 5 mL of 0.1 M $Cu(NO_3)_2$ to each tube. Place a strip of zinc (Zn) in one tube and a strip of lead (Pb) in the other. Allow the tubes to stand for a few minutes. Record your observations.

3. Using two clean, dry test tubes, repeat the procedure in step 2 using 0.1 M Pb $(NO_3)_2$ and strips of copper (Cu) and zinc. Record your observations.

4. Repeat the procedure a third time, using 0.1 M $Zn(NO_3)_2$ and strips of Cu and Pb. After you have recorded your observations, discard the materials in the test tubes as instructed. Clean and rinse the tubes.

PART B   REACTIONS OF IRON METAL AND IRON IONS

5. Place 5 mL of 0.1 M $FeCl_3$ in a clean, dry test tube. Using a pipet, add $SnCl_2$ drop by drop until a change is observed. Record your observations.

6. Place a heaping microspatulaful of iron filings (Fe) into a clean, dry test tube. Add 5 mL of 6 M HCl. **CAUTION:** *Handle this acid very carefully. It can cause painful burns.* Using a test tube holder, warm the contents of the test tube *carefully* over a low burner flame. Allow the test tube to stand for several minutes. Record your observations.

Observations and Data

PART A

Observations

1. Cu + $AgNO_3$:   _____

   Ag + $Cu(NO_3)_2$:   _____

2. Zn + $Cu(NO_3)_2$:   _____

   Pb + $Cu(NO_3)_2$:   _____

3. Cu + $Pb(NO_3)_2$:   _____

   Zn + $Pb(NO_3)_2$:   _____

4. Cu + $Zn(NO_3)_2$:   _____

   Pb + $Zn(NO_3)_2$:   _____

PART B

5. Fe^{3+} + Sn^{2+}:   _____

6. Fe + HCl: _____

   _____

Equations

Write balanced chemical equations for each reaction that occurred in this experiment. Beneath each equation, write equations for the half-reactions, identifying each as an oxidation or reduction half-reaction.

Conclusions and Questions

Where necessary, refer to the Table of Standard Electrode Potentials in Appendix A to help you answer these questions.

1. List the order of activity of the metals Ag, Cu, Pb, and Zn as determined by your experimental results. Do these results agree with the positions of these metals in the table?

_____

_____

_____

2. Which metal listed in the Table of Standard Electrode Potentials will replace Fe^{2+} but will not replace Zn^{2+}? Explain, using the table.

_____

_____

_____

_____

41 Redox: Oxidation-Reduction Reactions (continued)

3. Define the following: oxidation; reduction; oxidizing agent; reducing agent.

_____

_____

_____

_____

_____

4. Study the chemical combinations listed below. Using the table, predict which combinations will produce a spontaneous redox reaction. For those redox reactions that will occur:

    (1) complete the balanced equation for the reaction;

    (2) write the half-reactions for each reaction and identify them as oxidation or reduction;

    (3) name the oxidizing and reducing agents in each reaction; and

    (4) calculate the net $E°$ for each reaction at standard conditions (1 molar ion concentration, 298 K, 101.3 kPa).

    a. Fe + $CuCl_2$

    b. Ag + H_2SO_4

    c. Al + $NaOH$

    d. F_2 + $CaCl_2$

Electrolysis

Lab 42

Text reference: **Chapter 20,** pp. 625–630

Pre-Lab Discussion

In **electrolysis**, an external source of electrical energy is used to induce a nonspontaneous redox reaction. The external voltage forces electrons to flow through a wire to the electrode where reduction takes place. This electrode, called the cathode, is the negative electrode in this cell. Oxidation takes place at the positive electrode, which is called the anode.

Electrolysis often is used to separate and isolate chemically active elements that are not found free in nature. For example, if an electric current is passed through a molten sample of an ionic compound, the positive ions are attracted to the cathode and the negative ions are attracted to the anode. The positive ions are reduced to free metal atoms and the negative ions are oxidized to free nonmetal atoms. If an electric current is passed through an aqueous solution of an ionic compound, the water, rather than the metallic ion, may be reduced. This is determined by the reduction potentials of the two substances. Whichever has the higher reduction potential will take part in the reduction half-reaction.

In this experiment, an aqueous solution of the ionic compound potassium iodide, KI, will be electrolyzed, and various indicators will be used to identify the products. This experiment will promote a better understanding of oxidation-reduction reactions and the process of electrolysis.

Purpose

Demonstrate electrolysis of an aqueous solution of an ionic compound.

Equipment

U-tube
ring stand
utility clamp
D.C. power source, 12-volt
electrodes, graphite (2)

alligator clips and wire leads (2)
dropper pipet
safety goggles
lab apron or coat

Materials

0.5 M potassium iodide (KI)
phenolphthalein
starch solution

Safety

Do not handle electrical apparatus with wet hands. Note the caution alert symbols here and with certain steps in the "Procedure." Refer to page xi for the specific precautions associated with each symbol. Always wear safety goggles and a lab coat or apron when working in the lab.

Procedure

1. Clamp the U-tube to a ring stand as shown in Figure 42-1. Fill the tube about three-fourths full of 0.5 *M* KI solution. Using a dropper pipet, add about three drops of phenolphthalein into each arm of the U-tube.

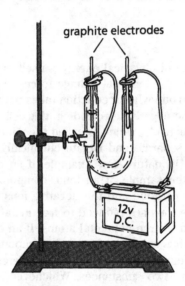

graphite electrodes

12v D.C.

Figure 42-1

2. Connect alligator clips and wire leads to two graphite electrodes. Insert one electrode into each arm of the U-tube as shown in Figure 42-1. Attach the leads to the terminals of a 12-volt D.C. source.

3. Allow the current to flow for 10-15 minutes. Note and record all observations.

4. Break the circuit. **Do this by disconnecting the leads at the battery first.** Then remove the electrodes from the U-tube carefully to avoid agitating the solution. Carefully smell the two openings of the U-tube to detect any telltale odors. Record your observations.

5. Add about 2 ml of starch solution to each arm of the U-tube. Record your observations.

Observations and Data

Anode (oxidation) side of the U-tube:

_____

_____

_____

Cathode (reduction) side of the U-tube:

_____

_____

_____

42 Electrolysis (continued)

Conclusions and Questions

1. Write the equation for the oxidation half-reaction, which occurred at the anode.

_____

2. Write the equation for the reduction half-reaction, which occurred at the cathode.

_____

3. Write the balanced redox equation for the overall reaction.

_____

4. Referring to the Table of Standard Electrode Potentials, Appendix A, explain why the water was reduced rather than the K^+ ions from the solution.

_____

_____

_____

5. If you wish to electroplate an object with silver metal, to what terminal of the D.C. power source must the object be attached? What ion must be present in the solution? Write the equation for the reduction half-reaction in this electrolysis.

_____

_____

_____

_____

Electrochemical Cells

Lab 43

Text reference: **Chapter 22,** pp. 653–655

Pre-Lab Discussion

In many redox reactions, there is a complete transfer of electrons from the substance being oxidized to the substance being reduced. If the electrons can be made to travel through an external conductor during this transfer, an electric current will be established in the conductor. This can be accomplished using an arrangement like the one shown in Figure 43-1.

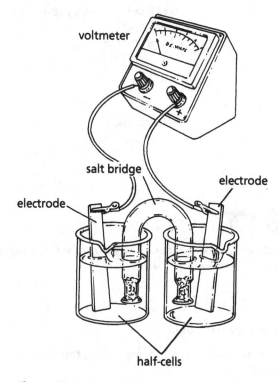

Figure 43-1

In this arrangement, the two half-reactions—oxidation and reduction— are carried out in separate vessels, called half-cells. The two half-cells are connected externally by metal wire attached to the two electrodes. In order to have a complete electrical circuit, ions must be free to flow from one half-cell to the other. This is made possible by connecting the solutions in the two half-cells with a salt bridge. The complete system is called an **electrochemical cell,** or simply a **chemical cell**.

In this experiment, you will observe several electrochemical cells, using different combinations of metal electrodes. In each of these cells, the electrode consisting of the more active metal will be oxidized. This will be the oxidation half-cell. Electrons will flow from this electrode through the wire conductor to the reduction half-cell. There, the less active metal electrode will be built up because of reduction of ions of that metal. The relative activities of the various metals can be determined by checking their positions on the table of standard electrode potentials. A voltmeter will be used to detect the presence of an electric current through the conductor.

This lab will aid in the understanding of redox reactions and electrochemical cells.

Purpose

Set up and test the voltage of several different electrochemical cells.

Equipment

beakers, 250-mL (3)
glass U-tube
cotton
D.C. voltmeter
alligator clips (2)

copper wire, insulated
steel wool or emery paper
safety goggles
lab apron or coat

Materials

0.5 M solutions of:
  $Cu(NO_3)_2$
  $Zn(NO_3)_2$
  $Pb(NO_3)_2$
  KNO_3

metal strips:
  Cu, Zn, Pb

Safety

Follow all normal lab safety procedures. Always wear safety goggles and a lab apron or coat when working in the lab.

Procedure

PART A Cu/Cu²⁺ AND Zn/Zn²⁺ CELL

1. Using steel wool or emery paper, clean the strips of copper, zinc, and lead.

2. Half-fill a 250-mL beaker with 0.5 M $Cu(NO_3)_2$ solution. Place a clean copper strip in the beaker as shown in Figure 43-2.

3. Half-fill a second 250-mL beaker with 0.5 M $Zn(NO_3)_2$ solution and place a clean zinc strip in the beaker.

4. Using alligator clips, connect the wire leads to the metal strips as illustrated in Figure 43-2.

5. Fill a U-tube with 0.5 M KNO_3 and stopper the ends with cotton. Invert the tube and place the ends of the U in the two beakers as shown.

6. *Immediately* touch the ends of the wire leads to the voltmeter terminals. If the voltmeter needle is deflected in the wrong direction, reverse the leads on the voltmeter.

43 Electrochemical Cells (continued)

7. Attach the leads to the proper terminals and read and record the voltage immediately. Disconnect the leads from the voltmeter.

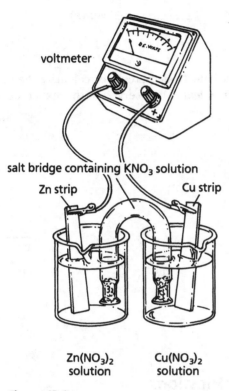

voltmeter

salt bridge containing KNO_3 solution

Zn strip   Cu strip

$Zn(NO_3)_2$ $Cu(NO_3)_2$
solution   solution

Figure 43-2

PART B Cu/Cu^{2+} AND Pb/Pb^{2+} CELL

8. Half-fill a third 250-mL beaker with 0.5 M $Pb(NO_3)_2$ solution and place a lead strip in the beaker. Remove the wire lead from the zinc strip and attach it to the lead strip.

9. Place the salt bridge between this lead half-cell and the copper half-cell. Connect the ends of the wire leads to the proper voltmeter terminals. Read and record the voltage. Disconnect the leads from the voltmeter.

PART C Pb/Pb^{2+} AND Zn/Zn^{2+} CELL

10. Remove the wire lead from the copper strip and connect it to the zinc strip.

11. Place the salt bridge between the lead half-cell and the zinc half-cell. Connect the leads to the proper voltmeter terminals. Read and record the voltage. Disconnect the leads from the voltmeter.

Observations and Data

Cell	Voltage
Cu/Cu^{2+} and Zn/Zn^{2+}	_____ volt(s)
Cu/Cu^{2+} and Pb/Pb^{2+}	_____ volt(s)
Pb/Pb^{2+} and Zn/Zn^{2+}	_____ volt(s)

Calculations

Using the table of standard electrode potentials, calculate the theoretical voltage for each electrochemical cell observed in this experiment.

Cell	Voltage
(1) Cu/Cu^{2+} and Zn/Zn^{2+}	_____
(2) Cu/Cu^{2+} and Pb/Pb^{2+}	_____
(3) Pb/Pb^{2+} and Zn/Zn^{2+}	_____

Conclusions and Questions

1. For each cell studied in this experiment, show:
   a. the oxidation half-reaction and the reduction half-reaction.
   b. the overall redox reaction.
   c. the oxidizing and reducing agents

43 Electrochemical Cells (continued)

2. Identify the electrode where oxidation takes place and the electrode where reduction takes place for each cell studied in this experiment. Indicate the direction of the flow of electrons.

_____

_____

_____

_____

_____

_____

_____

3. How did the experimental voltages compare with the theoretical voltages calculated from the table? Explain any differences.

_____

_____

_____

_____

_____

_____

_____

_____

4. Describe three conditions under which the voltmeter reading will be 0.

_____

_____

_____

5. Discuss an electrochemical cell in which the half-cells are Ag/Ag^+ and Cu/Cu^{2+}. Write the oxidation and reduction half-reactions and the overall redox reaction. Name the oxidizing and reducing agents and calculate the theoretical net electrode potential.

_____

_____

_____

_____

_____

_____

_____

Corrosion of Iron

Lab 44

Text reference: **Chapter 22,** pp. 655–660

Pre-Lab Discussion

Corrosion is a redox reaction in which a free metal is oxidized, or "corroded," by some oxidizing agent. In nature, the oxidizing agent is frequently atmospheric oxygen dissolved in water. Perhaps the most familiar example of corrosion is the rusting of iron. In this reaction, free iron, Fe, is oxidized to Fe^{2+} and Fe^{3+} ions. In the reduction half-reaction, oxygen, O_2, reacts with water to form OH^- ions.

The rusting of iron usually is considered to be a destructive change, and considerable time and money are expended to prevent it. One method, which you will observe in this experiment, makes use of a "sacrificial" metal. If iron is placed in contact with a more active metal (one that is more easily oxidized), the more active metal will be corroded instead of the iron. Metals situated below iron on the table of standard electrode potentials can function as sacrificial metals.

In this experiment, indicators will be used to signal the formation of Fe^{2+} ions and OH^- ions as products of the corrosion of iron. One such indicator, the hexacyanoferrate(III) ion, turns blue in the presence of Fe^{2+} ions. The other, phenolphthalein, turns pink in the presence of OH^- ions. This experiment should help promote a better understanding of corrosion and of oxidation-reduction reactions.

Purpose

Observe the corrosion of iron and investigate conditions related to corrosion.

Equipment

balance	glass stirring rod
burner	dropper pipet
graduated cylinder, 100-mL	petri dishes (2)
beaker, 250-mL	steel wool or emery paper
ring stand	metric ruler
iron ring	safety goggles
wire gauze	lab apron or coat

Materials

0.1 *M* $K_3Fe(CN)_6$ [potassium hexacyanoferrate(III)]

agar powder	copper wire, 5-cm
1% phenolphthalein solution	zinc strip, 5-cm
distilled water	iron nails (4)

Safety

Observe all general lab safety precautions. Always wear safety goggles and a lab coat or apron when working in the lab.

Procedure

1. Set up a ring stand, ring, and wire gauze. Add 200 mL of distilled water to the 250-mL beaker and heat to boiling. While the water is being heated, clean four iron nails with steel wool or emery paper.

2. Using the balance, measure out 2.0 g of agar powder. When the water is boiling vigorously, put out the flame and slowly add the agar to the water, stirring constantly. When the agar has dissolved, add 10 drops of 0.1 M $K_3Fe(CN)_6$. Rinse the dropper pipet and add five drops of phenolphthalein solution.

3. Place one bent iron nail and one straight iron nail into one of the petri dishes. Be sure the nails do not touch and are positioned as shown in Figure 44-1(a).

(a) 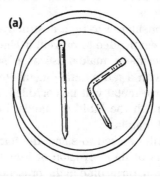 (b)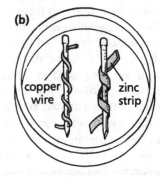

Figure 44-1

4. Tightly wrap one of the remaining nails with copper wire and the other with the zinc strip. Place these nails in the other petri dish, as shown in Figure 44-1(b).

5. When the agar solution is cool enough, pour it into each petri dish to a depth of 0.5 cm. Make and record observations in the time remaining. At the end of the lab period, place the dishes in your drawer to be observed on the following day.

Observations and Data

Petri dish (a):

_____

_____

_____

_____

_____

Petri dish (b):

_____

_____

_____

_____

44 Corrosion of Iron (continued)

Conclusions and Questions

1. Explain why corrosion occurred at the sites indicated by the blue color in petri dish (a).

_____

_____

_____

_____

2. What is the whitish material surrounding the zinc-wrapped nail in petri dish (b)?

_____

3. Explain why the zinc-wrapped nail showed no evidence of corrosion, while the copper-wrapped nail did.

_____

_____

_____

_____

4. Would a magnesium wrapping prevent the corrosion of iron? Explain.

_____

_____

_____

_____

5. Why would sodium metal not be appropriate as a sacrificial metal in this experiment?

_____

_____

_____

Allotropes of Sulfur

(Demonstration)

Text reference: **Chapter 23**, pp. 680–682

Pre-Lab Discussion

Allotropes are different structural forms of the same element. In the case of solids, differences in form result from differences in crystalline structure. In other cases, differences in form may result from differences in the number of atoms in a molecule of the substance, as in oxygen gas (O_2) and ozone gas (O_3).

In this experiment, you will prepare three allotropic forms of sulfur, observe their structures, and test their properties. These three forms are rhombic, monoclinic, and amorphous (plastic) sulfur. The different forms of this element will be produced by changing the conditions under which the sulfur crystals develop.

Purpose

Prepare and investigate the structure and properties of three allotropic forms of sulfur. Observe the conditions under which each of the forms develops.

Equipment

test tubes, 13×100-mm (5)
test tube holder
lab burner
ring stand
iron ring
beaker, 250-mL
microspatula

watch glass
magnifying glass
forceps
funnel
safety goggles
lab apron or coat

Materials

sulfur, powdered (S_8)
toluene (C_7H_8)
ethanol (C_2H_5OH)

copper foil (Cu)
filter paper

Safety

This experiment is to be conducted under a properly functioning fume hood. Do not inhale the vapors of any substance used, except as directed. When noting the odor of sulfur dioxide (step 9), waft some of the gas toward your nose and sniff gently. Note the caution alert symbols here and with certain steps in the "Procedure." Refer to page xi to review the specific precautions associated with each symbol. Always wear safety goggles and a lab coat or apron when working in the lab. Tie back long hair and secure loose clothing when working with an open flame.

Procedure

PART A RHOMBIC SULFUR

1. Pour about 5 mL of toluene (C_7H_8) into a test tube. Dissolve about 1 microspatula of sulfur (S_8) in the toluene.

2. Pour the clear liquid into a watch glass and leave the glass *under the hood.* Allow the solution to stand until all of the liquid has evaporated. You may proceed with Part B of this experiment and return later to examine the solid left behind on the watch glass. Record your observations upon examination of the solid.

PART B MONOCLINIC SULFUR

NOTE: Parts B and C should be done in the fume hood *well away* from toluene and other flammable liquids.

3. Prepare a filter paper cone in a funnel and set up the apparatus as shown in Figure 45-1.

Figure 45-1

4. Place two heaping microspatulas of sulfur into a test tube. Using a test tube holder, heat the test tube slowly until all the sulfur has melted to form a viscous, pale-yellow liquid.

5. Pour the molten sulfur into the filter paper cone as shown in Figure 45-2. *Immediately* unfold the filter paper and observe the crystal formation. Examine the crystals with a magnifier and record your observations.

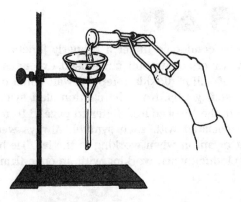

Figure 45-2

45 Allotropes of Sulfur (continued)

PART C AMORPHOUS (PLASTIC) SULFUR

6. Half-fill a 250-mL beaker with tap water and set it to one side. Using the same test tube as in Part B, add two heaping microspatulas of sulfur. Heat the sulfur to boiling (dark red color).

7. As soon as the sulfur is boiling, extinguish the burner and pour the hot sulfur into the beaker of water, as shown in Figure 45-3. The sulfur may start to burn. If this happens, continue pouring until the test tube is empty. Then extinguish any sulfur that is still burning by smothering the flames with a damp towel.

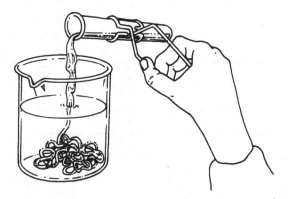

Figure 45-3

8. Examine the solid formed in the beaker of water and record your observations.

PART D PROPERTIES

9. Burn a spatulaful of sulfur under the fume hood. Gently waft some of the gas formed toward your nose and note its odor. *Do not smell the fumes directly.*

10. Add 10 mL of tap water to one test tube and 10 mL ethanol to a second test tube. Add a spatula of sulfur to each tube and try to dissolve the sulfur. Record your observations.

11. Under the fume hood, heat two or three spatulas of sulfur in a test tube until it begins to boil. Using a forceps, hold a piece of copper foil in the hot vapors near the top of the tube while continuing to heat the sulfur gently. Examine the copper and record your observations.

Observations and Data

PART A

_____

_____

_____

_____

PART B

_____

_____

_____

_____

PART C

_____

_____

_____

_____

PART D

_____

_____

_____

_____

_____

_____

Illustrations

Sketch the crystal form of rhombic and monoclinic sulfur as they appear
to you under magnification.

45 Allotropes of Sulfur (continued)

Conclusions and Questions

1. Write a balanced equation for the reaction between sulfur and copper.

_____

2. Name some allotropes of the elements carbon, oxygen, and phosphorus.

_____

_____

_____

_____

3. How does the meaning of the term allotrope differ from that of the term isotope?

_____

_____

_____

4. Briefly describe the different conditions under which the three allotropic forms of sulfur were formed in this experiment.

_____

_____

_____

_____

5. Based on evidence from this experiment, what do you think the relationship is between rate of cooling and crystal size?

_____

_____

Oxygen: Its Properties

Lab 46

Text reference: **Chapter 23**, pp. 678–680

Pre-Lab Discussion

Oxygen is one of the most abundant of all elements. It is found in the earth's crust combined with other elements. It is also present in elemental (diatomic) form in the atmosphere. In addition to being plentiful, oxygen is a highly reactive element. It combines with most other elements by gaining or sharing two electrons.

In this experiment, you will observe some of the properties of oxygen.

Purpose

Investigate some of the properties of oxygen.

Equipment

lab burner
trough
small gas-collecting bottles, (2)
glass plates (3)
wooden splints
crucible tongs
microspatula
safety goggles
lab apron or coat

Materials

oxygen gas
sulfur powder (S_8)
"steel" wool (Fe)

Safety

Tie back long hair and secure loose clothing when working with an open flame. Observe all normal safety precautions when observing the properties of O_2 gas. Be sure to waft just a small amount of the gas produced in step 5 to your nose. Note the caution alert symbols here and with certain steps in the "Procedure." Follow the precautions associated with each symbol. Always wear safety goggles and a lab coat or apron when working in the lab.

Procedure

1. Your teacher will collect and dispense two small gas-collecting bottles of oxygen to each student team. See Figure 46-1.

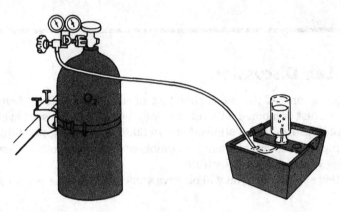

Figure 46-1

2. At your lab station, insert a *glowing* (not burning) splint into one of the bottles of oxygen gas. Record your observations.

3. Place a glowing splint on the bench surface and "pour" oxygen onto it from the same bottle. Record your observations.

4. Light the burner and, using crucible tongs, hold a small piece of "steel" wool in the flame until it glows. Thrust the glowing metal into the second bottle of oxygen. Turn off the burner and record your observations.

5. **TEACHER DEMONSTRATION.** Your teacher will do the following in the fume hood and have you note the odor of the gas produced. Using a match, your teacher will ignite a small amount of sulfur powder on a microspatula, then thrust the burning sulfur into a bottle of oxygen. Then you should *carefully* smell the gas produced by wafting it toward your nose. *Do not smell the gas directly.* Record your observations.

Observations and Data

Step 2:

_____

_____

Step 3:

_____

_____

Step 4:

_____

_____

Step 5:

_____

_____

46 Oxygen: Its Properties (continued)

Conclusions and Questions

1. What property of oxygen gas is illustrated by the procedure in step 2 of this experiment?

_____

2. What other properties of oxygen are illustrated in the steps of this experiment?

_____

_____

_____

_____

_____

3. Describe what is meant by collecting a gas by the "downward displacement of water."

_____

_____

_____

_____

_____

4. What property of a gas would make the gas unsatisfactory to collect by the downward displacement of water?

_____

_____

_____

Hydrogen: Preparation and Properties

Lab 47

(Demonstration)

Text reference: **Chapter 23**, pp. 678–680

Pre-Lab Discussion

Hydrogen is unique among the elements in that it does not really belong to any particular group of the periodic table. In some versions of the table, hydrogen is separated from the main body of elements.

Although hydrogen is classified as a nonmetal, it combines with almost all elements. The hydrogen atom consists of a single proton and one electron that is situated very close to the nucleus. It forms covalent compounds with other nonmetals by sharing its one electron. In such compounds, the oxidation state of hydrogen is 1+. Hydrogen also combines with some Group 1 and Group 2 metals to form ionic compounds, called metal hydrides, in which it has an oxidation state of 1−.

In this lab, either you or your teacher will prepare hydrogen gas by reacting an active metal with an acid. The gas will be collected by water displacement, and several properties of hydrogen will be investigated.

Purpose

Prepare hydrogen and investigate some of its properties.

Equipment

ring stand	delivery tubing, rubber or plastic
clamp	gas-collecting bottles, small (3)
Erlenmeyer flask, 250-mL	trough
thistle tube	glass squares (2)
rubber stopper, 2-hole (for flask)	safety goggles
glass tubing	lab apron or coat

Materials

zinc, mossy (Zn)
18 M sulfuric acid (H_2SO_4)
wooden splints

Safety

Hydrogen gas mixed with air can be highly explosive. There should be no open flames in the lab when hydrogen is being prepared. Handle concentrated sulfuric acid with extreme care. You should wear rubber gloves when dispensing this acid. Avoid spills on your skin or clothing. Rinse any spills at once with cool water and $NaHCO_3$ solution and report them to your teacher. Note the caution alert symbols here and with certain steps in the "Procedure." Refer to page xi to review the specific precautions associated with each symbol. Always wear safety goggles and a lab apron or coat when working in the lab.

Procedure

1. Place three or four pieces of mossy zinc in a 250-mL Erlenmeyer flask. Add sufficient water to the flask to just cover the zinc. Clamp the flask to a ring stand as shown in Figure 47-1.

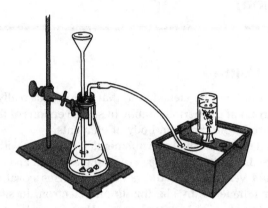

Figure 47-1

2. Fit the thistle tube and one of the curved pieces of glass tubing into a 2-hole rubber stopper. Place the stopper securely in the flask, *making sure that the end of the thistle tube extends*

3. Fill the trough with water. Fill two gas-collecting bottles with water and leave them upside-down in the trough. Attach the delivery tubing.

4. *Slowly and carefully* add 2.0 mL of 18 *M* sulfuric acid (H_2SO_4) through the thistle tube. **CAUTION:** *Handle this acid carefully. It will cause painful burns if it comes in contact with the skin.*

5. Allow the bubbles to escape into the trough for about 30 seconds. Then, place a gas-collecting bottle (filled with water) mouth down over the end of the delivery tube. Fill the bottle with hydrogen gas.

6. When the bottle is filled, lift the bottle *slightly*, and slide a glass square over the mouth of the bottle under water. Holding the glass square in place, lift the bottle out of the water and place it *mouth down* on the lab bench, with the glass square still in place.

7. In the same manner, collect another bottle of hydrogen gas.

8. Disconnect the rubber stopper and remove the tube from the trough. Unclamp the flask and carefully fill the flask with cold tap water. Discard the liquid and any remaining zinc as instructed.

9. Keeping the bottle mouth down, lift one of the bottles of hydrogen gas and insert a burning splint up into the bottle. Record your observations.

10. Keeping the glass square in place over the mouth of the bottle, turn the second bottle of hydrogen gas over. Place an inverted "empty" gas-collecting bottle on the glass square so that

47 Hydrogen: Preparation and Properties (continued)

the two bottles are mouth-to-mouth. Slide the glass square away, leaving the two bottle mouths resting against each other. After about 30 seconds, test both bottles for hydrogen with a burning splint. Record your observations.

Observations and Data

Step 9:

_____

_____

_____

_____

_____

_____

Step 10:

_____

_____

_____

_____

Conclusions and Questions

1. Why is it important to have the end of the thistle tube extend below the surface of the liquid in the flask?

_____

_____

_____

2. Why is the generator allowed to operate for 30 seconds *before* starting to collect the hydrogen gas?

_____

_____

_____

3. Write a balanced equation for the reaction used to produce hydrogen gas in this experiment.

_____

_____

4. What product results from the burning of hydrogen? Write a balanced equation for the reaction.

_____

_____

5. Based on observations from this experiment, describe the solubility of hydrogen gas in water and describe its relative density.

_____

_____

_____

_____

_____

_____

Melting Point Determination of an Organic Compound

Text reference: **Chapter 24,** pp. 693–696

Pre-Lab Discussion

Substances are identified by their properties. Many substances have the same property, but no two substances have the same *set* of properties. For example, a number of substances boil at 61°C, and a number of other substances freeze at −63.5°C, but very few *both* boil at 61°C and freeze at −63.5°C. And there is only one substance (chloroform) that boils at 61°C, freezes at −63.5°C, and has a density of 1.48 grams per milliliter at 20°C. Several properties of a substance, not just one or two, must be known to positively differentiate one substance from another.

In identifying solids, melting point is commonly one of the properties measured. This is particularly true with organic solids, which generally are characterized as having relatively low melting points. Organic compounds are covalently bonded. Only weak forces exist between one organic molecule and those surrounding it in the same sample. Relatively low temperatures are needed to overcome these forces. As a result, almost all organic compounds melt at temperatures below 400°C, a temperature easily attained in a laboratory having a gas burner as its primary heat source. By contrast, inorganic solids generally have much higher melting points. This is because such solids are ionically bonded, and high temperatures are required to disrupt the bonds during melting. Sodium chloride, for example, melts at 801°C. Most high school laboratories are not equipped to determine the high melting points of inorganic solids.

In this experiment, you will conduct a procedure that is commonly used for determining melting points of organic solids.

Purpose

Demonstrate the technique for determining the melting point of organic solids. Determine the melting points of several organic solids.

Equipment

ring stand	rubber band
iron ring	watch glass
wire gauze	microspatula
Erlenmeyer flask, 125-mL	capillary tubes (4)
rubber stopper, 1-hole	safety goggles
thermometer, −10°C to 200°C	lab apron or coat
burner	

Materials

mineral oil	tannic acid
maleic acid	urea
salicylic acid	

Safety

Tie back long hair and secure loose clothing when working with an open flame. Take care when inserting the thermometer into the rubber stopper to avoid breakage. Note the caution alert symbols here and with certain steps in the "Procedure." Follow the precautions associated with each symbol. Always wear safety goggles and a lab apron or coat when working in the lab.

Procedure

1. Seal one end of a capillary tube by holding it in a burner flame.

 2. Using a microspatula, place on a watch glass a small quantity of the organic solid to be studied. Gently push the open end of a capillary tube into the solid. Invert the tube and tap it gently on the bench top. Continue this procedure until a column of solid about 2 cm long is in the capillary tube.

 3. Lubricate the thermometer and insert it into the 1-hole rubber stopper. Attach the capillary tube to the thermometer with a rubber band, as shown in Figure 48-1.

4. Half fill a 125-mL Erlenmeyer flask with mineral oil. Set up the melting-point apparatus as shown in Figure 48-2. The thermometer should extend about 3 cm below the surface of the mineral oil.

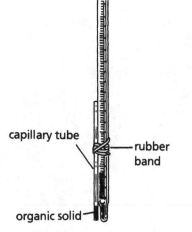

capillary tube

rubber band

organic solid

Figure 48-1

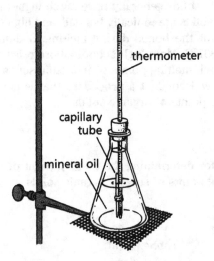

thermometer

capillary tube

mineral oil

Figure 48-2

 5. Using a low flame, heat the oil slowly. Hold the burner in your hand and move it slowly back and forth to ensure even heating.

6. Record the temperature at which the organic solid in the tube starts to melt.

7. Repeat the procedure for each organic solid to be tested.

48 Melting Point Determination of an Organic Compound
(continued)

Observations and Data

Organic Solids	Melting Point (°C)
maleic acid	_____
salicylic acid	_____
tannic acid	_____
urea	_____

Conclusions and Questions

1. Define the term melting point.

_____

_____

_____

2. Explain why organic solids generally have lower melting points than do inorganic solids.

_____

_____

_____

_____

_____

3. Explain why water is unsuitable for use as a liquid bath in this experiment.

_____

_____

_____

4. In terms of its boiling point and vapor pressure, explain why mineral oil is a suitable liquid for use in this experiment.

_____

_____

_____

_____

_____

Esters (Demonstration)

Lab 49

Text reference: **Chapter 24,** pp. 724–726

Pre-Lab Discussion

Esters are organic compounds formed by the reaction of an alcohol with an organic acid. This process, called **esterification,** can be represented by the general equation:

$$R_1OH + R_2COOH \rightarrow R_2COOR_1 + H_2O$$
$$\text{alcohol} \quad \text{acid} \quad\quad \text{ester} \quad \text{water}$$

where R_1 and R_2 represent hydrocarbon radicals that may be the same or different.

The name of the ester formed is derived from the names of the alcohol and acid that react. For example, the ester formed from ethyl alcohol (ethanol) and acetic acid is called *ethyl acetate*. The first part of the name comes from the alcohol and the second part from the acid. The names of all esters end in the suffix -*ate*. The molecular equation for this reaction is

$$C_2H_5OH + CH_3COOH \rightarrow CH_3COOC_2H_5 + H_2O$$
$$\text{ethyl alcohol} \quad \text{acetic acid} \quad \text{ethyl acetate} \quad \text{water}$$

Notice that in the formula for the ester, the acid portion is written first. The structural arrangement of the atoms in ethyl acetate is:

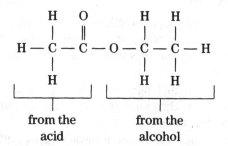

from the acid   from the alcohol

Esters are liquids that have characteristic odors that resemble those of fruits or flowers. For this reason, they are used extensively in the manufacture of deodorizers, perfumes, and other products that have a fragrance.

This experiment will demonstrate the preparation of esters. Three esters will be prepared and their odors noted.

Purpose

Prepare several esters.

Equipment

graduated cylinder, 10-mL
beaker, 250-mL
ring stand
iron ring
utility clamps (2)
microspatula
burner

test tubes, 25×200-mm (3)
rubber stopper, 1-hole (for test tube)
10-mm glass tubing (50 cm)
dropper pipet
safety goggles
lab apron or coat

Materials

ethanol
methanol
amyl alcohol (n-pentyl alchohol)

acetic acid, glacial
salicylic acid
18 M sulfuric acid

Safety

Because of the flammability of the alcohols and esters and the irritating quality of the ester vapors, this experiment should be conducted in a properly functioning fume hood. Handle concentrated sulfuric acid with extreme care, and always wear rubber gloves when dispensing it. Tie back long hair and secure loose clothing when working with an open flame. Note the caution alert symbols here and with certain steps in the "Procedure." Refer to page xi to review the specific precautions associated with each symbol. Always wear safety goggles and a lab coat or apron when working in the lab.

Procedure

PART A ETHYL ACETATE

1. Place 5 mL each of ethanol and glacial acetic acid in a 25×200-mm test tube. Add eight drops of 18 M H_2SO_4. **CAUTION:** *Handle this acid very carefully.* Note the odor of the mixture.

2. Insert a 50-cm length of 10-mm glass tubing into a 1-hole rubber stopper. The end of the tubing should extend very slightly below the bottom of the stopper.

3. Fill a 250-mL beaker about three-fourths full of tap water. Set up the apparatus as shown in Figure 49-1. Gently heat the water to boiling. Once the water boils, reduce the heat and allow the water to simmer gently. DO NOT HEAT THE TEST TUBE DIRECTLY.

4. Heat for about 15 minutes. Turn off the flame and remove the test tube from the water bath. Allow the liquid in the tube to cool and then note and record its odor.

PART B AMYL ACETATE

5. Repeat the procedure followed in Part A using 5 mL of amyl (n-pentyl) alcohol, 5 mL of glacial acetic acid, and eight drops of 18 M H_2SO_4. Note and record the odor of the ester.

49 Esters (continued)

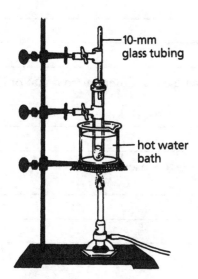

10-mm glass tubing

hot water bath

Figure 49-1

PART C   METHYL SALICYLATE

6. Repeat the procedure again, this time using a spatulaful of salicylic acid, 5 mL of methanol, and eight drops of 18 M H_2SO_4. Note and record the odor of the ester.

Observations

Ester	Odor
ethyl acetate	_____
amyl acetate	_____
methyl salicylate	_____

Conclusions and Questions

1. Write the equations for the three esterification reactions.

PART A

_____

PART B

_____

PART C

_____

2. What is the role of the H_2SO_4 in these reactions?

_____

_____

_____

_____

3. How is the $-OH$ radical of an alcohol different from that of an inorganic compound (a base)?

_____

_____

4. In what types of products are esters used?

_____

_____

_____

Saponification

Text reference: **Chapter 25,** pp. 740–742

Pre-Lab Discussion

Fats are esters formed from glycerol (an alcohol) and a long-chain organic acid (a long-chain fatty acid). The formation of a fat can be represented by the equation:

Soaps are metallic salts of fatty acids. Soaps are made by boiling solid fats or liquid fats (oils) with a solution of a strong base. This reaction is called **saponification.** If the fat from the equation above reacts with a strong base, such as NaOH, a soap and glycerol are formed:

In condensed form, this equation can be written:

$$(RCOO)_3C_3H_5 + 3NaOH \rightarrow 3RCOONa + C_3H_5(OH)_3$$

In this experiment, soap will be made by reacting a liquid fat with sodium hydroxide dissolved in ethanol.

Purpose

Prepare soap from liquid fat and a strong base.

Equipment

beaker, 25-mL
graduated cylinders, 10-mL and 100-mL
evaporating dish
ring stand
iron ring
wire gauze
microspatula
test tube, 13×100-mm

glass stirring rod
funnel
burner
watch glass
cork
rubber gloves
safety goggles
lab apron or coat

Materials

oil, cottonseed or olive
ethanol
30% NaOH solution
distilled water

saturated NaCl solution
litmus paper
filter paper

Safety

Sodium hydroxide solution is corrosive. Wear rubber gloves, handle it with care, and avoid spills on your skin or clothing. Flush any spills with cool water and report them to your teacher. To protect against spattering, carry out the experiment with a watch glass on top of the evaporating dish. Tie back long hair and secure loose clothing when working with an open flame. Ethanol is flammable; keep the burner flame away from it. Note the caution alert symbols here and with certain steps in the "Procedure." Refer to page xi to review the specific precautions associated with each symbol. Always wear safety goggles and a lab apron or coat when working in the lab.

Procedure

 1. Measure out 4.0 mL of cottonseed or olive oil and pour it into a clean, dry evaporating dish. Add 4.0 mL of ethanol and 2.0 mL of 30% NaOH solution to the oil. **CAUTION:** *Handle this solution carefully.*

 2. Set up the ring stand, wire gauze, evaporating dish, watch glass, and burner as shown in Figure 50-1. Heat the mixture *gently* with a *very low* flame. **CAUTION:** *Keep the flame away from the ethanol, which is highly flammable.*

50 Saponification (continued)

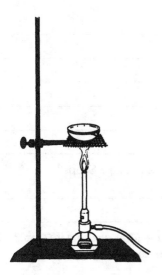

Figure 50-1

3. Continue heating for 10 minutes. Stop heating when the odor of fat has disappeared and the oil has dissolved.

4. Allow the mixture to cool. During this time, place 10.0 mL of distilled water in a 25-mL beaker and heat to just below boiling.

5. When the evaporating dish is cool enough to touch, add the hot water to the mixture in the dish. Then add 12.5 mL of saturated NaCl solution and stir the mixture.

6. Filter the mixture, collecting the liquid in the beaker. Discard the liquid and keep the solid on the filter paper.

7. In a test tube, dissolve 1 microspatula of your soap in 10.0 mL of distilled water. Test the solution with litmus paper and record your observations.

8. Add about 1.0 mL of tap water to the solution in the test tube. Cork the mouth of the tube and shake vigorously. Record your observations.

Observations

Litmus test:

_____

_____

Shaking test:

_____

_____

_____

_____

_____

_____

Conclusions and Questions

1. What do the processes of saponification and esterification have in common? How do these processes differ?

_____

_____

_____

_____

_____

2. To what class of compounds do fats belong? Soaps?

_____

_____

3. Describe the contents of the test tube after shaking it (step 8). Did any white precipitate (scum) appear? If so, explain its presence.

_____

_____

_____

_____

_____

4. The formula for the hydrocarbon radical (R—) in the fat glycerol stearate is $C_{17}H_{35}$. Write an equation showing the reaction of glycerol stearate with sodium hydroxide to produce the soap sodium stearate.

_____

5. How are soaps treated commercially before they are marketed?

_____

_____

_____

Radioactivity (Demonstration)

Lab 51

Text reference: **Chapter 26,** pp. 755–757

Pre-Lab Discussion

The nuclei of most atoms are extremely stable. Even when these atoms are involved in chemical reactions, their nuclei are unaffected. However, the nuclei of certain elements *do* undergo changes, even though they do not take part in chemical reactions. Changes that involve the nuclei of atoms are called nuclear reactions.

Radioactivity is a type of nuclear change in which the nuclei of an element spontaneously disintegrate, or decay, to produce another element (or elements). Such a change of an element into an entirely different element or elements is called transmutation. Nuclear disintegration is accompanied by radiation—the emission of particles and rays from the nucleus. Three types of radiation are alpha particles, beta particles, and gamma rays. An alpha particle is essentially a helium nucleus. Consisting of 2 protons and 2 neutrons, an alpha particle carries a charge of 2 + and has a mass of 4 atomic mass units. A beta particle is a fast-moving electron with a charge of 1 − and negligible mass. Gamma rays are a form of electromagnetic radiation. They are similar to X rays, but have even shorter wavelengths.

Alpha particles, beta particles, and gamma rays have different penetrating powers. A stream of alpha particles can be stopped by a single sheet of paper. Beta particles will pass through a sheet of paper, but can be stopped by a thin sheet of aluminum. It takes several centimeters of lead to stop gamma rays.

In this experiment you will study some methods used to detect radiation and the effects of distance and various materials on the intensity and passage of radiation.

Purpose

Gain familiarity in the methods of detecting radiation, determining its intensity, and testing materials for the purpose of shielding radiation.

Equipment

Geiger counter
meter stick
cardboard sheets (12)
aluminum sheets (12)

lead sheets (12)
safety goggles
lab apron or coat

Materials

beta emitters, low energy (5 or 6)

Safety

Handle the beta emitters with care, as instructed by your teacher. Note the caution alert symbols here and with certain steps in the "Procedure."

Refer to page xi for the specific precautions associated with each symbol. Always wear safety goggles and a lab apron or coat when working in the lab.

Procedure

PART A USING A GEIGER COUNTER

1. Open the beta window of the Geiger counter and get a background count. Record this in Data Table A.

2. Place one of the radioactive samples as close to the tube as possible. **CAUTION:** *The radioactive samples used in this experiment are weak emitters and present no health risk with normal use. However, like all potentially dangerous materials, these samples should be handled with considerable care.* Record the voltage and the number of counts per minute as indicated by the Geiger counter.

3. Repeat step 2 with as many different radioactive samples as are available.

PART B SHIELDING EFFECTS OF DIFFERENT MATERIALS

4. Place the Geiger counter tube on a flat surface facing out from the Geiger counter. Open the beta window and place a radioactive sample 10 cm from the tube. Read and record the voltage and number of counts per minute in Data Table B.

5. Place a single sheet of cardboard between the tube opening and the radioactive sample (see Figure 51-1). Read and record the data with the cardboard in place.

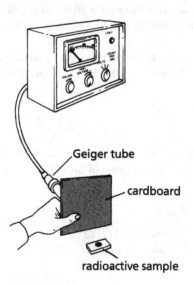

Figure 51-1

6. Add another sheet of cardboard to the first. Read and record the data with the two sheets in place.

7. Repeat step 6, adding one sheet of cardboard at a time, until all 12 sheets have been used. After each sheet is added, read and record the data.

51 Radioactivity (continued)

8. Repeat steps 5 through 7 using aluminum in place of cardboard.

9. Repeat steps 5 through 7 using lead in place of cardboard.

PART C RELATIONSHIP BETWEEN DISTANCE AND RADIATION

10. Set up the Geiger counter and meter stick as shown in Figure 51-2. Place a radioactive sample 2 cm from the Geiger counter tube. Note and record the exact distance and the reading on the Geiger counter in Data Table C.

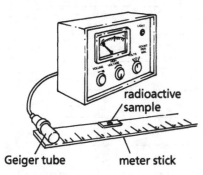

radioactive sample

Geiger tube   meter stick

Figure 51-2

11. Move the radioactive sample 4 cm farther from the tube (6 cm total distance). Note and record the distance and Geiger counter reading.

12. Continue to move the sample away from the tube at 4-cm intervals until it is about 30 cm from the tube. Note and record the distance and Geiger counter reading after each move.

Observations and Data

PART A

DATA TABLE A

Background count _____ **Voltage** _____

Sample	Counts per minute

PART B

DATA TABLE B

Voltage _____

Number of sheets	Counts per minute		
	cardboard	aluminum	lead
1			
2			
3			
4			
5			
6			
7			
8			
9			
10			
11			
12			

PART C

DATA TABLE C

Distance (cm)	Counts per minute
2	
6	
10	
14	
18	
22	
26	
30	

51 Radioactivity (continued)

Graphing Data

1. Plot data from Part B on the grid of Figure 51-3. Plot the number of sheets of each different material used versus the count per minute. Plot all three curves on the same grid, using different colors for each curve.

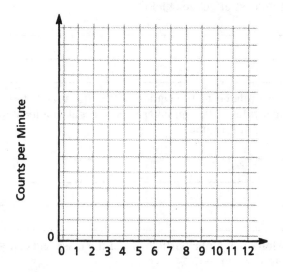

Number of Sheets

Figure 51-3

2. Plot data from Part C on the grid of Figure 51-4.

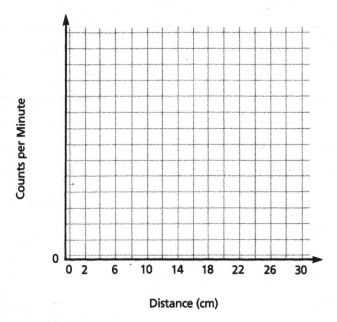

Distance (cm)

Figure 51-4

Conclusions and Questions

1. What causes the background count?

_____

_____

_____

2. Which material provides the most effective shield against beta particles? Which provides the least effective shield?

_____

_____

_____

3. Counts per minute are related to the square of the distance between the source and the Geiger tube. Is this an inverse or a direct relationship? Express this relationship in a formula.

_____

_____

_____

_____

4. How does the emission of an alpha particle affect the mass and charge of the atom from which it is emitted?

_____

_____

_____

5. State one way in which a nuclear equation showing radioactivity differs from a regular chemical equation. Give an example to illustrate your answer.

_____

_____

_____

_____

_____

_____

_____

Determining Half-life

(Demonstration)

Lab 52

Text reference: **Chapter 26,** pp. 757–763

Pre-Lab Discussion

The rate at which nuclear decay takes place is fixed and constant for each kind of radioactive nucleus. The time it takes for half of the atoms in a given radioactive sample to decay is called the half-life of that isotope. Each radioactive isotope has its own unique half-life, which is totally unaffected by temperature, pressure, and all other factors.

The half-life of a radioactive isotope is related to the original and final masses of a sample of that isotope by the formula $M_f = M_o(\frac{1}{2})^n$, where M_f is the final mass, M_o is the original mass, and n is the number of half-life periods. Using this formula and the known half-lives of various isotopes, scientists can determine the ages of rock samples and ancient objects containing a given radioactive isotope.

In this experiment, the radiation emitted by two different radioactive isotopes will be observed and recorded over extended periods of time. The intensity of the radiation at the end of a given period of time will be compared with the intensity of radiation emitted by the same sample at the beginning of the experiment. The difference in the intensity will provide some information about the half-life of the radioactive isotope.

Purpose

Determine the half-life of two different radioactive isotopes.

Equipment

Geiger counter
ring stand
clamp
meter stick
safety goggles
lab apron or coat

Materials

iodine-131, 10 microcuries
phosphorus-32, 10 microcuries

Safety

Handle the radioactive isotopes with care, as instructed by your teacher. Note the caution alert symbols here and with certain steps in the "Procedure." Refer to page xi for the specific precautions associated with each symbol. Always wear safety goggles and a lab apron or coat when working in the lab.

Procedure

PART A   HALF-LIFE OF IODINE-131

1. Clamp the Geiger tube to a ring stand as shown in Figure 52-1. **NOTE:** Once the apparatus is set up, it should remain undisturbed throughout the period of this experiment.

2. Close the beta shield over the window of the tube. Measure and record the background count for gamma radiation in Data Table A, Column (1).

 3. Place a 10-microcurie sample of the isotope iodine-131 (I-131) close enough to the tube to produce a high reading on the counter. Carefully note the position of the sample and measure the distance between the sample and the tube. *These conditions should be reproduced each time the sample is checked.*

4. Record the day and time in Data Table A. Take a reading of the count produced by the I-131 sample and record it in Data Table A, Column (2). Subtract the background count from the reading and record the difference, (2) − (1), in the table. Return the I-131 sample to its container.

5. Repeat steps 2–4 at the same time every day for 2 weeks.

PART B   HALF-LIFE OF PHOSPHORUS-32

6. Open the beta shield and measure and record the background count for beta radiation in Column (1) of Data Table B.

7. With the beta window open, repeat steps 3 and 4, using a 10-microcurie sample of phosphorus-32 (P-32) in place of I-131. Readings should be made every day at the same time for a period of 3 to 4 weeks.

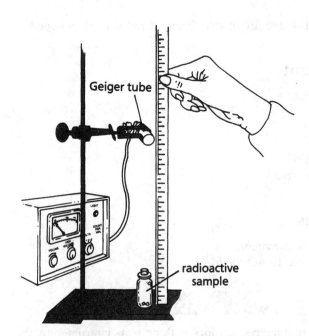

Figure 52-1

52 Determining Half-life (continued)

Observations and Data

DATA TABLE A—IODINE-131

Day	Time	(1) Background count	(2) Geiger counter reading	(2) − (1) Net count I-131

DATA TABLE B—PHOSPHORUS-32

Day	Time	(1) Background count	(2) Geiger counter reading	(2) − (1) Net count P-32

Graphing Data

1. On the grid provided (Figure 52-2), plot the net count (*y*-axis) versus the day (*x*-axis) for each of the radioisotopes used. Label each curve to indicate the isotope it represents.

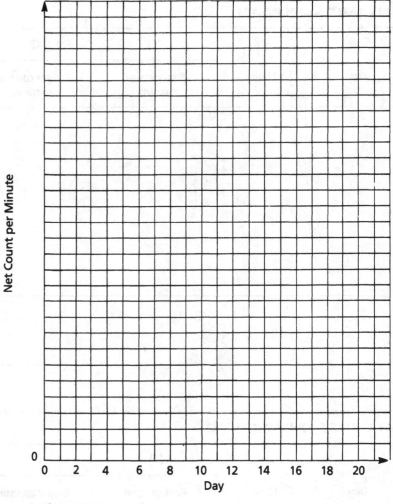

Figure 52-2

2. Once the curves are drawn, estimate the net count for each of the days on which no readings were available. Enter these estimates in your data tables.

Conclusions and Questions

1. Using the experimental data, determine the half-life of each of the radioisotopes. (Half-life = day that the net count is one-half that produced by the original sample.)

_____

_____

_____

_____

52 Determining Half-life (continued)

2. Using the experimental value for the half-life of I-131, find the number of days required for a 100-g sample of this radioisotope to decay to a mass of 25 g. Show both algebraic and graphic solutions.

3. A sample of P-32 has a mass of 80 g. Based on your experimental data, what mass of this radioisotope would remain after 42 days? Show both algebraic and graphic solutions.

4. Explain why, theoretically, the mass of a radioisotope never reaches zero.

_____
_____
_____

5. Why must the background count be measured and subtracted from the sample count each day?

_____
_____

6. How do archeologists use the half-life of carbon-14 to date organic material that they discover?

_____
_____
_____
_____
_____

Appendices

Appendix A   Standard Electrode Potentials

Ionic concentrations 1 M water at 25°C and 101.3 kPa	
Half-reaction	E^0 (volts)
$F_2(g) + 2e^- \rightarrow 2F^-$	+2.87
$8H^+ + MnO_4^- + 5e^- \rightarrow Mn^{2+} + 4H_2O$	+1.51
$Au^{3+} + 3e^- \rightarrow Au(s)$	+1.50
$Cl_2(g) + 2e^- \rightarrow 2Cl^-$	+1.36
$14H^+ + Cr_2O_7^{2-} + 6e^- \rightarrow 2Cr^{3+} + 7H_2O$	+1.23
$4H^+ + O_2(g) + 4e^- \rightarrow 2H_2O$	+1.23
$4H^+ + MnO_2(s) + 2e^- \rightarrow Mn^{2+} + 2H_2O$	+1.22
$Br_2(\ell) + 2e^- \rightarrow 2Br^-$	+1.09
$Hg^{2+} + 2e^- \rightarrow Hg(\ell)$	+0.85
$Ag^+ + e^- \rightarrow Ag(s)$	+0.80
$Hg_2^{2+} + 2e^- \rightarrow 2Hg(\ell)$	+0.80
$Fe^{3+} + e^- \rightarrow Fe^{2+}$	+0.77
$I_2(s) + 2e^- \rightarrow 2I^-$	+0.54
$Cu^+ + e^- \rightarrow Cu(s)$	+0.52
$Cu^{2+} + 2e^- \rightarrow Cu(s)$	+0.34
$4H^+ + SO_4^{2-} + 2e^- \rightarrow SO_2(aq) + 2H_2O$	+0.17
$Sn^{4+} + 2e^- \rightarrow Sn^{2+}$	+0.15
$2H^+ + 2e^- \rightarrow H_2(g)$	0.00
$Pb^{2+} + 2e^- \rightarrow Pb(s)$	−0.13
$Sn^{2+} + 2e^- \rightarrow Sn(s)$	−0.14
$Ni^{2+} + 2e^- \rightarrow Ni(s)$	−0.26
$Co^{2+} + 2e^- \rightarrow Co(s)$	−0.28
$Fe^{2+} + 2e^- \rightarrow Fe(s)$	−0.45
$Cr^{3+} + 3e^- \rightarrow Cr(s)$	−0.74
$Zn^{2+} + 2e^- \rightarrow Zn(s)$	−0.76
$2H_2O + 2e^- \rightarrow 2OH^- + H_2(g)$	−0.83
$Mn^{2+} + 2e^- \rightarrow Mn(s)$	−1.19
$Al^{3+} + 3e^- \rightarrow Al(s)$	−1.66
$Mg^{2+} + 2e^- \rightarrow Mg(s)$	−2.37
$Na^+ + e^- \rightarrow Na(s)$	−2.71
$Ca^{2+} + 2e^- \rightarrow Ca(s)$	−2.87
$Sr^{2+} + 2e^- \rightarrow Sr(s)$	−2.89
$Ba^{2+} + 2e^- \rightarrow Ba(s)$	−2.91
$Cs^+ + e^- \rightarrow Cs(s)$	−2.92
$K^+ + e^- \rightarrow K(s)$	−2.93
$Rb^+ + e^- \rightarrow Rb(s)$	−2.98
$Li^+ + e^- \rightarrow Li(s)$	−3.04

Appendix B Vapor Pressure of Water

Temperature (°C)	Pressure (mm Hg)	Temperature (°C)	Pressure (mm Hg)	Temperature (°C)	Pressure (mm Hg)
0	4.6	24	22.4	42	61.5
2.5	5.5	25	23.8	43	64.8
5	6.5	26	25.2	44	68.3
7.5	7.8	27	26.7	45	71.9
10	9.2	28	28.3	46	75.6
11	9.8	29	30.0	47	79.6
12	10.5	30	31.8	48	83.7
13	11.2	31	33.7	49	88.0
14	12.0	32	35.7	50	92.5
15	12.8	33	37.7	60	149.4
16	13.6	34	39.9	65	187.5
17	14.5	35	42.2	70	233.7
18	15.5	36	44.6	75	289.1
19	16.5	37	47.1	80	355.1
20	17.5	38	49.7	85	433.6
21	18.7	39	52.4	90	525.8
22	19.8	40	55.3	95	633.9
23	21.1	41	58.3	100	760.0

Appendix C   Solubility Product Constants (K_{sp}) at 25°C

Compound	Formula	K_{sp}
barium carbonate	$BaCO^3$	2×10^{-9}
barium chromate	$BaCrO_4$	8.5×10^{-11}
barium sulfate	$BaSO_4$	1.1×10^{-10}
cadmium sulfide	CdS	1.0×10^{-28}
calcium carbonate	$CaCO_3$	4.7×10^{-9}
calcium sulfate	$CaSO_4$	2.4×10^{-5}
copper(II) iodate	$Cu(IO_3)_2$	1.4×10^{-7}
copper(I) iodide	CuI	1.1×10^{-12}
copper(II) sulfide	CuS	6.3×10^{-36}
iron(II) sulfide	FeS	4×10^{-19}
lead chloride	$PbCl_2$	1.6×10^{-5}
lead chromate	$PbCrO_4$	2.8×10^{-13}
lead iodide	PbI_2	7.1×10^{-9}
lead sulfate	$PbSO_4$	1.3×10^{-8}
lead sulfide	PbS	7×10^{-29}
magnesium carbonate	$MgCO_3$	3.5×10^{-8}
magnesium hydroxide	$Mg(OH)_2$	1.8×10^{-11}
mercury(II) chloride	Hg_2Cl_2	1.3×10^{-18}
silver acetate	$AgC_2H_3O_2$	2.5×10^{-3}
silver bromide	$AgBr$	5.0×10^{-13}
silver chloride	$AgCl$	1.8×10^{-10}
silver chromate	Ag_2CrO_4	1.1×10^{-12}
silver iodide	AgI	8.3×10^{-17}
zinc sulfide	ZnS	1.2×10^{-23}

Appendix D Solubilities in Water

i — nearly insoluble ss — slightly soluble s — soluble d — decomposes n — not isolated	acetate	bromide	carbonate	chloride	chromate	hydroxide	iodide	nitrate	phosphate	sulfate	sulfide
Aluminum	ss	s	n	s	n	i	s	s	i	s	d
Ammonium	s	s	s	s	s	s	s	s	s	s	s
Barium	s	s	i	s	i	s	s	s	i	i	d
Calcium	s	s	i	s	s	ss	s	s	i	ss	d
Copper(II)	s	s	i	s	i	i	n	s	i	s	i
Iron(II)	s	s	i	s	n	i	s	s	i	s	i
Iron(III)	s	s	n	s	i	i	n	s	i	ss	d
Lead	s	ss	i	ss	i	i	ss	s	i	i	i
Magnesium	s	s	i	s	s	i	s	s	i	s	d
Mercury(I)	ss	i	i	i	ss	n	i	s	i	ss	i
Mercury(II)	s	ss	i	s	ss	i	i	s	i	d	i
Potassium	s	s	s	s	s	s	s	s	s	s	s
Silver	ss	i	i	i	ss	n	i	s	i	ss	i
Sodium	s	s	s	s	s	s	s	s	s	s	s
Zinc	s	s	i	s	s	i	s	s	i	s	i

How to use this table. The names of several metals that normally form positive ions (plus the ammonium ion, NH_4^+) are listed vertically at the left of the table. Across the top of the table are listed the names of several nonmetals and clusters of atoms that normally form negative ions. To obtain information about the solubility of any compound included in the table, find the box where the row for the positive ion and the column for the negative ion meet. The solubility information is in that box.

Appendix E   Solubility Curves for Selected Solutes

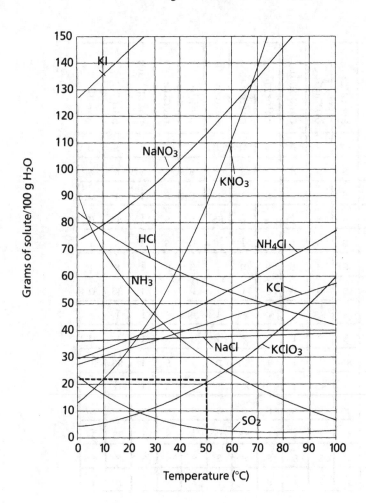

Appendix F Standard Energies of Formation of Compounds at 101.3 kPa and 25°C

Compound	Heat (Enthalpy) of Formation* kJ/mol (ΔH_f°)	Free Energy of Formation kJ/mol (ΔG_f°)
Aluminum oxide $Al_2O_3(s)$	−1676	−1582
Ammonia $NH_3(g)$	−46.0	−16
Barium sulfate $BaSO_4(s)$	−1473	−1362
Calcium hydroxide $Ca(OH)_2(s)$	−986.2	−898.7
Carbon dioxide $CO_2(g)$	−394	−395
Carbon monoxide $CO(g)$	−110	−137
Copper(II) sulfate $CuSO_4(s)$	−771.5	−661.9
Ethane $C_2H_6(g)$	−84.5	−33
Ethene (ethylene) $C_2H_4(g)$	52.3	68.2
Ethyne (acetylene) $C_2H_2(g)$	227	209
Hydrogen fluoride $HF(g)$	−271	−273
Hydrogen iodide $HI(g)$	26	1.7
Iodine chloride $ICl(g)$	18	−5.4
Lead(II) oxide $PbO(s)$	−215	−188
Magnesium oxide $MgO(s)$	−601.7	− 569.4
Nitrogen(II) oxide $NO(g)$	90.4	86.6
Nitrogen(IV) oxide $NO_2(g)$	33	51.5
Potassium chloride $KCl(s)$	−437	−409
Sodium chloride $NaCl(s)$	−411	−384
Sulfur dioxide $SO_2(g)$	−297	−300
Water $H_2O(g)$	−242	−228
Water $H_2O(l)$	−286	−237

Sample equations:

$$2Al(s) + \frac{3}{2} O_2(g) \rightarrow Al_2O_3(s) + 1676 \text{ kJ}$$

$$2Al(s) + \frac{3}{2} O_2(g) \rightarrow Al_2O_3(s) \quad \Delta H = -1676 \text{ kJ/mol}$$

*Minus sign indicates an exothermic reaction.

Appendix G Relative Strengths of Acids in Aqueous Solution at 101.3 kPa and 25°C

Conjugate Pairs		K_a
Acid	**Base**	
$HI = H^+ + I^-$		very large
$HBr = H^+ + Br^-$		very large
$HCl = H^+ + Cl^-$		very large
$HNO_3 = H^+ + NO_3^-$.		very large
$H_2SO_4 = H^+ + HSO_4^-$		large
$H_2O + SO_2 = H^+ + HSO_3^-$		1.5×10^{-2}
$HSO_4^- = H^+ + SO_4^{2-}$		1.2×10^{-2}
$H_3PO_4 = H^+ + H_2PO_4^-$		7.5×10^{-3}
$Fe(H_2O)_6^{3+} = H^+ + Fe(H_2O)_5(OH)^{2+}$		8.9×10^{-4}
$HNO_2 = H^+ + NO_2^-$		4.6×10^{-4}
$HF = H^+ + F^-$		3.5×10^{-4}
$Cr(H_2O)_6^{3+} = H^+ + Cr(H_2O)_5(OH)^{2+}$		1.0×10^{-4}
$CH_3COOH = H^+ + CH_3COO^-$		1.8×10^{-5}
$Al(H_2O)_6^{3+} = H^+ + Al(H_2O)_5(OH)^{2+}$		1.1×10^{-5}
$H_2O + CO_2 = H^+ + HCO_3^-$		4.3×10^{-7}
$HSO_3^- = H^+ + SO_3^{2-}$		1.1×10^{-7}
$H_2S = H^+ + HS^-$		9.5×10^{-8}
$H_2PO_4^- = H^+ + HPO_4^{2-}$		6.2×10^{-8}
$NH_4^+ = H^+ + NH_3$		5.7×10^{-10}
$HCO_3^- = H^+ + CO_3^{2-}$		5.6×10^{-11}
$HPO_4^{2-} = H^+ + PO_4^{3-}$		2.2×10^{-13}
$HS^- = H^+ + S^{2-}$		1.3×10^{-14}
$H_2O = H^+ + OH^-$		1.0×10^{-14}
$OH^- = H^+ + O^{2-}$		$< 10^{-36}$
$NH_3 = H^+ + NH_2^-$		very small

Sample equation: $HI + H_2O = H_3O^+ + I^-$

*Note: $H^+(aq) = H_3O^+$

Appendix H Physical Constants and Conversion Factors

Name	Symbol	Value(s)	Units
Angstrom unit	Å	1×10^{-10} m	meter
Avogadro number	N_A	6.02×10^{23} per mol	
Charge of electron	e	1.60×10^{-19} C	coulomb
Electron volt	eV	1.60×10^{-19} J	joule
Speed of light in vacuum	c	3.00×10^8 m/s	meters/second
Planck's constant	h	6.63×10^{-34} J $\cdot$ s	joule-second
Universal gas constant	R	0.0821 L $\cdot$ atm/mol $\cdot$ K	liter-atmosphere-mole-kelvin
		8.31 dm^3 $\cdot$ kPa/mol $\cdot$ K	cubic decimeters-kilopascals/mole-kelvin
		8.31 J/mol $\cdot$ K	joules/mole-kelvin
Atomic mass unit	u(amu)	1.66×10^{-24} g	gram
Volume standard, cubic decimeter	dm^3	1×10^3 cm^3 = 1 dm^3	cubic centimeters, cubic decimeter, liter
Standard pressure, atmosphere	atm	101.3 kPa	kilopascals
		760 mmHg	millimeters of mercury
Kilocalorie	kcal	4.18×10^3 J	joules

Physical Constants for H_2O

Molal freezing point depression .... 1.86°C

Molal boiling point elevation .... 0.52°C

Heat of fusion .... 333.5 J/g

Heat of vaporization .... 2257 J/g

Appendix I Densities and Boiling Points of Some Common Gases

Name		Density g/dm^3 (at STP*)	Boiling Point °C (at 101.3 kPa)
air	—	1.29	—
ammonia	NH_3	0.771	−33
carbon dioxide	CO_2	1.98	−78
carbon monoxide	CO	1.25	−191
chlorine	Cl_2	3.21	−35
hydrogen	H_2	0.0899	−253
hydrogen chloride	HCl	1.64	−85
hydrogen sulfide	H_2S	1.54	−61
methane	CH_4	0.716	−164
nitrogen	N_2	1.25	−196
nitrogen (II) oxide	NO	1.34	−152
oxygen	O_2	1.43	−183
sulfur dioxide	SO_2	2.92	−10

*STP is defined as 0°C and 101.3 kPa.

The Chemical Elements

(Atomic masses in this table are based on the atomic mass of carbon-12 being exactly 12.)

NAME	SYMBOL	ATOMIC NUMBER	ATOMIC MASS†	NAME	SYMBOL	ATOMIC NUMBER	ATOMIC MASS†
Actinium	Ac	89	(227)	Neon	Ne	10	20.2
Aluminum	Al	13	27.0	Neptunium	Np	93	(237)
Americium	Am	95	(243)	Nickel	Ni	28	58.7
Antimony	Sb	51	121.8	Niobium	Nb	41	92.9
Argon	Ar	18	39.9	Nitrogen	N	7	14.01
Arsenic	As	33	74.9	Nobelium	No	102	(255)
Astatine	At	85	(210)	Osmium	Os	76	190.2
Barium	Ba	56	137.3	Oxygen	O	8	16.00
Berkelium	Bk	97	(247)	Palladium	Pd	46	106.4
Beryllium	Be	4	9.01	Phosphorus	P	15	31.0
Bismuth	Bi	83	209.0	Platinum	Pt	78	195.1
Boron	B	5	10.8	Plutonium	Pu	94	(244)
Bromine	Br	35	79.9	Polonium	Po	84	(210)
Cadmium	Cd	48	112.4	Potassium	K	19	39.1
Calcium	Ca	20	40.1	Praseodymium	Pr	59	140.9
Californium	Cf	98	(251)	Promethium	Pm	61	(145)
Carbon	C	6	12.01	Protactinium	Pa	91	(231)
Cerium	Ce	58	140.1	Radium	Ra	88	(226)
Cesium	Cs	55	132.9	Radon	Rn	86	(222)
Chlorine	Cl	17	35.5	Rhenium	Re	75	186.2
Chromium	Cr	24	52.0	Rhodium	Rh	45	102.9
Cobalt	Co	27	58.9	Rubidium	Rb	37	85.5
Copper	Cu	29	63.5	Ruthenium	Ru	44	101.1
Curium	Cm	96	(247)	Samarium	Sm	62	150.4
Dysprosium	Dy	66	162.5	Scandium	Sc	21	45.0
Einsteinium	Es	99	(254)	Selenium	Se	34	79.0
Erbium	Er	68	167.3	Silicon	Si	14	28.1
Europium	Eu	63	152.0	Silver	Ag	47	107.9
Fermium	Fm	100	(257)	Sodium	Na	11	23.0
Fluorine	F	9	19.0	Strontium	Sr	38	87.6
Francium	Fr	87	(223)	Sulfur	S	16	32.1
Gadolinium	Gd	64	157.2	Tantalum	Ta	73	180.9
Gallium	Ga	31	69.7	Technetium	Tc	43	(97)
Germanium	Ge	32	72.6	Tellurium	Te	52	127.6
Gold	Au	79	197.0	Terbium	Tb	65	158.9
Hafnium	Hf	72	178.5	Thallium	Tl	81	204.4
Helium	He	2	4.00	Thorium	Th	90	232.0
Holmium	Ho	67	164.9	Thulium	Tm	69	168.9
Hydrogen	H	1	1.008	Tin	Sn	50	118.7
Indium	In	49	114.8	Titanium	Ti	22	47.9
Iodine	I	53	126.9	Tungsten	W	74	183.9
Iridium	Ir	77	192.2	Unnilennium	Une	109	(266?)
Iron	Fe	26	55.8	Unnilhexium	Unh	106	(263)
Krypton	Kr	36	83.8	Unniloctium	Uno	108	(265)
Lanthanum	La	57	138.9	Unnilpentium	Unp	105	(262)
Lawrencium	Lr	103	(256)	Unnilquadium	Unq	104	(261)
Lead	Pb	82	207.2	Unnilseptium	Uns	107	(262)
Lithium	Li	3	6.94	Uranium	U	92	238.0
Lutetium	Lu	71	175.0	Vanadium	V	23	50.9
Magnesium	Mg	12	24.3	Xenon	Xe	54	131.3
Manganese	Mn	25	54.9	Ytterbium	Yb	70	173.0
Mendelevium	Md	101	(258)	Yttrium	Y	39	88.9
Mercury	Hg	80	200.6	Zinc	Zn	30	65.4
Molybdenum	Mo	42	95.9	Zirconium	Zr	40	91.2
Neodymium	Nd	60	144.2				

†Numbers in parentheses give the mass number of the most stable isotope.

Periodic Table

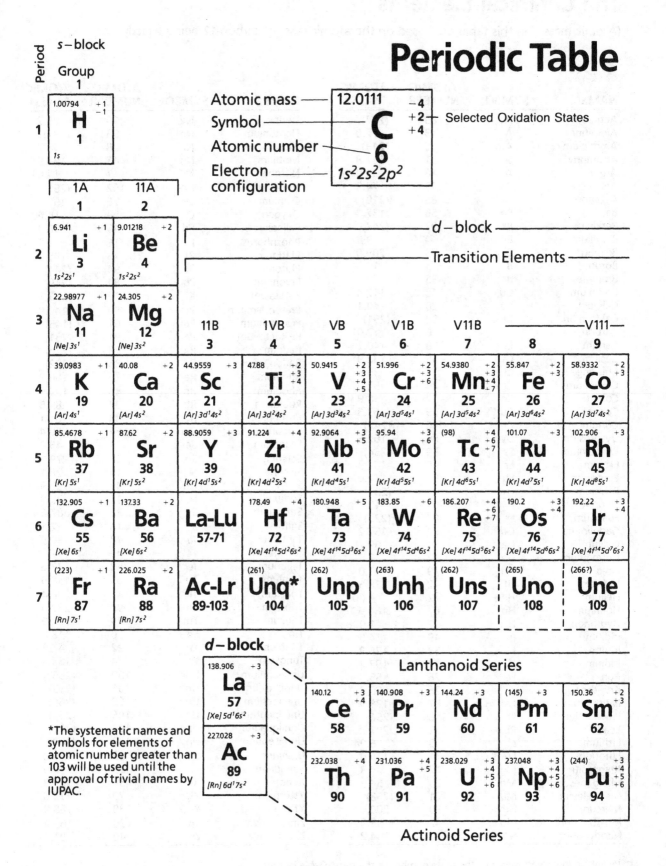

Period

s–block

Group 1

Legend:
Atomic mass — 12.0111
Symbol — C
Atomic number — 6
Electron configuration — $1s^2 2s^2 2p^2$
Selected Oxidation States: -4, +2, +4

Period / Group	1A (1)	11A (2)	3 (11B)	4 (1VB)	5 (VB)	6 (V1B)	7 (V11B)	8 (—V111—)	9
1	1.00794 +1 −1 **H** 1 $1s$								
2	6.941 +1 **Li** 3 $1s^2 2s^1$	9.01218 +2 **Be** 4 $1s^2 2s^2$							
3	22.98977 +1 **Na** 11 [Ne]$3s^1$	24.305 +2 **Mg** 12 [Ne]$3s^2$							
4	39.0983 +1 **K** 19 [Ar]$4s^1$	40.08 +2 **Ca** 20 [Ar]$4s^2$	44.9559 +3 **Sc** 21 [Ar]$3d^1 4s^2$	47.88 +2 +3 +4 **Ti** 22 [Ar]$3d^2 4s^2$	50.9415 +2 +3 +4 +5 **V** 23 [Ar]$3d^3 4s^2$	51.996 +2 +3 +6 **Cr** 24 [Ar]$3d^5 4s^1$	54.9380 +2 +3 +4 +7 **Mn** 25 [Ar]$3d^5 4s^2$	55.847 +2 +3 **Fe** 26 [Ar]$3d^6 4s^2$	58.9332 +2 +3 **Co** 27 [Ar]$3d^7 4s^2$
5	85.4678 +1 **Rb** 37 [Kr]$5s^1$	87.62 +2 **Sr** 38 [Kr]$5s^2$	88.9059 +3 **Y** 39 [Kr]$4d^1 5s^2$	91.224 +4 **Zr** 40 [Kr]$4d^2 5s^2$	92.9064 +3 +5 **Nb** 41 [Kr]$4d^4 5s^1$	95.94 +3 +6 **Mo** 42 [Kr]$4d^5 5s^1$	(98) +4 +6 +7 **Tc** 43 [Kr]$4d^6 5s^1$	101.07 +3 **Ru** 44 [Kr]$4d^7 5s^1$	102.906 +3 **Rh** 45 [Kr]$4d^8 5s^1$
6	132.905 +1 **Cs** 55 [Xe]$6s^1$	137.33 +2 **Ba** 56 [Xe]$6s^2$	**La-Lu** 57-71	178.49 +4 **Hf** 72 [Xe]$4f^{14} 5d^2 6s^2$	180.948 +5 **Ta** 73 [Xe]$4f^{14} 5d^3 6s^2$	183.85 +6 **W** 74 [Xe]$4f^{14} 5d^4 6s^2$	186.207 +4 +6 +7 **Re** 75 [Xe]$4f^{14} 5d^5 6s^2$	190.2 +3 +4 **Os** 76 [Xe]$4f^{14} 5d^6 6s^2$	192.22 +3 +4 **Ir** 77 [Xe]$4f^{14} 5d^7 6s^2$
7	(223) +1 **Fr** 87 [Rn]$7s^1$	226.025 +2 **Ra** 88 [Rn]$7s^2$	**Ac-Lr** 89-103	(261) **Unq*** 104	(262) **Unp** 105	(263) **Unh** 106	(262) **Uns** 107	(265) **Uno** 108	(266?) **Une** 109

d–block — Transition Elements

d–block

138.906 +3 **La** 57 [Xe]$5d^1 6s^2$

227.028 +3 **Ac** 89 [Rn]$6d^1 7s^2$

*The systematic names and symbols for elements of atomic number greater than 103 will be used until the approval of trivial names by IUPAC.

Lanthanoid Series

140.12 +3 +4 **Ce** 58	140.908 +3 **Pr** 59	144.24 +3 **Nd** 60	(145) +3 **Pm** 61	150.36 +2 +3 **Sm** 62

Actinoid Series

232.038 +4 **Th** 90	231.036 +4 +5 **Pa** 91	238.029 +3 +4 +5 +6 **U** 92	237.048 +3 +4 +5 +6 **Np** 93	(244) +3 +4 +5 +6 **Pu** 94